Tonbridge in the Early

Tonbridge Historical Society

The Society runs a regular annual programme which includes authoritative talks on varied aspects of local and general history, as well as visits to places of historical interest. Its Research Group has produced four books in addition to *Tonbridge in the Early Twentieth Century*, all of them edited by Dr Christopher Chalklin. *Early Victorian Tonbridge* (1975), *Mid-Victorian Tonbridge* (1983) and *Late Victorian & Edwardian Tonbridge* (1988) were published by Kent County Library, Maidstone. *Georgian Tonbridge* (1994) was published by the Society itself. For details of the Society's current programme, and information on how to join, please contact the Hon. Secretary, Tonbridge Historical Society, 8 Woodview Crescent, Hildenborough, Tonbridge, Kent TN11 9HD.

TONBRIDGE

in the Early Twentieth Century

edited by Christopher Chalklin

Tonbridge Historical Society

British Library Cataloguing-in-Publication Data
A catalogue record for this book is available from the British Library.

ISBN 0 9523563 1 7

Set in 9.5-point Galliard using WordPerfect and Pagemaker software.

Printed in England by Hobbs the Printers Limited, Totton, Hampshire.

Published by Tonbridge Historical Society, 8 Woodview Crescent, Hildenborough, Tonbridge, Kent TN11 9HD.

Cover photograph
Part of a postcard showing Tonbridge High Street before the First World War – see page 18.

Contents

List of Maps and Illustrations

The Contributors

Dr Christopher W. Chalklin comes from a Tonbridge family. He is a former Reader in History at Reading University. His writings include works on Kentish social and economic history, acting as editor of this Tonbridge series. He is Past President of the Tonbridge Historical Society (THS).

Mrs Pat Hopcroft has had a longstanding interest in local history, archaeology and the effect of building on the environment. She studied for a Certificate in Archaeology, and is a committee member and leader of the Pictorial Records Group of the THS.

Mr Peter Swan is a BA (Oxon) in Modern History. He had 30 years' service in public libraries, ending his career as Tonbridge Reference Librarian. He has been a committee member and is currently Vice Chairman of the THS. He recently obtained a Certificate in Local History from the University of Kent.

Dr Peter L. Humphries was at Hugh Christie School in Tonbridge, where he was a pupil of Dr John Ray. He gained a University of Kent MA and an Oxford University DPhil on Kentish political history in the eighteenth and early nineteenth centuries. He was a contributor to the previous book in this series, *Georgian Tonbridge*.

Mrs Alison Williams has a BA Honours degree, and a Diploma in Local History of the University of Kent. She taught for many years at Fosse Bank School in Tonbridge as Head of History. She is a committee member of the Hadlow Historical Society, having a special interest in the history of Tonbridge and Hadlow in the sixteenth century.

Mrs Gwenyth Hodge has a Diploma in Local History of the University of Kent. She was for many years Tonbridge Reference Librarian, and contributed to previous books in this series, and to *Archaeologia Cantiana*. She has been Hon. Secretary and Chairman and is a longstanding committee member of the THS.

Mr G. Laurence Johnson was at the Judd School in Tonbridge and played rugby football for the Old Juddians. His father was a chairman of the Tonbridge Sports Association. He has been Chairman of the THS.

Mrs Pat Mortlock has a BA Honours degree and is a former History mistress and Librarian at Tonbridge Grammar School for Girls. She contributed to *Early Victorian Tonbridge* in this series, and has lectured locally on the mid-nineteenth century censuses of Tonbridge. She has been Chairman and is currently Minutes Secretary of the THS.

Acknowledgements

The Committee of Tonbridge Historical Society would like to express its gratitude to the authors of these essays, to Christopher Chalklin whose guidance and leadership have brought the project to fruition, to Anthony Wilson who copy-edited and indexed the book, typeset it and saw it through the press, and to the staff of Tonbridge Reference Library who have helped in many ways over the years. The individual authors' more specific acknowledgements appear at the ends of their chapters.

Except where otherwise credited, the photographs in this book are from the Tonbridge Historical Society's photographic archive or from the Don Skinner postcard collection, now held by the Society.

A Note about Money

The purchasing power of the pound varied significantly during the period covered by this book, and has changed even more since. As a rough guide, based on data from the Government Statistical Service, £1 in 1914 had the same purchasing power as £56 today (1999), £1 in 1920 had the same purchasing power as £23 today, and £1 in the 1930s had the same purchasing power as £36 today.

Most readers of this book will be familiar with the pre-decimal system of pounds, shillings and pence, in which there were 12 pence to the shilling and 20 shillings to the pound. Those wishing to convert to decimal currency should proceed as follows: to convert sums in old pence (d) into new ones (p), divide by 2.4 – for example 6d becomes 2.5p; to convert sums in shillings (s) into new pence (p), multiply by 5 – for example 12s becomes 60p. Sums in pounds (£) remain unchanged.

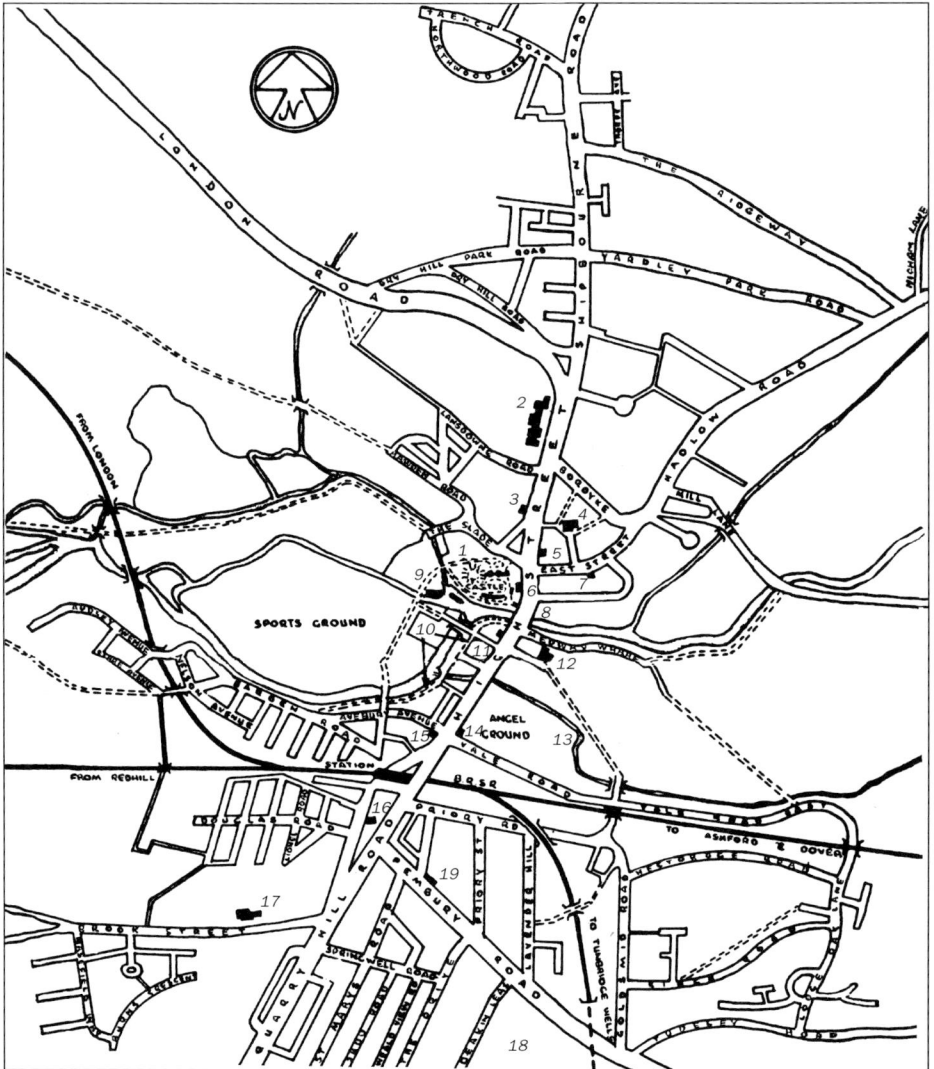

1	The Castle	7	Portreeve's House
2	Tonbridge School	8	Great Bridge
3	Capitol Cinema	9	Swimming Pool
4	Parish Church	10	River Walk
5	Rose & Crown Hotel	11	Medway Hall
6	Chequers Inn	12	Ritz Cinema
		13	Tonbridge Bowling Club

14	Angel Hotel
15	Library & Technical Institute
16	St Stephen's Church
17	Judd School
18	County School for Girls
19	Police Station

Street plan of Tonbridge as it was at the end of the period covered in this book
(from The Official Guide to Tonbridge and District, *c1950).*

Introduction

Dr Christopher Chalklin

Tonbridge was a medium-sized market town. Its shopkeepers, craftsmen and professional people served the surrounding countryside to a distance of five to eight miles, except in the south where Southborough and Tunbridge Wells played the urban role. The railway station and several industries gave additional work, and by the 1930s a few hundred residents were employed in London.

The town grew from 14,796 people in 1911 to 15,368 and 15,929 in 1919 and 1921 respectively. Expansion was tiny in the 1920s as the population was only 16,332 in 1931, and then a little faster with 'something over 17,000' in 1935 and about 18,000 in 1946. The boundaries were enlarged in 1928 and 1934 to include small parts of Hadlow parish on the north-east and Hildenborough on the north-west.

The normal development of local society was interrupted by two big outside events, the First World War, 1914-18, and the fall in exports by traditional industries between 1920 and 1939. While the German invasion of Belgium at the beginning of August 1914 was the pretext for the declaration of war, its fundamental cause was the need to stop the defeat of France, a friendly power since 1904, and the consequent dominance of the Continent by Germany, a military power. Although the slump in overseas sales of coal, cotton textiles, steel and shipping in the 1920s and 1930s hit the north of England, Clydeside and South Wales hardest, the rest of the country also suffered unemployment.

Work and Income

The nature of work changed gradually except for the sharp transformation during the Great War. The causes were the coming of buses, vans and motor cars using petrol engines, the further slow replacement of local handicrafts by mass-produced goods from factories in the North and West, the expansion of London which encouraged the siting of works and housing within 30 or 40 miles, improved real wages and salaries, and a lower unemployment level in the 1920s and 1930s than outside south-east England. Some of these influences were general to Britain and others peculiar to the Home Counties and adjoining areas.

Among occupations which were general to English towns, shop work either as manager or assistant was one of the two most common forms of employment. Shops varied from the individually run business such as that of tobacconist or beer retailer to the department or multiple store with 12 or 20 people. Frank East was still the leading department store, the stock of which included higher quality drapery, and to earlier multiples such as Freeman, Hardy and Willis, and Home and Colonial were added Sainsbury and Woolworth. There were flourishing businesses of one shop such as Nelson Gale for shoes, Thomas Vane the family grocer and John Angell jeweller. Food and clothing and shoe shops were numerous. Although goods were increasingly supplied by wholesalers and directly by manufacturers rather than made by craftsmen-retailers, bootmakers survived and suits were often made to order.

Higher living standards and technical innovation were responsible for photographers, car and cycle suppliers, toy and sports dealers. Presumably the High Street multiples with cheap, standard goods including canned food attracted working-class trade from small one-person dealers in neighbouring lesser roads such as Priory Street and parts of Shipbourne Road. Altogether goods had a bigger price range, were more varied despite standard brands, and were sold increasingly by bigger shops and businesses. There was also a weekly produce market, and an important wholesale stock market. The numerous public houses and hotels had bartenders, grooms and vehicle attendants, and there were carrier services linking the station and shops with neighbouring villages. Shop work also involved contact with regular customers at home, both to take orders and to deliver, as well as by careful attendance to the special needs of the more well-to-do clients when they called at the shop. There was also street selling by women with flowers and men with matches and other cheap goods. Rag and bone men and door-to-door salesmen were also common.

Much work was still provided in middle-class homes. The low wage level and considerable unemployment meant that maid service and daily cleaning indoors, and gardening was still usual. The biggest source of skilled manual work in the open air was building, still largely unmechanised. Council houses were erected in the 1920s and private building flourished afterwards, bricklayers and carpenters being especially numerous. Several builders had large workforces, such as George Baker with a High Street office and premises at the Slade with 'foremen and workmen skilled in each branch of the building trade' in January 1911, while other employees were in firms of four or five men, such as that of C. M. Hewitt, 'plumber, painter and glazier' of 2 Castle Street in 1911. Some trading was also done in the roads and at house doors, as already mentioned. Road upkeep, refuse disposal, the gas, water and sewage works used much general labour, and a few miscellaneous skilled workers included chimney sweeps and sign writers.

Another occupational group were those supplying professional services. They included solicitors and doctors, typically in partnerships, numerous elementary teachers in private and state schools, and many secondary masters and mistresses on account of Tonbridge School with its boarders, the girls' and boys' grammar schools, and the Technical Institute. Clergy continued to serve the parish churches, Free Churches and the Roman Catholics, and there were auctioneers and estate agents, bank managers, insurance officials and more Council administrators. Growing real earnings expanded the number of professional people and clerks. The absence of free medicine and dentistry restricted these two professions. According to *Kelly's Directory* in 1919 there were only 8 doctors and 2 dentists, compared with 18 solicitors, although chemists also drew teeth.

The biggest single employer was the station, owned by the South Eastern Railway Company and from 1922 the Southern Railway Company. On 3 June 1932 the *Tonbridge Free Press (TFP)* stated that there were 650 railway workers, some of whom lived in railway cottages. Cheap land and easy transport links with London were responsible for the establishment and growth of factories making specialised goods. The Crystalate Gramophone Record Manufacturing Company under the local management of W. C. Chalklin, had 40 employees when the Postern Lane works were built in 1917, and by 1932

W. C. Chalklin, photographed on his retirement as manager of the Crystalate Co. in 1933 (author's photograph).

there were 390 or 400, sending records all over England and abroad, according to the *TFP* on 19 February 1932 and 2 June 1933. The manager of Whitefriars Press, A. E. Minton, has written that the firm had nearly 400 employees in 1926. Printing was probably the biggest source of work throughout the period. In September 1934 the Tonbridge Chamber of Trade was told that about 700 people were fully employed, with 370 at the Whitefriars Press, 230 at Dowgate, and 100 at other works. Our contributor Peter Swan mentions (page 55) the short-lived motor manufacturing works of Storey Brothers, created by the boom and shortage of cars in 1919, and killed by the recession at the end of 1920. Other firms made cricket bats and balls, and the Acme Chemical Company made 'weed killer, lawn sand, worm killer and fertilisers'.

Unemployment may have affected 200 or 300 people before 1914. Pauper orphan children and elderly were still sent to Pembury Workhouse until 1929, numbers falling on account of small old age pensions from 1909 which were improved later. The War gave everybody work, 3,000 serving (one in every five of the population) and 346 being killed. From 1916 the local Military Tribunal dealt firmly with claims for exemption on the grounds of disability or essential work. Schoolmasters enlisted, and in 1918 Judd's Commercial School had two women teachers, excluded from the Masters' Common Room! There were jobs in the town from the service of troops stationed locally, the Voluntary Aid Detachment Hospital for the wounded at Quarry Hill House, which by February 1916 had over 500 patients, and administrative expansion. Home entertainment and 'socials' for the soldiers were also provided, and local people contributed to organising sports and concerts. In addition to labour saving, vacancies in shops, offices and places of entertainment were filled by women, some of whom had been domestic servants or had not worked before. Evening and weekend work included the cultivation of allotments, rearing of chickens and rabbits, and pig keeping by the Council, especially during the food shortages in 1917 and 1918, when the number of allotments showed a remarkable increase.

In the brief post-war boom, men resumed former jobs or joined new or expanding firms. By late 1920 recession set in, and the *TFP* noted 400 unemployed on 4 February and 484 on 8 July 1921. Nationally, unemployment was highest in 1921-22 and 1931-33. In Tonbridge it affected 764 men and 96 women on 5 February and 746 men and 91 women on 26 February 1932, and next year on 13 and 27 January 994 men and 94 women and 975 and 89 respectively, according to the *TFP*. Although unemployment eased a little in 1934 as private house building rose, and the closure of the Leigh Powder Mills affecting 60 Tonbridge families was balanced by a new factory for synthetic alcohol and more work at the Crystalate, the making of gramophone records was transferred elsewhere a year or two later. There were 366 unemployed in January 1937 and 688 men and 225 women out of work on 10 February 1939 during a harsh winter. Casual work was extensive so that bad weather deprived many outside workers of employment temporarily.

Public schemes of work brought temporary relief. In 1933 the Council borrowed £2,000 to make the Woodland Walk using men out of work, and like other councils searched for schemes to relieve unemployment. Private charity helped in crises. According to Minton a fire burnt half the Whitefriars Press Works on 22 June 1926 and many of the printers had to survive on national insurance and trade union funds; a relief fund was started by the Chairman of the Council, F. G. P. Neve (an auctioneer) and the solicitor Henry Cogger. Help for the poor at Christmas continued through the period, so that on 20 January 1939 the *TFP* reported that the 'Advance' Christmas Coal Fund had realized £23 8s 9d, and coal had been sent to 176 families 'in great need of warmth during the very severe Christmas season'. Begging, often under the guise of some entertainment such as singing, was rife in the High Street, a natural result of heavy unemployment and relatively lax police supervision of the streets. Early in 1932 hundreds of men were said to be hanging round the Labour Exchange in winter months, and a Social and Occupational Centre was opened in 1932 with training in basic crafts such as bootmaking, though only a small minority of unemployed went to it.

There is little information about local earnings. In September 1934 Tonbridge printers were earning wages which were 120 per cent more than in 1914. Down to 1920 wages in England rose several times, rather faster than costs; then they declined as prices fell, and average prices dropped slowly until 1939. Working people benefited. According to Perkin and Glyn and Oxborrow wages roughly doubled between 1911-13 and 1938, salaries rose 71 and prices 56 per cent. In the 1920s and 1930s urban manual workers earned £2 10s or £3 a week. In 1920 unemployment relief which had begun for insured workers in 1911 was extended to all out of work, though rates of under a £1 for single men were low. Fortunately unemployment in the south-east was half the national average.

Among professional people some evidence exists of teachers' earnings. In 1921 the *TFP* reported on 3 March that 43 elementary masters and mistresses received an average of £285 a year, or between £5 and £6 weekly. The Headmaster of the Judd School giving secondary education for boys earned £650 in 1928, his salary rising by £25 annual increments to £800. Elementary teachers' salaries were among the lowest received in the professions, and the highest earners such as solicitors and doctors took £1,000 or £1,500. On the whole middle class earnings rose more slowly than those of manual workers.

Retired people and those of independent means still drew much of their income from local sources, such as holdings in local businesses or housing. Although owner-occupation was spreading among the middle class, clerks and better-paid skilled workers by the 1930s, the majority of dwellings were rented. On 6 January 1911 Neve and Son of 1 Bank Street, 'auctioneers, house and estate agents', who handled insurances, valuations, rent collection and estate management like other property agents, advertised that '£100 will purchase the equity of good Tonbridge cottages, bringing in £9 9s a year clear', and another agent, Ernest Sanderson, had 'unfurnished houses to let from £52 per annum upwards' on 6 January 1939.

While real income was higher, two factors affected its disposal. Consumption was reduced by bigger taxes and rates. Taxes rose from 1s 2d (6 per cent) in 1910 to 6s in 1919 on account of the War; then transfer payments such as national insurance benefits, old age pensions and rising interest on the National Debt, and 'social' payments for education and housing kept taxes at 4s in 1926-30, and 5s 6d in the 1930s, when there was also rearmament. Very few wage earners paid tax, although payments became gradually more common among other occupied people, especially if they did not have children. Rates also rose to pay for greater local authority work, that is, in the case of Tonbridge, by the County Council and Urban District Council. On the other hand family size declined as births fell from the 1910s, and members of households had proportionately more money to spend.

The Standard of Living

A basic result of higher incomes, improved local and national transport, greater factory and mass-production bringing machine-made garments, shoes, canned and powdered foods, and more multiple stores with refrigerators, was consumption of better quality, more varied and a greater quantity of food and clothing. Although eating had improved since the mid nineteenth century, and free school meals were given after 1907 to elementary school children who had deficient home diets, malnutrition survived particularly in big, working-class families before 1914. Food consumption was steady during the War, with more margarine and lard and less butter, some saccharine instead of sugar, and bacon and ham replacing some of the butchers' meat. Rationing in 1918 reduced the quality of the abundant and varied middle class diets and improved consumption by the families of manual workers.

According to J. Burnett in *Plenty and Want*, in the 1920s and 1930s 'protective' or health foods were eaten more by wage earners, such as meat, butter, eggs, especially fruit and vegetables and even chocolate and crisps, compared with cheaper cereals or energy foods. Imported tropical fruits, refrigerated apples and pears, butter, eggs and chilled meat helped to provide a more varied diet throughout the year. Eating out spread to the lower middle classes, helped by the use of the private motor car, as shown locally by the popularity of town restaurants and the Old Barn, Hildenborough. Eating among the more numerous middle class people was becoming more economical and lighter, with less domestic help and a busier life. By 1939 it was still of higher quality and more varied than that of manual workers, especially with children, many of whom had a diet below the standard needed for health, from choice and tradition as well as necessity. By then the poorest children had free meals and milk at school, and health departments gave milk, cod liver oil, iron and vitamin products for mothers and children with malnutrition. The greater public and private middle-class concern about health standards is shown by a local inquiry about school milk. At the end of 1938 the Ratepayers Association queried its quality in a letter to the Council, and the Kent Education Committee wrote subsequently that 11 samples had been satisfactory, the matter being reported by the Health Committee of Tonbridge Council and published by the *TFP* on 10 February. Standard quality factory-made shoes and clothes also helped the less well-off.

Better education also contributed to rising living standards. Schooling was compulsory until the age of 14 from 1919. Ninety or ninety-five per cent of the children went to state schools. In 1938 there were 2002 at nine elementary schools, with classes averaging about 30. Secondary education was at the County School for Girls, with over 200 in 1917, and the Judd

School for Boys (244 in 1917, 355 in 1939), both drawing pupils from outside the town. Alison Williams discusses (page 143) the growth of private education, which served numerous boarders. Better teaching helped post-school training, including that for professional work. Reading of books and newspapers and sensible understanding of local and national issues were encouraged. On 30 July 1937 Tonbridge Library had 5,181 borrowers in a population of about 17,500, almost 30 per cent.

Three million private houses and a million council dwellings were erected in England in the 1920s and especially the 1930s. Although population grew slowly, households rose fast as child numbers fell. Building declined after 1910 with the introduction of Land Values Duties, and only 50,000 houses were erected in the War. There was a huge shortage by the beginning of the 1920s, particularly of smaller property, as rent control deterred private landlord building. From 1919 a series of acts provided for state and local authority subsidisation of council houses let at rents manual workers could afford, and grants for private building. In the 1930s rising real earnings, a fall in building costs including lower interest rates, and easier building society terms all stimulated private building, according to Burnett's *Social History of Housing*.

Scarcely any houses were built in Tonbridge between 1910 and 1919 apart from 20 by the Railway Company. Like other local authorities Tonbridge began council house building with attention and over-optimism. Estates were planned at Barden and North End. Houses on the Barden scheme began to be finished in blocks of four in January 1921; on 5 August 86 were reported to be built or building, with 34 planned for completion by 31 July 1922. Originally 500 were suggested, but the failure of Storey's works and of one or two other prospective big manufacturing concerns, and a cut in government support led to the abandonment of the North End Estate and the reduction of the Barden project from 236 to 210, then 176 and finally 120 dwellings, mostly with three bedrooms without parlours. The cost was said to be £784 11s 4d per house, with the town contributing the proceeds of a penny rate as elsewhere. They used direct labour first, then private builders by contract. By March 1932 the Council had built 517 houses for £219,312, with loans repaid by rents (£14,500 to date), a government subsidy of £8,000 annually, and £2,000 each year from rates. The Hectorage Estate was being finished with 26 houses, and there was an estate at Cage Green. Unlike older cottage property these houses had internal toilets and were equipped with baths. The Council had also advanced £108,900 to enable 257 people to buy under the Small Dwellings Acquisitions Act. There is much other evidence in the *TFP* on Council building.

Private building prospered in the 1930s, output booming in 1934 and 1935. Important areas of development included the south-eastern upland off Pembury Road, near The Ridgeway to the north and Hadlow Road and adjoining streets on the north-east. As before nearby meadows subject to flooding to the east of the town centre and on the east side of the Hadlow Road were not used, and the sports grounds, Castle site and Tonbridge School playing fields blocked westward expansion. The new houses were detached, semi-detached (the most popular) and bungalows, without the terrace form; houses lined roads at least several hundred yards long, gardens were usually ample and deep, and by the 1930s garages and garage sites were often provided. Some of the largest houses were built on the north side, in Yardley Park Road and The Ridgeway, roads which linked two of the major thoroughfares. To the north of The Ridgeway two long rows of bungalows were built in Thorpe Avenue at the beginning of the 1930s. In the *TFP* on 3 March 1933 semi-detached houses with three or four bedrooms, bathroom, two reception rooms and offices with a garage space were being sold in Deakin Leas on the south-eastern edge of the town for £720, £740 or £775. The attractive terms may be illustrated by the advertisement on 19 May 1933 of new 'modern houses' on the Fox Bush Building Estate beyond the town's boundary in Hildenborough, 'price £575 or £75, and balance by arrangement with Building society (about 15s 6d per week)'. Detached houses with four or five bedrooms cost £900 or £1,000 upwards. The expanding townscape is discussed at length by Pat Hopcroft.

Services such as gas, electricity and main drainage were general. By the 1930s most houses had electricity for lighting and power supplied by the Council-owned electricity works. Its use grew as houses, businesses and streets increased. Between October and December 1938 there were 85 new connections, 49 reconnections and 189 extensions, and 19 public lamps were connected. Gas fitting grew and became normal. According to the *TFP* on 2 March 1928 it was noted at the Annual General Meeting of the local Gas Company that £8,071 had been spent on appliances up to 1917, then £16,084 until 1927. During 1927, 250 new consumers were connected, with a record in new appliances, including 324 cookers, 301 fires and 66 geysers for hot water. Fewer resident staff such as cooks and maids and the absence of daily cleaners from many semi-detached dwellings had two effects: houses were planned to be 'labour-saving', especially in regard to the kitchen layout, and work was reduced by consumer durables such as hoovers, irons, washing-machines and refrigerators.

The widespread use of radios and the coming of television in a few homes by 1939 did not stop outside evening entertainment and culture, of which this was a golden age. According to Tapsell's *Memoirs of Kent Cinemas*, two cinemas and a skating rink opened in 1910. In the 1920s and 1930s there were two or three cinemas, a theatre and skating rink, entry charges of a few pence upwards opening them to general use. The *TFP* mentions three cinemas, the Star, Empire Picture Palace and New Theatre on 13 January 1928. The New Theatre run by F. West had an orchestra and its seats cost 6d, 9d, and 1s downstairs and 1s 3d and 1s 6d in the circle with children at 3d and 6d, and showing 'the great all-British production, a Daughter in Revolt'. The buildings were decorated lavishly and had plush seats. The last and biggest, the Ritz, from 1937, had a restaurant. The huge popularity of the cinema is shown by the visit of 8 or 9 thousand people to the Capitol Cinema to see 'Snow White' in December 1938; probably they represented one in three townspeople and others from the vicinity, according to the *TFP* on 13 January 1939.

Numerous plays, concerts, whist drives, dances and dinners, sometimes helping charities, were arranged, in addition to society meetings on various subjects. The Constitutional Club, Tonbridge Club and Working Men's Club and Institute obviously appealed to different social levels. An Amateur Dramatic Society and Orchestral Society appeared in the 1920s, according to *Kelly's Directory*. Two societies in 1919 were discussing philosophical subjects: on 3 January the *TFP* reported a lecture to the Tonbridge Theosophical Lodge by Philip Tillard on 'Chance', and a talk to the Brotherhood by Mr Hailstone of Hadlow (a dentist and Methodist Lay Preacher) on 'The Great Things and Small Things of Life'. On 13 January 1928 a discussion on employer-employee relationships was reported. Masonry was represented by the Freemasons' Medway Lodge (at the Masonic Hall) and International Order of Good Templars' True Unity Lodge in the Temperance Hall.

Sports were flourishing before the Great War, and expanded in the 1920s and 1930s. Games reached a peak during the six days in June when the Kent County Cricket Club played two matches on the Angel Ground in the town centre, owned by the Tonbridge Cricket Club. Fireworks, plays, concerts and a river fête were held at the same time. At first a golf club played near the Hadlow Road, and in 1920 a company was formed with a course off Pembury Road; by 1934 there were two courses and 200 members. The River made possible boating and angling, and the Tonbridge Angling Society had 149 members in 1936 and 166 in 1937.

There was indoor and outdoor bowling, hockey, soccer and rugby football; tennis became especially popular for women as well as men, with club courts and lawns in some of the larger house properties, and there was a Council swimming pool from 1910, which Gwenyth Hodge discusses (page 173), used by a swimming club with 120 male and female members in 1937 and 130 in 1938. Much sport was unorganised, such as cycling and motorcycling, the latter sometimes being of the daredevil kind. Youngsters bathed in the River and several big water-filled pits. During the War farming and allotments were organised in societies, and later gardening and horticulture were represented similarly. In general most kinds of entertainment and sport were fostered by higher real earnings which made possible the payment of more annual subscriptions and entry fees.

The Great War temporarily and the permanent rising living standards brought growing public regulation and expenditure. Conscription came in 1916 and food rationing two years later, accompanied by higher taxation and rates. Between 1919 and 1939 Tonbridge was changed by public expenditure through the central government, County Council (responsible for roads, education and police) and the Town Council. As already mentioned, national and local funds paid part of the cost of housing, and the Council sports ground provided cricket, tennis, football and bowls partly at ratepayers' expense, as is shown by the minutes of the Tonbridge Ratepayers Association on 22 April 1938. For its work the Council had 18 (by 1939, 20) elected members who met monthly for three years, with a new chairman each year. In 1919 there were 12 permanent committees, for the sewage work and farm, highways and lighting, general purposes, health, housing, electricity, bye laws, parks and museum and baths, the Shop Act, public library, allotments, and finance, and also *ad hoc* committees. As elsewhere committee discussions and decisions were included in the monthly reports to the Council which approved them or returned them for further consideration. The Council was spending £12,500 of which at least £8,000 was used for public works and roads.

Social relations also changed, quickly during the War and slowly thereafter. Geographical mobility was growing and a few Tonbridge residents came from the North in search of a better livelihood and perhaps a warmer climate. The Councillor and Chairman Donald Clark and the managing director of the Gas Company between 1917 and 1933, James Donaldson, were Scots, and others came from Lancashire and Yorkshire, such as Charles J. Fowler (died January 1939) who was born in Leeds and came to Tonbridge before 1900, where he designed houses in Goldsmid Road and the Barden Housing Scheme, and was a friend of Councillor Worrin as a member of the Medway Club. More came from London, like Councillor Angell the jeweller, and George Walter Blatchley, the manager of Freeman, Hardy and Willis between 1905 and 1934, a keen sportsman and club member. People of local families were still numerous, such as Mrs Francis Caroline Smith, daughter of William Nye, of 4 Lawn Road, wife of the verger of St Stephens Church and for many years a Sunday School teacher and active church member, who died aged 73 in January 1939.

The Great War brought greater equality of the sexes as women took over men's work. Women gained the parliamentary vote in 1918 and 1928 and were able to become solicitors and accountants. The first female councillor (Mrs J. B. Darling) appeared in 1919 and there were at least five in the 1930s.

Richard Norton, a printer, elected to the Council in 1922 and made Chairman in 1932 (from The Month in Tonbridge, 1932).

Women's social activities gradually became more prominent. Despite the effect of the hierarchical system of rank in the armed forces Tonbridge men fought together on the Western Front and elsewhere. Rather fewer women were household employees and more worked in shops, offices and places of entertainment. There was more mixing of different social classes as the sports and cinemas expanded. Although motor car ownership and occupation of council houses were perhaps socially divisive, the self-confidence of working families grew with better food, living conditions and more leisure. Even so, much talent was still wasted as few children of manual workers attended the grammar schools. Rarely did people of humble background become leaders in Tonbridge life, like

Councillor Norton who worked in the Whitefriars Press after leaving elementary school at 13 and had to 'burn the candle at both ends in order to obtain a little extra education', in his words. Among the other better known local figures were the shopkeepers, business and professional men who filled the Council and gave leadership in the sporting and cultural societies, and to the masons and church congregations. The town had to wait for the Second World War, the legislation of the Labour Government after 1945, and the accompanying full employment to bring decisive social change.

Sources

The *Tonbridge Free Press* and *Kent and Sussex Courier* newspapers and *Kelly's Directories* hold enormous amounts of information. The minutes of the Council and of the Ratepayers Association are also available. The physical growth of Tonbridge is shown on the 6-inch and 25-inch *Ordnance Survey Maps*. All this material is held in the Tonbridge Reference Library. The minutes and other relevant records of the committees of the Kent County Council may be seen at the Centre for Kentish Studies at Maidstone.

For social and economic changes in England as a whole one may read:

Marwick, A., *The Explosion of British Society 1914-1970*

Stevenson, J., *British Society 1914-1945,* and

Glynn, S. and Oxborrow, J., *Inter War Britain: a Social and Economic History*.

Particular themes are discussed in:

Jones, S. G., *Workers at Play: a Social and Economic History of Leisure 1918-1939*

Burnett, J., *A Social History of Housing*

Burnett, J., *Plenty and Want: a Social History of Diet in England from 1815 to the Present Day*, and

Perkin, H., *The Rise of Professional Society: England since 1880*.

E. Melling's *A History of Kent County Council 1889-1974* helps to place the work of the Tonbridge Council in perspective.

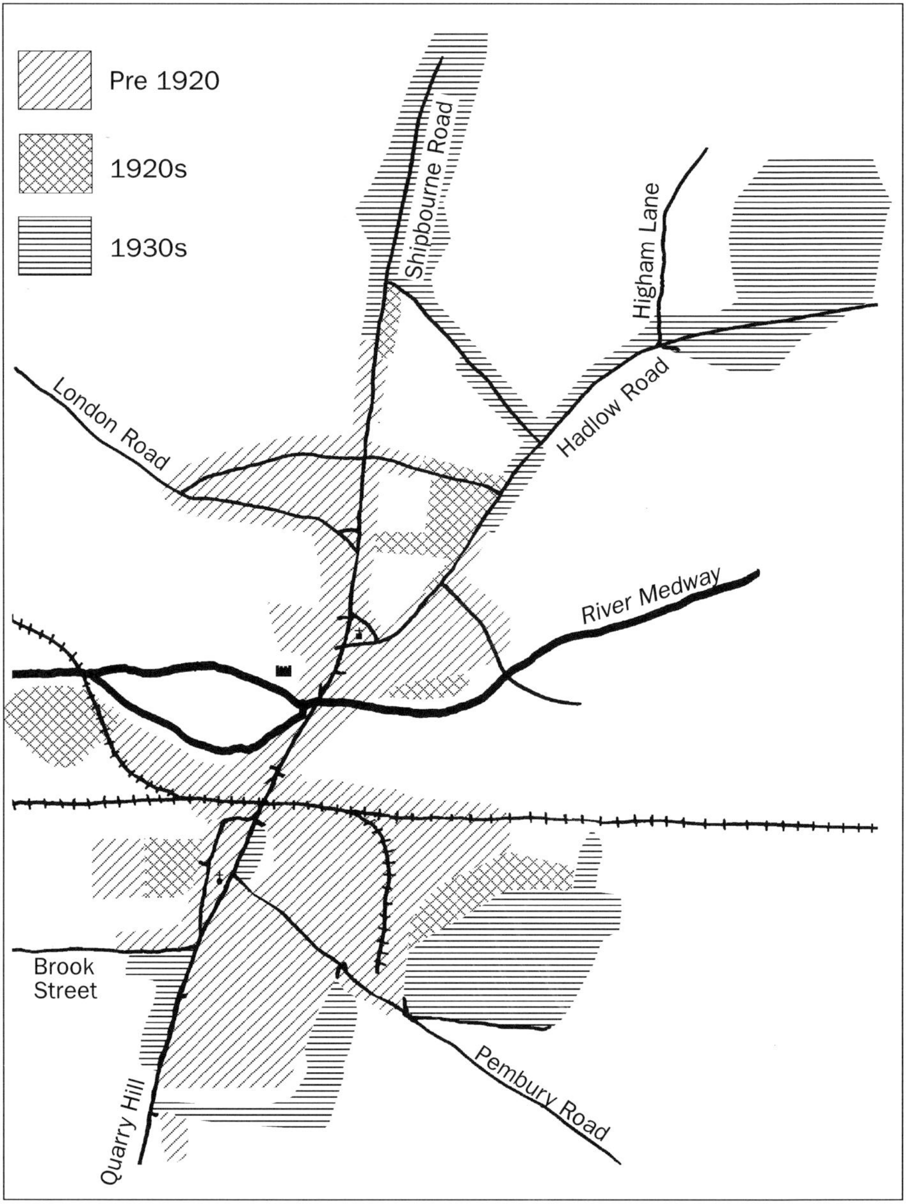
Pre 1920
1920s
1930s
Shipbourne Road
Higham Lane
London Road
Hadlow Road
River Medway
Brook Street
Pembury Road
Quarry Hill

How Tonbridge grew in the 1920s and 30s.

The Changing Appearance of the Town

P. A. Hopcroft

In 1910 Tonbridge was a busy market town with the housing mainly clustered close to each end of the central High Street. A relatively small number of men, including landlords and councillors, tended to control the destiny of the community. Family businesses and specialist craftsmen drew their custom locally and most of the inhabitants were educated, employed and entertained here. There were strong social distinctions related to occupation and area, or even street of residence, that were well respected and everyone knew their place.

These factors may not seem important with regard to the appearance of the town, but they did influence the changes that were made. New initiatives like council housing and increased home ownership added an element of social mobility which continued to grow. There was a frequent and fast train service bringing daily newspapers from London and manufactured goods from the Midlands and the North to be sold in the new multiple stores, like Liptons Ltd, The International Tea Co., The Singer Sewing Machine Co. and Freeman Hardy and Willis, as well as the more traditional shops. Motor buses and even private cars were becoming a more usual sight in the area.

By 1939, Tonbridge was part of a wider network, as improved transport systems and telephone communications were changing the way in which transactions and businesses were conducted. Other influences such as radio and films altered social attitudes during the period from 1910 to 1939 and people became more willing to accept new ideas. There was a growing number of home owners and there was increasing choice for everyone. Residents were now able to commute daily to London and in Tonbridge there was now a wide range of shops.

The role of the town seems to have changed significantly during these years but the framework, the road system and most of the buildings, altered little. In 1939, important features of the townscape like the castle, the parish church, many of the grand buildings including Tonbridge School in its spacious setting in the north of the town, looked much as they had in 1910. So did long stretches of the High Street.

By comparing the 1906/7 Ordnance Survey 25-inch maps with mid 1930s editions it is possible to establish the changes in the extent of the development, whilst the pattern of the new roads and housing give clues to the type of building which took place. This growth can be dated more precisely by reference to the local directories which are available for some of the intermediate years. These directories classify the businesses and list the streets that existed when they were compiled, together with the houses that were occupied at the time.

The minutes of Tonbridge Urban District Council meetings provide information about the planning processes involved in changing the structure of the town and the way in which these changes were executed. In particular, they document the housing schemes that were undertaken by the Council following the First World War. Any changes to the appearance of Tonbridge, such as the introduction of this council housing or improvements to the roads to accommodate the increasing amount of traffic, must be seen against the background of changing social and economic issues affecting the country as a whole because these wider implications have a direct influence on the changes that occurred in our town.

Although the period from 1910 to 1939 is within living memory of many Tonbridge residents it is still difficult to appreciate what the town was really like in 1910, because of the cumulative effect of what were, in some cases, very minor changes.

The best evidence for the appearance of the town comes from old photographs but many are not accurately dated and must be used in conjunction with other records. Photography provides a clear visual record of the past beginning with a very limited number of prints when first introduced in the mid nineteenth century and expanding to the prolific reproduction techniques available today. Initially, the images portrayed eminent Victorians and show lifeless houses and empty streets. Later prints record notable events and picturesque scenes, so that Tonbridge has a legacy of photographs showing the Castle, the Old Town Hall, the Great Bridge and the Medway, as well as many and varied views of the High Street. By the beginning of the period under review here, there is a huge increase in the amount of photographic material but more importantly faster films were capturing incidents of people going about their daily lives against a background of the town that was very slowly changing. Although most of these photographs still focus on the centre of the town, those covering other aspects of life especially sporting events or the floods sometimes accidentally include informative and evocative glimpses of forgotten features.

Over the years there have been several books published which use this wealth of photographs to illustrate the past in Tonbridge. Many of the pictures are old postcards and these are important because they can often be dated, as well as adding an element of social history. The pictorial record held by the Tonbridge Historical Society provides a compact source of reference for the local historian.

The structures and the appearance are recorded in pictures, but we must pause if we are to consider other aspects of the town as it developed between the wars. When comparing photographs of the same subject it becomes apparent that perspective and scale can be deceptive. Some buildings, for instance The Bull Hotel which stood at No. 65 on the east side of the High Street appears large in some photographs, but reference to an adjacent shop which still remains, show how modest this building must have been.

Smells and sounds of a bygone age are difficult to recapture but played an important part in the atmosphere of the place. This was a time when most people walked or travelled to work by bicycle and real horse power was gradually replaced by the motorized variety. A cocktail of smells filled the air, that of the horse nowhere more pungent than near the railway goods yards where many worked the wagons. Coal dust was free to blow about in the breeze and sulphurous smoke poured from the industrial premises, steam trains and domestic fires.

The evidence from maps, aerial photographs and the occasional wide-angled shot show that the skyline was broken by many tall chimneys as well as the gasholders which are still with us today. These chimneys belonged to the brewery, the electricity and water works, the brickworks and the iron foundries. They were prominent features of the town but the photographers nearly always managed to exclude them from their viewfinder. The sawmills in woodyards on the wharves beside the river must have added the sounds of screeching saws, clanking cranes and hoists, as baulks of timber were moved around and cut to size.

The traffic, which included livestock on the hoof going to and from the market, moved slowly. The heavy horse shoes and solid wheels would crush

The High Street before the First World War, showing window displays, enamel signs, and the Central Picture Hall beside the Little Bridge.

the loose road surface as they passed along the High Street and over the bridge. The weather too, must have affected the senses more dramatically than it does today, as a shower of rain would change the smell of the damp sawdust, whilst turning the dusty streets to mud.

The High Street – 1910 to the early 1920s

Photographs of the town before the First World War show a busy High Street with the carriageway full of carts and wagons of all descriptions. They included many hand carts on which the local tradesmen carried things like ladders and other tools of their trade. Close inspection of the images can reveal changes to the individual buildings, the shop fronts and the way in which retailers displayed their goods. The town had a rather cluttered appearance with a haphazard array of signs and advertisements hanging outside the shops. The popular enamelled signs, advertising the expanding ranges of manufactured goods becoming available, were so durable that they often appear in photographs many years apart. Each shop window contained a display of almost everything sold by the store, with the goods often spread out onto the pavement when the shop was open. Awnings feature prominently in many of the views; they appear to have been essential for protecting the merchandise from the elements although the pictures may not provide a true representation of their use because the photographers would obviously choose bright sunny conditions for the best results.

By 1910, the town possessed a high percentage of new purpose-built shop premises due to the total redevelopment on the west side of the High Street south of the Great Bridge. There is an interesting account of the progress of this undertaking by M. Barker Read in the Tonbridge Historical Society's publication *Late Victorian and Edwardian Tonbridge*.

This rebuilding scheme had significantly changed the appearance of this part of town because sections of the roadway had been almost doubled in width and the irregular frontage line of the former buildings was now straightened out. Work commenced at the station end of the High Street in 1893 and was still in progress two decades later. The final section, between New Wharf Road and the river, was dominated by the Dartford Brewery Co. and its 'tap', The Loggerheads, and as the buildings here were replaced they were set back to the new building line. The pair of shops, Nos 88 and 90 were built before 1912 in a style similar to other shop premises in the rebuilding scheme although they have now had the tops of the gable ends repaired in less decorative style. Only a few of the splendid terra cotta finials which adorned many of these new gable ends still survive today; some had already gone by 1939.

At No. 92 there was an older two-storey glass fronted building for H. E. Hall's Automobile Engineers, who had occupied this site since the turn of the century. The large plate glass windows of their building reflect a different construction technique from those used to build other contemporary shops and provided a wide flexible trading space especially useful for the motor trade. This building was replaced in the mid 1930s by a pair of shops and interestingly the entrance at No. 92 which became James Walker Ltd. the jewellers now has steps up to the ground floor. The increasing use of structural steel in new shops made it possible to do away with intermediate supporting walls and advantage was taken of this when rebuilding Nos 86 and 84. A wide expanse of window across the facade lit the premises of Seale, Austen and Barnes the Ironmongers, whose ironfoundry was in Botany, but whose retail outlet was based on this site for many years.

A postcard of a Church Parade dated January 1915 shows that the final bottleneck in the High Street south of the river had been removed; temporary boarding surrounds the empty site of the Loggerheads where the new General Post Office was soon to be built. The original proposal for this new building was put before the Council in October 1914 and the design is fairly typical of other main Post Offices elsewhere. The ground floor of this large four-storey brick building has wide bands of raised coursed brickwork on a sandstone plinth and a prominent stone cornice above the third storey. Tall sash windows are an important feature of the design and it has the royal cypher inscribed beneath the pediment over the entrance door. Next to the Post Office, at No. 96, a new shop was opened for J. Sainsbury's in 1923 and the shop at No. 98 was completed two years later.

The Midland Bank bought the site nearest the river and plans for the building, which was single-storey until the 1960s were put before the Council in August 1922. This brick building has a considerable amount of stone dressing and was built with a decorative balustrade around the roof. The banking hall occupied a prestigious site beside the river walk and was designed to display the image of security that this type of institution wishes to foster.

48242 TONBRIDGE: POST OFFICE.

The new Post Office (right) in c1920, before the adjacent garage was replaced by Sainsburys.

The development of River Walk

When redevelopment on the west side of the High Street as far as the bridge was completed, attention became directed to the area of land between the rear of these High Street shops and the river bank, which had become the site of small boatyards and storehouses. A change in the economic climate, in which the role of the river as a highway had seriously declined, together with frequent flooding left many of these premises derelict. Access to this area and the Water Works was improved by upgrading Bradford Street and New Wharf Road, although the latter remained very narrow and mainly served as an entrance to the yards behind the shops, not so very different from the way it appears today. It was in this part of the town and along the river side that the most notable changes occurred in the years following the first World War.

The Council had acquired much of the land along the bank of the Medway before the war and they planned a riverside feature with a pedestrian walkway through to River Lawn and Avebury Avenue. Work eventually started on this scheme in December 1920 but because of the acute unemployment situation at the time, the scheme was modified to use local unskilled labour. The first stage of the project between the Great Bridge and Buley's weir involved filling in the small streams, levelling the ground and then laying out the pathways, lawns and flowerbeds. The cost of the work, which was completed in 1922, was £2,500 and the extension on towards Barden Road cost a further £700.

Improved public access to this area made it a good centre for pleasure activities. The nearby outdoor swimming pool had opened in 1910 and two venues of public entertainment in Bradford Street had also opened that year. The Empire Skating Rink in a large single story wooden structure stood on the site of the present car park beside the Ebenezer Chapel; it was popular with the younger members of society until it closed in 1939. It later become a secondhand furniture store before it was ruined in the 1968 flooding.

On the opposite side of the road was the Star cinema housed in a brick warehouse that had an entrance lobby built on the side nearest the town. Large lettering painted onto the brickwork of the Bradford Street elevation of the building read 'Star Picture House' and the name was repeated over the entrance, where posters displayed the forthcoming programme. Although the cinema was frequently flooded it too served Tonbridge until 1939.

Early Cinemas like the Star were not normally purpose-built and any large-volume halls, particularly redundant chapels, were often converted to show films. In Tonbridge in 1910 films were shown occasionally in the Public Hall at the north end of the town, which has functioned as a Bingo Hall until recently gutted by fire, and in the Central Picture Hall which was next to the little bridge. The Central Picture Hall was originally built as a chapel, and the hall survived the High Street demolition scheme when the porch was removed to widen the road. A bold new facade somewhat taller than the hall, fronted the High Street and fitted the Central Hall for its new role. In 1914 a new cinema, the Empire Picture Palace in Avebury Avenue, was added to this list. The New Theatre, also in Avebury Avenue, was converted from a warehouse in 1921 and became a cinema later, in 1929.

Long term planning was not given serious consideration in the years following the war and even temporary buildings were encouraged. A large wooden hall, the Medway Hall, was erected at the junction with New Wharf Road and Bradford Street on the site of the present supermarket car park. Opened in 1922 it was a venue for meetings, shows and dancing and it was obviously not photogenic as the only views to be found of this hall are aerial shots showing the roof; as one picture also includes Crown Building which bears a date of 1952, the hall must have stood there for some 30 years.

Phil's Café by the river bank will be well remembered as part of the pleasure scene with its structure formed from two corrugated iron huts. This building may once been painted brown or black because these were the most durable colours available during the 1920s and 1930s and therefore very popular, but in later years it became dark green. A verandah along one side stored the outside tables when they were not in use. Nearby were the timber clad buildings of Doust's yard with pleasure boats stacked beside the river.

A series of photographs taken from an aeroplane in 1920 show the line of the High Street and the extent of the built up area behind the shops. These views were published as postcards and are almost clear enough to see individual premises. One shows that the Great Bridge had then become the next obstacle to the traffic, and as it was the County Council's intention to continue the road widening scheme further up the High Street, the bridge itself was widened in 1927. The shops, north of the bridge, under threat from the road widening scheme were not lost until the 1960s; up to that time they caused the road to be narrow near the bridge. There was also a row of small shops opposite the Ivy House enclosing the north end of the High Street, which tended to emphasize the spacious central part near the Rose & Crown. The town seems to have remained relatively unchanged for several years and it was not until the end of the 1920s that any further rebuilding took place in the High Street. It was in the growth of the housing that fundamental changes were occurring.

The residential area in 1910

In 1910 the built up area of housing lay close around the town centre. It extended northwards to include most of the larger houses in Dry Hill Park, the London Road and a few properties at the top end of Yardley Park Road. There were terraces of cottages in Uridge Road and Dernier Road and along the Shipbourne Road to just beyond the cemetery. On the Hadlow Road building finished opposite the Mitre public house on the west side and on the east side continued as terraces and semi-detached villas as far as Alexandra Villas next to the track leading to Tonbridge School old swimming pool. Beyond this built up area were orchards, hopgardens and meadows with some houses and isolated groups of cottages along the country roads.

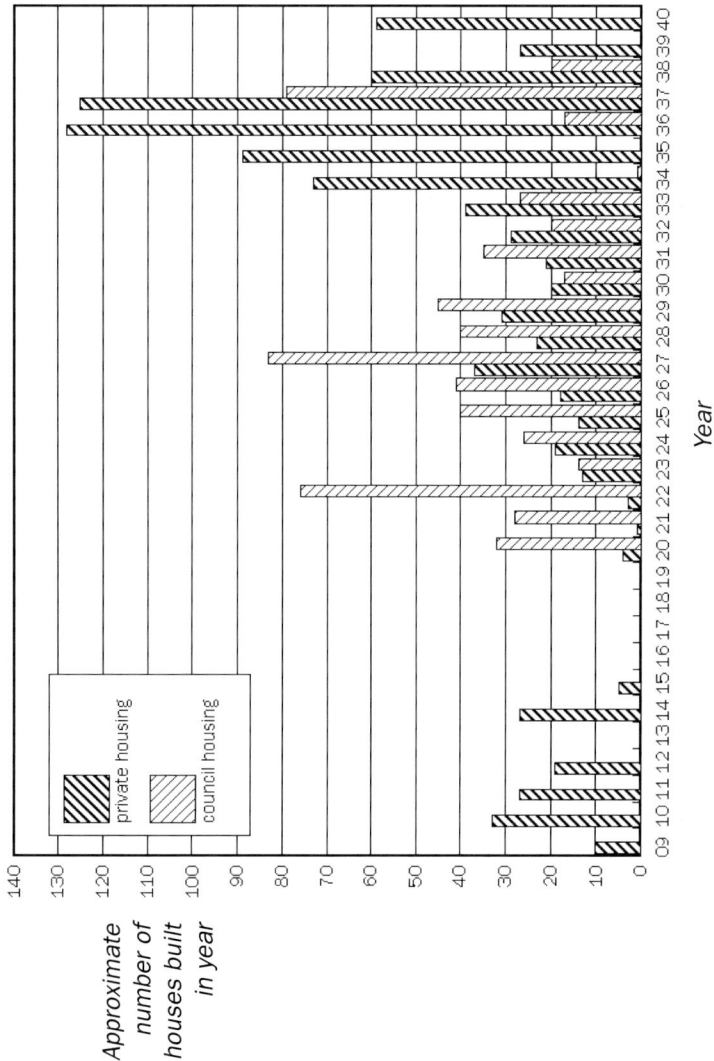

Approximate
number of
houses built
in year

private housing

council housing

Year

House-building in Tonbridge, 1909-40

Based on the number of occupation certificates issued, and occupied houses listed in Kelly's Directories.

Nearer to the town, the basic pattern of the development was already well established, although there were still spaces that became filled later. A few years before 1910, Stafford Road had been formed across an orchard at the bottom of the Slade and over the Fosse to give a more convenient access to the Houselands Estate.

To the south, where the expansion had been linked to the arrival of the railway, lay the spread of mid to late Victorian properties. This housing included the compact development between the railway line and the river around Barden Road. In the Priory Road area, housing extended to include properties at the bottom of Hectorage Road, with some along the newly created Goldsmid Road.

On the southern main roads, the Pembury Road had continuous housing almost to the top of the hill but Quarry Hill had been developed on the east side only as far as Baltic Road, the western side belonging to the Mabledon Estate. Although quite a lot of development had already taken place before 1910 on the land between these two main routes, this was one of the areas where houses continued to be built towards the higher ground away from the town.

In the Douglas Road area, the road structure had been completed before 1910. Building began at the far end, where it was related to the already established Brown, Knight and Truscott printing works and the school. Most of the houses in Sussex Road, Chichester Road and many of those in Mabledon Road and Meadow Road were built before the First World War, along with the Mission Church that was erected in 1912, but the houses towards the Waterloo Road end are of a style that appeared at the end of the 1920s.

This then was the situation at the beginning of the period under review and most of this housing stock still survives. There have been minor alterations, in the form of extensions and replacement doors and windows, that have kept the properties fashionable but the basic structures remain. Although the individual houses may look much as they did when they were new, the streets along which they are aligned now have a different appearance. There are few photographs from this period showing the residential roads in Tonbridge but one very noticeable feature in some of these early streets was the dominant iron railings, around the Victorian properties, that were removed during the Second World War. The front boundaries of many houses were decorated with this ironwork, which was often quite high, imparting a more confined feel to spaces around the homes than the remaining low walls on which they were fixed.

The streets appear to us rather empty as there were no parked cars or road markings. The surface of most residential roads was crushed stone which was rolled regularly to maintain a firm finish and the footpaths were made up with paving slabs or bricks. Lamp standards lined the pavements and, as photographic views of Pembury Road, Dry Hill Road and the lower end of Quarry Hill show, many of the roads were lined with trees.

We read, in the Council Minutes in November 1910, that the Town Wardens agreed to advance funding for a considerable number of lime trees to enhance some of the existing roads. These included Chichester Road, Mabledon Road, Stafford Road and several roads in the Barden area. The trees were duly planted, and surrounded with neat brick curbs. However the following year it was reported that some of the trees had died and it was suggested that leaky gas mains could be the cause. A few of these trees and their replacements still struggle to survive today but do not impart the same leafy qualities that were originally intended.

The amenities and features provided for these streets came under the guidance of the local council members who would have influenced the decisions taken by the committees on which they served. Since these members were mostly local business men, the amenities they were keen to promote, probably reflected their own commercial interests.

Changes in residential properties after 1910

Changes in towns occur in two significant areas, the loss of old property for redevelopment and the expansion of the limits of the town at the expense of the surrounding countryside. Growth, or decline, of our towns is a continuous process and any changes have to take account of what already exists. So that we find that most development, whether it involves demolition and reuse of a plot or a fresh project on a green field site, generally respects the boundaries already imposed upon the land by manmade or natural features.

In Tonbridge, redevelopment has resulted in the removal of many small properties from the centre of the town, and along the main thoroughfares. Waterloo Road, the old route to Tunbridge Wells, had the Good Intent public house on the corner opposite Albert Road and several other old cottages. In the Shipbourne Road, cottages in front of St Stephen's Church Hall, beside Elm Lane, were cleared away in the 1930s and replaced by the present house and shop. Others near the junction with Dry Hill Park Road were taken down when alterations were made to the road.

Short rows of cottages, such as Church Row, Kinnings Row, and Skinners Row, and some of the mid nineteenth century housing along Vale Road and in the Priory Road area, no longer exist. In Lamberts Yard 10 properties are listed in the 1909 *Kelly's Directory* but only the corn merchant is listed a decade later. However there were other residents: the Council Minutes of 5th July 1922 record that 11 pigs were kept there unlawfully and the owner was given two months to dispose of them.

Many of these older homes were the subject of inspection under the 1930 Housing Act, and a report to the Housing Committee dated November 1933 lists structural defects that include bulging walls and extensive dampness. Vermin were a serious problem as there was often inadequate rubbish storage space and no regular refuse collection service. The Council considered that some of these houses were not valued by the owners because the cost of reconditioning would be too high. Although some of the houses under investigation were condemned as substandard and demolished during the 1930s, others survived well into more recent times.

Because these tiny cottages seldom feature in the photographs, the only remaining evidence of them comes from lines on maps and directory entries or newspaper stories. Just occasionally a hint of their existence is revealed in the photographic record, as in one view of the south end of town, where the roof profile of Skinners Row can be glimpsed behind Webber's Greenhouse and Salford Terrace.

Government legislation, such as measures designed to raise the standard of the housing stock which eventually resulted in the loss of these substandard dwellings, was only one of the many changes that affected the appearance of Tonbridge during the 30 years after 1910. Any form of property development involves capital expenditure to meet an expected need but it also has to be economically worthwhile. Therefore land and property suitable for a change of use must be in the control of individuals with vision who are prepared to invest. In Tonbridge useful new building land close to the centre was limited, partly because of the problems associated with flooding but also the restrictions already imposed on the town by the river, railway, and existing road pattern.

During the period under review here, planning applications made to the Council came under the umbrella of the Health Committee. This was because earlier the planning controls were under the Public Health Acts with a view to improving the sanitary conditions of homes. The pattern of development was not seriously controlled and seems to have been led by builders and developers who applied for permission to put up one or two houses at a time. The Council Minutes show that applications to build new properties were usually followed a few months later by a certificate of occupation.

New houses were not necessarily built consecutively along the streets and Goldsmid Road is perhaps the best example in Tonbridge of the kind of development produced when houses of different dates are built in between already existing properties. This road demonstrates the changes in housing style as there are Victorian Villas, 1920s Cottage Style, 1930s semi-detached and later post-war houses interbuilt. These styles reflect the changing social attitudes through these periods.

The Victorian villa with its wide variety of decorative detail was based on a design that had been refined for over 40 years. The villa style is repeated in terraces, small rows and pairs across Britain. One feature of this late Victorian housing was the rear extension containing the scullery and washroom and often a small bedroom above. This rear extension had developed from a desire to increase accommodation without the inconvenience of three storeys. It had the advantage of space within the rear wall for a window to light the back rooms with access into the yard through a door from the scullery. In the poorer quality housing it was only this extension that contained any plumbing, keeping the damp smells from leaking joints away from the living space.

New housing between 1910 and 1920

In Tonbridge, villa style homes were still being built during the first decade of this century in Goldsmid Road, The Drive, Hectorage Road, Baltic Road, St. Mary's Road and the Douglas Road area, as well as along some of the main roads out of town. When this period of rapid expansion came to an end about 1909, comparatively few new houses were built until after the war. The railway financed some housing for its workers and other projects were started but put on hold until the 1920s. In Nelson Avenue, the terrace of eight cottages backing onto the railway, built in 1911, have small rear extensions.

At the front, the roof above the bay window on the ground floor extends to form a porch to each cottage so that it makes a continuous feature along the terrace. Nearby, in the new Barden Park Road, three pairs of villas were completed in 1912, in a style that would now be referred to as 'semi-detached' although this term was not coined until much later.

In 1914, 20 more houses were built, again for railway workers, in Hectorage Road. These homes were much more substantial than the Nelson Avenue terrace and consists of two blocks of six dwellings either side of a centre group of eight. The symmetry of the development is disguised by a wealth of architectural and decorative features which include tile hanging, rendering with timber or tile patterns which are repeated in different combinations throughout the blocks. Some houses are set forward from the main building line while others have large square bays. The exterior finish is brick or render and some have prominent coloured quoins. The front elevations are topped with varying size gables in a design which breaks up the roof line. These houses contrast with plain brick facades of those built opposite by Elkingtons in 1924.

Hectorage Road was only about 150 m (166 yards) long when first built and was extended as necessary to give access to these new homes. Many residential roads remained private; most new ones, like Wincliffe Road and Woodlands Road, created in 1911, were small and poorly constructed and surfaced. New roads were expensive to create so it is not surprising that most of the new houses were built along existing roads where ever possible. Goldsmid Road had been developed on the Somerhill Estate and the Council charged d'Avigdor Goldsmid for any repairs they carried out. Roads, theoretically, had to meet a high standard if they were to be adopted by the Council, and were required to be 'sewered, levelled, paved, metaled, flagged, channelled, made good and lighted'.

One speculative development designed to meet this council 'standard' involved land between the top end of the High Street and the Hadlow Road. Presumably Portman Park was conceived following the tradition of Dry Hill Park and Yardley Park as a site for quality housing. In August 1913 the proposal for a new road terminating in a circular drive met the council minimum requirement of 40 foot (12.2 m) width and the plans were passed for its adoption by the Committee although the Lovers' Walk footpath was considered too narrow at 8 feet (2.4m). However in conjunction with this planning application, the Council did agree to make up a section of footpath along the

Hadlow Road which had recently been widened and where homes were constructed after the war. Progress was slow in this ill-timed venture because apart from an existing timber cottage in Reed's Lane immediately behind houses on the Shipbourne Road, the first new house in Portman Park dates to 1915, but it was not until the 1920s that others followed and then the type of buildings erected were dictated by a very different economic and social climate.

New homes after the First World War

All wars are a catalyst for social change and by the early 1920s many traditional values had been turned aside. Family units became smaller and few people could afford to retain servants. One effect of this change was the introduction of the new cottage-style housing which was influenced by the earlier Garden City developments. The homes were thoughtfully designed for easy maintenance, with individual rooms often sharing more than one aspect, and great importance was placed on establishing pleasant healthy surroundings. Large gardens were provided for growing vegetables and the surrounding area was landscaped.

Throughout the war, rents and interest rates did not rise to keep pace with the relative monetary values and as a result property to let was no longer a worthwhile investment. Consequently, by the end of the war there were not enough houses and a shortage of labourers and building materials raised building costs. The problem was addressed by central government with generous grants to local authorities under the Addison Act in 1919 and the country set about creating homes for heroes.

A meeting of Tonbridge Urban District Council's Housing Committee on 6th November 1918 sanctioned the building of 20 new homes immediately, with a further fifty after the war. They also commissioned a report which suggested that a total of 300 new houses would be needed over the following years. The report added that local builders might be employed to work on a scheduled scheme and that brickworks at Lavender Hill and Baltic Road could be operated to overcome the shortage of building materials. Three suitable locations were chosen and the initial development began on a 20 acre site at Barden Park.

The Council chose to control the building operation themselves and

*Early Council Houses
in the Barden Road area*

employed a direct labour scheme in which groups of men worked on separate stages of the construction, moving on the next block of dwellings as the work progressed. By June 1921, 60 houses were in various stages of completion along Barden Road and Barden Park Road.

This first group of new council homes was designed to the high standard, as outlined in the government's 'Tudor Walters Report', and commanded higher rents than the subsequent council developments at Hectorage Road and Shipbourne Road. They are also the largest of the cottage-style homes with a parlour, a living room and either three or four bedrooms, kitchen and bathroom. The houses are arranged mainly in blocks of two or four and some are rendered externally. Variety is created by using a limited number of basic styles but they display similar design features. At the junction of Barden Road and Barden Park Road we can appreciate the 'garden suburbs' influence as a spacious effect is created by setting the corner pair of houses at an angle to the road. The gardens are wide and are easily reached from within the house; they form an integral part of the scheme, emphasizing the light and airy aspect of the whole development.

It soon become apparent that this form of development was expensive and a more realistic approach was then adopted by the Council, who scaled down the standard required and employed local builders for the work. The houses at the far end of the Barden Estate, beyond the railway bridge, are plain straightforward homes like the first Hectorage Road housing scheme that followed from 1923 onwards. They are arranged in blocks of two, four or six under a pitched roof with string courses of coloured bricks and small tiled porches as the only outstanding decorative features.

The Council bought 4.5 acres of Cage Green Farm land beside the Shipbourne Road in April 1925. The first 40 homes built on this site, south of what was to become The Ridgeway, are characterized by a return to the part-rendered cottage style featuring small gables and dormer windows. These homes were built using local bricks and tiles and although these are traditional materials, the grouping and the design set these homes apart from other properties in the Shipbourne Road at that time. The houses cost £1,132 for a pair of the larger parlour design and £1,909 for a block of four houses. All the dwellings were built with three bedrooms and were separated from the road by a wide grass strip planted with oak trees. The houses north of The Ridgeway were built next; one of the builders involved was Lewis Thorpe who also successfully tendered to build 43 pairs of council houses in the Hectorage Road area.

The early council housing was concentrated at Barden, Cage Green and Hectorage Road, extending to include Lodge Oak Lane and Somerhill Road later. There then followed a new site at Baltic Road commencing in 1929.

Later Council Housing

On average, 30 new homes a year were added to the council housing stock between 1929 and 1933 but only two three-bedroom council homes, those recently serving as offices on River Walk, were built in 1934. After a short break, the schemes recommenced in 1936 with the first of 92 homes on the Little Trench Estate. Here the development included eight one-bedroom bungalows as well as some four-bedroomed homes.

The council estates were built as cohesive units and the design of the houses did not alter dramatically over these years. The external appearance was maintained although internal improvements were made from time to time.

New private housing between 1920 and 1929

Private sector housing was slow to pick up after the war. The builders faced the same problems that the councils were struggling with, a shortage of money, materials and skilled labour. Many local builders were involved in building estates for the Council and this experience eventually led some of them to develop their own estates. Before the war houses were mainly built to let, then when rents and interest rates were held at pre-war levels new investment was slow. The government introduced subsidies in 1919 and again in 1923 to boost the housing stock but this initiative produced homes that were often of poor quality because these subsidies were only available on homes cheap enough to be affordable by ordinary working people.

Although there were several houses built during the first four years from 1920, only significant numbers of new homes were built in Yardley Park Road, where there were 12, and six in Portman Park. In Bourne Lane a completely new development of 10 properties, considered by some residents to be superior homes, commenced in 1923. Additional housing during the following years was mainly confined to the established built-up area, and new homes were added in Goldsmid Road, The Drive and Yardley Park Road.

The shortage of traditional building materials in the early 1920s encouraged new forms of construction using cheaper alternatives. Many of the sheet materials then used, such as early types of plasterboard, have not proved long-lasting but these lightweight materials, including the asbestos cement tiles that were so popular at this time, could be supported on a minimal frame work. Of six small cottages built in Cannon Lane in 1924, four have not survived.

The typical 1920s housing presents a very square box-like appearance and is often partly pebbledashed. Window frames had become heavy, with small opening top lights. Timber work on the small square bays and gable ends was often false, but painted to mimic a struc–tural purpose. From 1924 onwards bung–alows became popular and many examples exist in the town. They were relatively economic to build as land prices at this time were low. At sites in Lyons Crescent and at the

1920s-style housing

lower end of Yardley Park Road bungalows are partly rendered under a large roof. Often double fronted, with a recessed central doorway, these buildings demonstrate many features of this housing including the popular diamond-shaped asbestos cement roof tiles. In the Douglas Road area building began again in 1927, initially with bungalows, followed by the more uniform housing with small square ground floor bay windows.

New private housing between 1930 and 1939

During the mid 1930s there was an escalation in the number of new houses being built in the private sector. This was partly due to economic changes and was especially linked to the rise of building societies, as tax advantages favoured this form of investment. For the first time people could more easily get mortgages to buy their own property. The cost of the mortgage was not much greater than the rents of the time and families were encouraged by the social aspirations of the age to become home owners.

At the beginning of the 1930s, the built-up area around Tonbridge was expanding slowly. New properties were built for sale beyond the already existing properties along the Hadlow Road, and a little later along the Shipbourne Road. These new houses were built one or two at a time by small building firms whose financial arrangements were such that they needed a sale before they could commence the next pair. The houses display the individual characteristics that were designed to appeal to buyers. Even in the late 1920s there were signs of a new style emerging as the houses built in the Hadlow Road between Kendal Drive and Yardley Park Road show. The cement rendering was often enhanced by decoration and there was an increasing use of curved lines for bays and porches adding form to this new image. Moving further out of town, the later 1930s houses show that this fashion developed into the elaborate Mock Tudor appearance of the more expensive properties, where many non-structural timber beams were added to all the other decoration.

Development at this time was along the existing roads and this tended to leave areas of land behind the houses without adequate access. These awkward plots came to be developed later when the value of land made it worthwhile, but often they were used as sites for allotments or playing fields. In Tonbridge the road pattern and the relatively slow growth left few undeveloped areas isolated behind the housing. To access this back land behind the Shipbourne Road, Hadlow Road, Cornwallis Avenue and near Tilebarn Corner, advantage was taken of the undeveloped plots along the main roads. In the south, Hillview School was built on the farm site behind Hectorage Road, and entrance to it has never been easy.

By forming new roads, like the development initiated by Mr Thorpe when he built the avenue which bears his name, a site can be laid out economically. The Ordnance Survey Map shows how the very linear plan of the Thorpe Avenue site unexpectedly cuts across several field boundaries; it is however aligned to the council housing along the Shipbourne Road, which it abuts and which Mr Thorpe had built for the Council. This Southborough builder had been awarded tenders for work on the council housing and would have been well aware of the implications involved with such a project. The new road did not link with White Cottage Road but ended in a cul-de-sac on the brow of the rising land. Mr Thorpe applied for permission to build the first 28 bungalows in 1929 and must have borne the initial cost of installing the road and services. Occupation Certificates were issued for 10 homes in 1930 followed by six and seven in subsequent years, with further planning applications to complete the development. These bungalows were built in two different styles; those with a central porch had three bedrooms and faced the smaller two-bedroomed bungalows across a straight tree-lined road.

Another new road to the south of the town, Deakin Leas, received approval about this time but unlike Thorpe Avenue this was not the work of a single builder. The houses here are typical 1930s style, mainly semi-detached, and give the appearance of uniformity. But close inspection reveals many different shapes and features that indicate the work of local firms such as Elkington and Punnetts who were engaged in building here. The entrances in particular are very stylish with the arches over the door taken to a full horseshoe in some cases. By 1932 there were 18 houses completed, with the numbers increasing to 94 by the outbreak of war.

Mid-1930s housing

The area of the town, as built up before the 1930s, had the advantage that the land drained down towards the sewage works at Walters Farm. The provision of this service was a major consideration for any further development of the town. The extension of the housing towards Hadlow was only possible after the installation of a new pumping station at the low point of the Hadlow Road, together with the upgrading of the sewage works when new filter beds were added in 1931.

The creation of Cornwallis Avenue in 1930, as a bypass to the narrow winding Old Hadlow Road, together with the new drainage system, mark the beginning of a new phase which was eventually to change many acres of farmland in north Tonbridge into housing estates. Higham Lane at this time was still very narrow and dipped steeply where it crossed the stream. Most of the properties here were built after the road was improved in 1956.

During the 1930s, the area to the north of the town tended to attract a more expensive type of housing development, including some architect-designed properties. The early houses were widely spaced in a new road, The Ridgeway, and along the Hadlow Road towards Higham Lane and Cornwallis Avenue. Good examples of the 'modern movement' architecture are rare in Tonbridge but include 'Four Winds' by Frank Scarlett in Cornwallis Avenue. Features of this style can seen in other properties. Several houses have flat roofs and further horizontal lines are added by the metal windows, which had become wide and low, often continuing round the external corners of the building. The boldly coloured, green and blue roof tiles date from this period but the majority of the home owners preferred the more conventional materials. Tudor-style housing on a grand scale was popular along the Hadlow Road, the black and white effect of timbers against painted cement render picking out details of bays and other projections. The individual character of these mid 1930s houses is reinforced by the use of many different building materials set in decorative and interesting patterns. The brickwork contains a variety of bonding styles including herringbone, and tiles are built into the walls to form arches or bands. Again, the numbers of houses involved was very small, rather less than half a dozen per year in each of these roads, from 1930 until 1936. So the change from farmland to housing proceeded at a slow pace as new properties were built further from the town centre.

By the second half of the 1930s the pace of change increased as the building industry flourished. Improved transportation increased the availability of the new manufactured components for house building. Using concrete roof tiles, steel beams and lintels with other mass-produced items like window-frames, estates of new houses were quickly constructed on green fields around most the larger towns in the south-east.

In Tonbridge, the small curved roads leading off Cornwallis Avenue are part of this expansion. This development was planned in 1934 on land of the Greentrees Estate and by 1937 a total of 98 homes had been completed. The change here was halted by the war, leaving Estridge Way, Greentrees Avenue and Orchard Drive unfinished with 92, 29 and 13 dwellings respectively. Only after 1946 were the roads properly surfaced and the estate completed.

The properties in Estridge Way are mainly houses, but the bulk of the development of the Greentrees Estate is in the form of bungalows, which again show the economic advantages of these low rise structures which were cheap to build when land was readily available. The bungalows have enormous barn-like roofs, weighed down under a sea of concrete tiles, and these tend to dominate the estate. In Greentrees Avenue pairs of brick-built bungalows alternate in style with hipped or gable-end roof above a bay window. Very few of the original heavy wooden window-frames survive, while fewer still retain the small diamond panes at the top. Only a small proportion of the properties were built with garages; most were added later. These estates are a long way from the town. Local shops and services in the area were rather sparse and families living here must have relied heavily on tradesmen delivering goods. There were limited facilities near the Hadlow Road, which at various times had included an athletics ground and a small golf course and later a shop, garage and tea garden.

At the other end of Tonbridge, the familiar view of the housing covering the lower slopes of the hill to the south was well established. The slate on the roof of the older properties nearer to the town giving way to the dominating red of brick and tiles on the higher ground. The growth here continued with additional private housing in Deakin Leas and in the roads that run up towards Baltic Road. The Kings Road and Mountfield Park development added a further 73 new houses just prior to the outbreak of the Second World War in 1939.

Another area where new housing made a significant change to the locality in which it was set, was around the junction of Quarry Hill and Brook Street. When the new houses were built on the south side of Brook Street in 1935, the high banks of the narrow lane were cut back to widen the road. This led to improved access to Judd School and other properties nearby.

Around the corner, in Quarry Rise, the development represents affordable quality housing built around 1936. These properties are spacious and substantial, mainly semi-detached, with four bedrooms and two receptions room. Although they are all basically one design, they have a variety of individual features and were initially offered for sale as labour-saving homes costing £1,020 with garage or £975 without. This Quarry Rise development includes the first service road built in Tonbridge, and other early examples in the area include Barclay Avenue where 9 houses were built in 1939 and Foxbush in Hildenborough. The concept of separating houses from the main thoroughfares as introduced with these service roads was not new, of course, but examples like the council housing built along Shipbourne Road, during the 1920s, were first served by footpaths and did not initially have vehicular access. The service roads, which were introduced after 1935, were part of a continuing progression of measures designed to improve road safety.

Changes due to increasing traffic

The rise in car ownership changed the appearance of new properties by adding garages and driveways and also changed the relationship between the property and the main roads. Along the Hadlow Road and the Shipbourne Road we can see how this relationship changed, especially in the 1930s. The early houses have gardens and drives near the road but the later houses are set well back with wide grass verges allowing good sight lines to see the approaching traffic. Service roads reduced the number of access points onto the busy routes.

The Council spent more time considering the management of traffic and its effect on the town. Parking and provision for vehicles became part of the planning process. Most early garages were free standing and constructed of timber or sheet materials like metal and asbestos. A change in the legislation in 1935 required fire-resisting materials to be used if the garages formed an integral part of the dwelling. The first purpose-built garage mentioned in the Council Minutes during the period under review, was for a house in Ashburnham Road in 1920, although several of the larger Victorian properties already had coach houses and other types of outhouse that were used to store cars.

Small petrol filling stations appeared on all the main roads, often on the edge of the development beyond the housing. The garages along the London Road, Hadlow Road, Pembury Road and Shipbourne Road were often associated with refreshment stops that catered for the weekend trade, as 'day trippers' found the freedom of the open road with their cycles, cars and motor bikes. The Boiling Kettle and The Green Rabbit were on the A21 in Hildenborough, and in the Shipbourne Road the Sun Dial café stood beside St Bernard's Garage. This site was between Brickyard Cottages and St Bernard's Road, well beyond the residential expansion which ended prior to the dip in which York Parade was later built.

Changes in the High Street

As well as at these new garages, petrol was also available at outlets within the town. Pumps stood on the pavement outside the premises of Charles Baker's Cycle and Motor works in the High Street at Nos 150 and 152. This business was established before 1910 and by the mid 1930s prospering sufficiently to consider rebuilding the motor showroom in a modern style. Some of the impression of the Modern Movement influence can still be gained from the present shop front, with the horizontal roof line and bronze trim around the doors and windows. The shop front originally held curved glass that enhanced the display of the fine new cars which were otherwise difficult to view in the poor quality lighting available at that time. The Council had reservations about the proposal for the new building but planning permission was given on condition that the paintwork was brown to blend in with the surrounding shops. This is a notable contrast to the recent transformation of this building, which was painted vivid blue when first converted into a restaurant. Now this has been changed and also some decorative metal screens designed for

HIGH STREET, TONBRIDGE.   4811

The High Street showing later changes, including Burtons and James Walkers, as well as Sainsburys, the Post Office, a pedestrian refuge and a bus stop opposite Medway Wharf Road.

the windows, that helped to retain the character of the buiulding, have been removed.

Some of the other changes in the High Street during the 1930s were directly linked to the increasing number of vehicles. Pedestrians were given new central refuges in the road at busy crossing points and there was a general increase in the number of traffic signs and signals. The extra traffic did not create serious jams but rather little knots of vehicles, held up behind large lorries or buses negotiating the tight spaces within the town. To ease traffic flow, many awkward street corners were rounded off and several little buildings and parts of others were removed in this process. The road surfaces were considerably improved with a tarred and gravel finish.

During the inter-war years the number of shop premises in the High Street, or even elsewhere in the town, did not increase to the extent that might be expected, compared with the rising number of new homes. A few extra shops were built in Bradford Street and Lyons Crescent and some of the High Street houses, particularly the terraces at each end of the town, were converted by adding shops to fronts. Many of the existing shops were altered during the 1930s and there were changes in shopping patterns. Long-established family businesses continued to exist but the new multiple chain stores like W. H. Smith, Timothy Whites, Dewhursts and MacFisheries were becoming increasingly popular. Advertising played a major role in attracting custom, and shop windows were carefully arranged to draw attention to certain items of merchandise. There must have been great excitement, especially among the younger generation, when Woolworths Bazaar came to Tonbridge. We have an example of one of their stores built in 1929, on the site of Hubbies the bakers and a hairdressers. We can judge how the building line has been set back a little here and although the shop has been extended and the front altered many times, the first floor facade appears to retain the original metal framed windows.

Many of the national stores opening shops in Tonbridge High Street introduced a corporate image by rebuilding premises to their own style. Boots the Chemist is one example, they already had a shop in town but they combined with the adjoining property, replacing the facade of the double unit at Nos 26 and 28. The horizontal roof line and brick banding show the 1930s style and the decorative motif showing a pestle and mortar, that is still to be seen in the brickwork, indicates that they then had every intention of staying.

Another example was at No. 60 High Street which used to be a splendid shop for Burtons the tailors. Burtons plans to rebuild on the site of the Central Hall were submitted in 1936. The building sits awkwardly on this streamside site but its classical facade is impressive with pilasters topped by a heavy brick parapet. This classical trade mark is typical of many Burton shops but unlike some other towns where their stores are to be found, in Tonbridge they failed to achieve planning permission for a public hall above the trading floor, although it was later used as a social club.

One area of the High Street where several changes were made to buildings lies between East Street and Lyons Crescent. Beginning in 1929, plans were submitted to replace a bootmakers shop at No. 105 with the new Barclays Bank building. Then about 1937, the adjoining property was rebuilt as a showroom for the Tonbridge Urban District Council Electricity Supply Department, with offices above. The facade of the Electricity Showroom, at No. 111, was similar in size to the three-storey Georgian house that it replaced. However, the scale of another development nearby, on the corner of East Street, was drastically altered when it was rebuilt about the same time. Whites Ironmongers shop, which was a small two-storey, brick-faced timber-framed building, occupied part of the site. When this was redeveloped, the corner of the new building was splayed, giving a little extra width at the road junction but the new three-storey building must have seemed large to those already familiar with the town. This area, opposite the Chequers, has some typical 1930s-style shop and office developments with classical-type features and decorative details that are remarkably similar on both the Electricity showroom and on the building at the corner of East Street.

All change at the Station

Regular visitors to the town would have noticed these new buildings and other alterations when business updated or changed hands. If they arrived by train they would also be aware of the changes to the station. The Victorian facade of this brick-built structure presented three pairs of arched windows each side of the central doorway. There was a pediment above this door and a decorative balustrade at the roofline. The building was topped by two high chimneys. New glossy faience tiles covered the front of the building after plans to modernize the image of the station were put before the Council in

February 1930. The pairs of windows remained but they were now square with small metal panes instead of wooden sashes. There was a canopy over the entrance with the name of the station in bold letters centered above it.

Modernisation of the station seems to have added a new vitality to the south end of the town and with it the first real sign of additional shopping facilities. Before Quarry Hill Parade was built, this was the site of Webber's Nursery and it provided an open aspect towards the First World War memorial which stood in the middle of the road at the junction of Quarry Hill and Pembury Road. The nursery moved to a new site in Brook Street, although Mr Webber continued trading nearby where he had a greenhouse and shop next to Salford Terrace. Single-storey extensions for shops were added to the front of several houses on Salford Terrace and a new parade of shops was built opposite. Plans for the new Quarry Hill Parade were submitted to the Council in October 1935. This development with its black and white Tudor-style decoration was the first in Tonbridge to introduce the new customer parking bays but these have since become part of the bus stop. The new parade of shops had flats above, and included tobacconist, hairdresser, wool shop, café and baker.

On the adjacent site, at the corner of Quarry Hill and Priory Road, a new showroom and workshop for Tonbridge Motor Services, Speedwell House, was a fine example of 1930s architecture with very angular detailing and large metal window frames emphasizing the horizontal lines. Like so many other new buildings of this period, it was only the public face that was impressive with little consideration given to the rear elevations.

The Ritz cinema which opened in July 1937 is another example, but here it was the interior that tended to be glitzy and sparkling whilst the outside was a rather dull brick edifice, with some horizontal banding, which concealed the structural frame.

Steel and concrete construction techniques were becoming widely used and the Ritz and Speedwell House were among a long list of structures that were regularly inspected by the Council Engineer's and Surveyor's Department. The list also included shops like Boots, Burtons and Frank East, who had made internal alterations to their premises, but increasingly featured industrial properties because these buildings tended to be on a larger scale. New works for South East Tar Distillers and The Distillers Company were among many buildings sited along Vale Road. Avebury Avenue was another area expanding in this period. Here, the new 1930s buildings included Bakers Garage, The Territorial Army Centre and the Telephone Exchange, as well as alterations to accommodate a new bus garage at the corner of Holford Street.

The telephone exchange, which was opened in 1939, is evidence of the broadening horizon of our market town but by this time, attention was focused on the impending war rather than on any further development. The Council Committees organised the air raid precautions and made preparations to construct air raid shelters for the inhabitants as well as allocating additional ground for burial if the need arose.

Summary of the growth and changing appearance in Tonbridge

The properties which existed in 1910 were the product of centuries of growth and consequently displayed a range of architectural styles. The old photographs show that the town centre buildings varied in size and shape as well as style, giving the High Street an irregular appearance. The methods of construction varied according to the age and type of property, but because the stone, timber and bricks were mainly local, these introduced a subtle harmony to the scene. By the late nineteenth century brick had become the most popular building material but there were still many timber-framed buildings including several small ones faced with shiplap boarding that was often tarred or whitewashed.

The changes to the appearance of Tonbridge during the years from 1910 to 1939 were many but they were not all dramatic. Small alterations were more usual. In the town centre, the demolition of the brewery with other riverside industry leading to the creation of River Walk marks one major change.

Shopping patterns changed too. The Victorians had founded small shops amongst their houses. These continued to thrive but hardly any new corner shops were included in the 1920s and 1930s developments. The town centre shops became relatively more important as they drew their custom from a wider area and became more specialized. Several shop premises were rebuilt, often to a larger scale and the addition of Quarry Hill Parade improved the shopping south of the station. Increasing competition in the High Street encouraged shopkeepers to mount attractive window displays to sell their goods and the work of signwriters was everywhere to be seen. Not only did the names painted on the fascias grow larger and bolder over these years with improved new paints and materials, but any blank area of brickwork on buildings within view of the town was likely to get covered with advertisements.

In 1910 the residential area associated with the town was situated within a one mile radius of the centre. The existing road system (with a few additions) gave a framework for further development until the council schemes commenced. The introduction of the council estates was significant in several ways, they expanded the boundaries of the built-up area with groups of homes that formed blocks within the landscape and introduced a new role for the Council, as landlords. The new private housing grew slowly at first, filling the vacant plots along the streets, but then developments extended to include new roads. Until the end of the 1930s these roads were often straight, but later they were planned to make economical use of a more extensive site with perhaps just a single exit on to the main road.

There were about 3,300 houses in the town in 1910 and, although there were some changes to the boundaries and many small properties were demolished, this number had risen to over 5,400 homes, including 661 council houses, by the end of the 1930s. The style of the new housing changed throughout this period, the early examples following the Victorian tradition both in the form of layout, as villas or terraces, and in the applied decoration. By 1920 the housing became more square and boxlike, but apart from the new council estates they were only built in very small numbers, whereas in the 1930s the tendency was to build larger groups often in estates.

By 1939 the extent of the built-up area was still within a one and a half mile radius of the town centre, even though there was considerable linear development towards the north covering many acres of land. Most of the new homes were sited to the south and the south-east and on more spacious plots north of the town. The development along the Shipbourne Road and the Hadlow Road, extended to include new roads, The Ridgeway, Cornwallis Avenue and the Greentrees Park Estate, which intruded into the farmland behind. Inter-war 'ribbon development' is absent to the south of the town where many residential roads already existed. Here some of the new housing forms discrete blocks, as in the Douglas Road area. In the areas bounded by Deakin Leas and Baltic Road and on the land rising towards Lodge Oak Lane, the development included council and private homes which formed compact neighbourhoods.

Early in this period many industries were located within the town. Some workshops and businesses were situated behind the High Street shops where the products were sold, but most industry was related to the river and the railway. During the 1920s and to a greater extent throughout the 1930s, industries relocated to Vale Road, Cannon Lane and Avebury Avenue, where there were several new purpose-built premises. Printing and publishing remained a major industry in the town, but there was a growing trend towards road and transport related trades including tar distillers.

The changeover from horse-drawn to powered vehicles increased the transport available for people and goods. Many new features such as road signs, petrol stations and car repair workshops were introduced. The roads had to change to accommodate the extra traffic and most of the main routes within the built-up area were widened during this time. A revolution in roadbuilding techniques, including the use of concrete, improved the surfaces making them more suitable for the increasing traffic. Laybys, street parking and service roads were all introduced in response to the growing number of vehicles.

Over the years Tonbridge has experienced some major changes and a host of more subtle alterations as it has adapted to the requirements of each new generation. Before 1910 there were sweeping changes when the whole west side of the lower High Street was redeveloped at the turn of the century, but these buildings remained largely unaltered throughout the period under review. Generally the changes in the town between 1910 and 1939 are less obvious than those in the periods before and after. The hallmark of this period seems to be a general lack of regulation to control the many changes that did occur.

Sources

Ordnance Survey Maps, 25-inch, 1907-09, and 1933-36

Kelly's Directories for the years 1909,1919, 1929, 1934, 1939 and 1940

Chalklin, C. (ed.), *Late Victorian and Edwardian Tonbridge* (Kent County Library, 1988)

Tapsell, M., *Memories of Kent Cinemas*, (Plateway Press, 1987)

Barrett, H. and Phillips, J., *Suburban Style – The British Home 1840-1960*, (Macdonald, 1987)

Tonbridge Urban District Council Minute Books, Ref UD/To/Am 18-27 (1910-39)

Tonbridge Urban District Council Year Books 1911, 1914, 1921, 1931, 1934, 1936

Tonbridge Urban District Council Engineer's and Surveyor's Dept Reports 1905-30, 1935-38, Works in hand August 1939

Photographs from the collection of the Tonbridge Historical Society

Acknowledgements

I am grateful to Sydney Simmons for help and advice and Derek Hopcroft for line drawings.

Boating on the Medway, near the Big Bridge, in the early years of the Twentieth Century.

Transport and Travel
Part 1: River, Roads and Private Cars

Peter Swan

Over a period of two hundred years the population of Tonbridge has grown from some 2,000 in 1800 to 15 times that figure at the time of writing. The forms of public conveyance seen on our streets have progressed from stagecoach to modern minibus, by way of horse-bus and motor omnibus.

The network and number of the streets themselves have evolved, with Tonbridge High Street in particular subject to changing theories of town planning. The successive widening schemes begun in the 1890s have now been put in reverse, amid much controversy, by the introduction of traffic calming and pinch-points in the 1990s.

The advent of the railway in 1842 had led to marked alteration in the nature of the local community, and supplanted the River Medway as Tonbridge's primary artery for trade and commerce. In due course a growing section of the town's working population was to commute to the capital by rail. Similarly, between the wars, the bus and the motor car accelerated social change in rural Kent. Village life became less isolated when inhabitants were able to share employment and leisure opportunities in nearby or distant towns.

In this chapter and the next we shall examine the infrastructure and modes of transport and travel in and around Tonbridge, viewing them as appropriate against the background of developments nationwide.

The River Medway

The Medway provided one means of pleasurable transport for the people of Tonbridge and visitors to the town. In his 1922 report to the Urban District Council the Surveyor, L. W. Nott, wrote, 'If opinion is divided on the question of navigation, one thing is clear – that the river above the Great Bridge to the Weir Hole is a great asset to the town, to be ... preserved, and to be possessed for its recreative value'.

The local guidebooks of the period point to the River Medway as one of our major tourist attractions. That of 1930 well described its appeal: 'The view from the river or the new riverside promenade just above the Great Bridge, with the historic castle opposite and the woodland around, is unique … The Medway, with its tributaries, completely encircles the town's recently acquired sports ground of 50 acres'.

As a locked river the Upper Medway lent itself to boating and canoeing in rural surroundings, and still does so today. In addition to several boathouses with fleets for private hire, the Tonbridge Boating Club had its base at New Wharf, owning craft for both recreation and racing. The pen of water below Cannon Bridge was used by Tonbridge School for competitions with other public schools. Annual events held on the river included a regatta on Skinners' Day, and the hugely entertaining Venetian Fête.

Between the wars the Urban District Council was responsible for issuing pleasure boat licences. In May 1923 the Council resolved that 'all boats plying for hire on the portion of river in this Council's district be licensed at a fee of 2s 6d each for this season'. In subsequent years the Minutes show a concern to avoid raising fees to a point where boating for pleasure became too costly for owner and hirer alike.

Apart from much 'messing about on the river' and some serious competition, what part did this considerable artery of transportation play in the economy of Tonbridge between the wars? It certainly presented a constant threat of flooding, but was no longer the working river of earlier times when 'hufflers' rather than horses pulled barges laden with hops, coal and timber, manpower being used due to the lack of a proper tow-path along the Medway.

The advent of rivalry from the railway from the 1840s onwards had led to a decline in river trade, and damaging neglect was to follow. In 1910 the East Farleigh lock collapsed, closing the river to navigation for several years. Although reconstruction did take place, enabling boats to pass through again by 1915, the River Medway was never to recover its commercial and economic importance to Tonbridge.

Following the failure of the 170-year-old Medway Company in 1911, Kent County Council (KCC) promoted legislation which created the Upper Medway Navigation and Conservancy Board to maintain the river. It was the 'Medway Conservators' who undertook the major rebuilding in 1915, including new weirs (as at the town lock) and the renewal of Cannon Bridge. The original estimate of £30,000 was less than a third of the final cost, but a partially successful flood relief scheme for Tonbridge accompanied the re-opening of the Medway for navigation.

The official opening on 31 August 1915 featured a tug and barge trip from Maidstone to Tonbridge. The event was held amid great celebration and what proved to be gross over-optimism. In its issue of September 3, the *Tonbridge Free Press (TFP)* predicted that 'from a commercial point of view there are now immense possibilities. At any rate the local trader will not be so much at the mercy of the railway companies'. But in the event the First World War and the rapid development of road transport which followed conspired with the old enemy to prevent the revival of trade by river to an economically viable level. In 1924 timber was still being brought to the Baltic Saw Mills and coal to the Tonbridge Gas Works by sailing barges, but the last regular commercial delivery was in 1927. When control passed to the River Medway Catchment Board in 1934 the leisure facility alone survived.

On Foot and by Bike

Walking and cycling were essential means of reaching their place of work for many during the 1920s and 1930s. For some they are still so today. These more gentle forms of travel also lend themselves to leisure activity, and were regular pastimes for enthusiasts in and around Tonbridge between the wars.

Kelly's Directory for 1934 listed in its commercial section no less than 29 local traders who earned a living from selling, making or repairing boots and shoes. There were four cycle retail/repair shops, including one belonging to the Woolley family of cricketing fame. During the First World War, Charles Baker & Co. in the High Street had advertised in the *TFP* for 28 April 1916 as follows: 'RALEIGH, the all steel bicycle, guaranteed for ever. Ride it and enjoy your week-ends'. There were 13 garages or motor engineers in the town by 1934. Such businesses would also have catered for countless motorcyclists. The needs of horse owners and riders around Tonbridge were met by a blacksmith, a saddler and a harness maker, while river craft could be hired and maintained at three or four boatyards on the Medway.

The healthy exercise of walking, given acres of adjacent countryside, has been a pleasure in every generation. It was further encouraged here by local council developments at both ends of the town during the inter-war period.

River Walk was constructed from 1920. A plaque on the Avebury Avenue bridge to the sports ground indicates that both were opened by Lord Hardinge of Penshurst on 23 June 1923. In the *Official Guide to Tonbridge* of 1930 the walk was described as a 'riverside promenade' following a route from the Great Bridge in the High Street to the junction of Avebury Avenue and Barden Road, via a river crossing at Buley's Weir. This project had helped to relieve the problem of unemployment during the winters of 1921-23.

In north Tonbridge, nothing like as built up then as now, Woodland Walk was developed in the early 1930s as a delightful footpath some one and a quarter miles in length running beside the Pen Stream from Shipbourne Road across to Higham Lane. The Minutes of the Urban District's 'Woodland Walk Committee' record an expenditure on the project of well over £1000 by October 1933, prior to the official opening some six months later.

Cycling, too, was a popular leisure pursuit at this time, whether informally enjoyed in ones and twos, or as a club activity. But those who used pedal power between the wars shared the highways with an increasing volume of motor traffic, unlike the slow moving horse power typically depicted in earlier local postcards. Subsequently a KCC document of 1948 entitled *Planning Basis for Kent* recommended that 'a bypass for Tonbridge should be provided to supplement the A21, with cycleways and footpaths.' A network of cycleways is only now becoming a somewhat controversial end-of-century reality.

Under the headline 'Enthusiasm runs high among Cyclists' the *TFP* of 9 March 1934 recorded the first annual dinner of the Southborough and District Wheelers as 'an organisation which caters for the Tonbridge district...' The list of annual awards indicated a competitive edge to the activities of this particular club.

Private Motoring

Between the wars the motorcar remained something of a middle-class luxury, largely for enjoyment at weekends. More economical motorcycles were popular with young men, but also for family transport with cyclecars attached. The working man and woman walked everywhere, or owned one of the ubiquitous bicycles (costing about £6) for day-to-day use. Buses brought workers and shoppers to the towns, enabling 14 per cent of the economically active residents of rural districts to reach employment in urban areas by 1921.

Many tradespeople made home deliveries between the wars, with delivery vans replacing the horse and cart. The first council houses were built in the 1920s with no provision for garages, and many communities grew through ribbon developments of semi-detached housing along the main roads into town.

Among Tonbridge's first private car owners, around the turn of the century, were Harry Beckett, William Arnold (whose East Peckham firm made early motor cars) and Alfred Cornell, a local jeweller and watchmaker. Only by the close of the nineteenth century had 'light locomotives' been allowed on the highway, with the condition that every motorcar be preceded by a man carrying a red flag to warn those still employing horse-power. By World War One lighting-up times were listed in the local newspaper.

Motorcar ownership was limited largely to professional people before the Great War, but by 1939 thousands on more modest incomes could afford a car. From 1921 taxation law favoured the small, cheaper vehicle; mass production was soon to offer the Austin Seven, Morris Cowley and Ford Model T. Statistics for cars registered in Kent underline the trend towards private motoring. There were only a few thousand across the county in 1908, over 20,000 in 1926 and approaching four times that many (80,000) by 1938.

Garages and Dealers

The provision of garage facilities, therefore, became increasingly important – not least the availability of petrol pumps. The Council Minutes indicate the regulatory role of the local authority in the granting (or otherwise) of petroleum licences. For example, in April 1919 the Anglo-American Oil Company was refused permission to increase its petrol storage capacity on railway premises near Lavender Hill from 1000 to 1500 gallons. In the early 1920s the same records show that petrol licences were granted to various garages for a year at a time (including Chas. Baker and the Ashbys) provided a quantity of dry sand was stored nearby as a safety measure. In July 1924 over 20 petroleum licences were renewed. In 1933 A. J. Ashby's plan to build a steel-framed garage between Wincliff Road and Albert Road was provisionally agreed, a location from which Renny's were trading by 1934. By the advent of the Second World War safety precautions had become more stringent, for in June 1939 the Council's General Purposes Committee recommended that all new

Ashby's premises on Quarry Hill in the 1920s (author's photograph).

petrol pumps licensed in future should be fitted with a 'cut-out' mechanism. As further confirmation of the spread of car ownership, numerous Tonbridge residents made successful application during this period to erect private garages on land adjoining their houses.

Car dealers advertising in the local press afford a valuable insight into the contemporary motor trade. H. E. Hall & Co. had been one of Woolley's competitors in the cycling market in the late 1800s. By 1913 Hall's (in the High Street opposite Botany – see photograph on page 21) were dealing in 20-25 horsepower Studebakers at £295, and a year later also offered Singer, Riley and Clyno cars.

The dominant Tonbridge car dealer between the wars, however, appears to have been Chas Baker & Co., near the former Post Office in the High Street. In 1913 they were agents for British, American and Continental models made by Ford, RCH, Humber, Swift, Delage and Hotchkiss, as well as selling motor and pedal-cycles. In the 1920s Baker promoted Morris cars; he also ran Tonbridge Taxi Cabs Limited.

*Advertisement by Chas Baker & Co. (*Tonbridge Free Press, *8 January 1937)*

Legislation was passed in 1934, and by 1935 the local paper advertised driving lessons: 'COMPULSORY DRIVING TEST – assure that you pass the official test by having competent instruction from Chas Baker and Co. of Tonbridge Ltd., 150 and 153 High Street' (*TFP*, 5 April 1935).

A Short Storey

Once upon a time motorcars were made here in Tonbridge ... but only for a couple of years around 1920. Jack Storey built his factory on the location of the Old Town Mills in Cannon Lane in 1919, where there are now modern DIY stores. He paid Tonbridge Urban District Council the sum of £3,000 for the 48 acre site.

The Storey family from London had a background in engineering. When their father died in 1913 Jack and Will took over the successful Storey Machine Tool Company at New Cross. The brothers sensed an opportunity to profit from the post-war motoring boom, so Jack attracted a workforce in Tonbridge by offering outstanding wages for the period.

Several different models were produced for the discerning motorist, the largest being a 20 horsepower, four-seater 'Tonbridge' saloon selling at £1,200. The customer could select from a choice of colours and upholstery. Every Storey car could be recognised by its distinctive oval radia-

Storey 'Tonbridge' saloon, 1920 (from Old Motor & Vintage Commercial, *1965).*

tor. Other models proudly presented at the Glasgow motor show in early 1920 were the 'London' coupé, the 'Kent' open two-seater coupé, and the 'Kent Tourer', all available with bespoke bodywork. For a time the prospects looked good, but sadly the operation was soon to collapse. Several hundred fine Storey cars had been made, but the slump of late 1920 undermined the ambitious venture. The future lay with the mass production of motor cars.

In more favourable financial times Jack Storey's limited company might have prospered. History records, however, that it was forced into liquidation when the bank withdrew its support. The fateful meeting at which the decision to close was taken took place at Hilden Manor on 7 December 1920. The manufacture of cars in Tonbridge came to an acrimonious halt, throwing dozens of local employees out of work. The Storey brothers retreated to London with heavy losses from their failed enterprise.

Roads and their Upkeep

The Urban District's engineers and surveyors had to plan, provide and maintain an adequate system of roads, paths and other facilities associated with town life in general, and travel in particular. I am indebted to one of their later twentieth century successors, Sydney Simmons, for much of the detail which follows. The remainder was found largely in the Minute Books of Tonbridge Urban District Council (TUDC) housed at the public library.

The Surveyor's staff in 1923 included a Road Foreman, whose wages were £4 10s 0d per week, later increased by five shillings in April 1929. Their task was complicated by repeated serious flooding. Wear and tear on the roads cannot have been helped by what at the time was described as an 'overdeveloped' bus service, on Quarry Hill in particular. The weekly cattle market and annual cattle fair in October were doubtless good for trade, but must have left their mark on the town's highways.

An on-going programme of road resurfacing was essential. For example, the lower half of Quarry Hill was resurfaced with Belgian granite in 1921 at a cost of about £1,000. In the same year TUDC bought a secondhand steam roller and a new tar boiler. The Surveyor's Report of 1922 indicated that horse power was still very much in use; the Council's five horses had a poor sickness record, due to overwork on main roads and unemployment schemes. Indeed, as late as July 1930 the then Surveyor, William L. Bradley, reported 'as soon as the motor vehicles are in commission we can dispense with three horses ... Now that the Council have 10 motor vehicles I think it would be advisable to have our own petrol pump, buying in bulk'.

In the early 1920s the Ministry of Transport and Kent County Council had classified the roads in Tonbridge. Rated as first class were London Road, High Street, Hadlow Road, Pembury Road, Shipbourne Road and Quarry Hill. Bordyke and Five Oak Green were ranked as second class roads. The cost of maintaining the first class roads was shared between the Ministry and KCC, with no contribution from the Urban District. According to contemporary reports from the town's Engineer and Surveyor, more than six miles of residential roads were made up and taken over between the years 1905 and 1930. The TUDC Yearbook indicates that in 1935 the local Council was responsible for 5.44 miles of delegated County roads and 19.10 miles of other (District) roads, making a total of 24.54 miles of carriageway.

At the close of the inter-war period the 'works in hand' included reconstruction and resurfacing on High Street, Quarry Hill and Pembury Road at an estimated cost of £6,970.

Road Schemes and Car Parking

Traffic congestion through the town centre led to serious consideration being given between the wars to the idea of a Tonbridge bypass, eventually to be constructed as recently as 1970. An inconclusive conference on the subject, involving the Ministry of Transport and Kent County Council, was held at the Castle in 1938. The County did not see such a scheme as a priority, whereas the Ministry favoured a bypass in view of increased traffic expected on completion of the Dartford Tunnel.

Instead, some road widening was progressed during the inter-war period. When KCC wrote to the local Council in late 1925, citing the 'Road Improvement Act' of the same year, Tonbridge Urban District Council was able to respond that widening was already in hand on the Hadlow and Shipbourne Roads. A decade or so later it was the turn of Brook Street and Lodge Oak Lane. A scheme to complete widening of the High Street up to the Chequers Inn and on Bordyke Corner was postponed; it was still considered 'an excellent main thoroughfare' by the author of the 1930 *Official Guide to Tonbridge*. In mid-December 1939 the General Committee reported that 'owing to the present national situation' the County Council has postponed carrying out improvements to Tonbridge High Street. These would have included the acquisition of certain properties required for widening of the High Street between 'Fosse Bank' and 'Graylings'.

Car parking was already a problem in Tonbridge between the wars. In 1928 the Surveyor was asked to report on the use of 'suitable portions of certain streets for the parking of cars'. He duly reported to the October meeting that parking at the Slade on market days could be both increased and improved by the provision of white lines to indicate the recognised parking area. At the same time the Surveyor informed council members that unauthorised parking in the High Street called for the introduction of white lines, a limit on the number of vehicles allowed, a short-stay system or even a total ban. The Surveyor's suggested accommodation for cars was as follows: Vale Road – 40 cars, Slade – 26, High Street – 13, Avebury Avenue – 10, making a total of 89. Other possible locations identified were Bradford Street (8), Botany (15) and possible use of River Lawn as a temporary car park for100 cars, which would be 'of great convenience for visitors to the Sports Ground'.

Despite attention to car parking provision at the Slade, adequate space for commercial vehicles appears to have been lacking. The Council received a petition in August 1937 from local residents 'protesting against the parking of lorries on market days'. Partly to ease the general congestion in that area when the market was in progress the Surveyor (now Mr Bertie Bishop) came up with a 1938 estimate of £290 (minimum) for laying out land in Medway Wharf Road for a car park, over which the Royal Automobile Club was to be consulted. Approval was given and the work completed in July of the same year, providing Tonbridge with a permanent off-road parking facility. However, the Baltic Saw Mills Co. Ltd. did extract an undertaking from TUDC that 'if and when river traffic is resumed and the land in question is required by the Company for the landing and unloading of barges ... then the Council will revoke the order constituting such land a place for the parking of cars'. We read nothing in the Minutes concerning payment for parking, which was a post-war development.

Traffic Control and Road Safety

Actual statistics for the volume of traffic in and through Tonbridge between the wars have proved elusive, although a yearly census does appear to have been taken on behalf of the Ministry of Transport during part of August.

Traffic control was fairly lax everywhere during the 1920s. We read that in 1922 the local council was not encouraged to introduce speed limits in the town, but standard warning signs were adopted. It was not until early 1935 that the Surveyor reported on a proposed national speed limit of 30 mph in built up areas.

We do, however, have some figures for road accidents in and around Tonbridge dating from the early 1930s, and an interesting insight concerning police views at the time. Superintendent W. Shepherd told the Highways Committee in late 1933 that the problem of traffic congestion in Tonbridge High Street could even be a blessing in disguise. He suggested that parked and stationary vehicles made the town centre a safer place by slowing down the traffic. His logic was supported by recent accident figures, not least the fact that the accident rate was markedly higher in the more rural parts of his area. In 1931, for example, there had been six fatal accidents (none in Tonbridge) and out of 251 cases of personal injury, only 15 took place in the High Street between the daytime hours of 9 a.m. and 6 p.m. We cannot be sure of the Superintendent's views on widening schemes (or pinch points) but must assume he would have favoured the latter.

By early 1934 the Surveyor was in a position to submit Ministry of Transport/KCC proposals for automatic traffic signals at the junction of

Pembury Road and Quarry Hill. These were duly approved by TUDC. Later the same year (1934) the Ministry raised the matter of pedestrian crossings, which led to a joint submission by the local Police Superintendent and Mr Bradley, the Surveyor. Five locations were suggested: 'near School House, opposite the Post Office, near the Angel Hotel, in Quarry Hill Road just north of the traffic signals, and in Pembury Road just west of St Mary's Road'.

In the following year, 1935, the Chamber of Trade wrote to the Council about 'the very poor lighting of the streets of this town, especially the main thoroughfare', and cited 'two recent fatal accidents'. The link between lighting and safety was soon underlined by a deputation from the National Union of Railwaymen urging councillors to keep all street lamps alight throughout the night during the winter months to assist people on their night-time journeys to and from work. In August 1935 further pressure was exerted by the local Ratepayers' Association, after which the Surveyor was instructed to approach KCC regarding the provision of pedestrian crossings at the Angel Hotel and at the Post Office on the High Street. Pedestrian crossings were clearly something of a mixed blessing. In March 1938 the Surveyor submitted a map and records showing the number of road accidents in the Urban District since the previous April. One outcome was the decision to improve the visibility of the three pedestrian crossings on the High Street affected by the reconstruction works 'by surfacing with asphalt of a contrasting colour to the adjoining road surface'.

When the Surveyor submitted accident statistics for the year 1938/9 in July 1939 the records and map demonstrated 'an unfortunate number of accidents at or near the pedestrian crossing at the Post Office, and at the junction of Avebury Avenue and the High Street'. This time the recommendation was for traffic islands with bollards at these crossings. The street furniture in Tonbridge was beginning to take on a distinctly modern look by the advent of World War Two, and already the seeds of later controversies were sown. The private motor car had been established as an important and increasingly affordable means of road transport, and the parking, garaging, and safety problems it created were a new feature of town life.

Sources and Acknowledgements

Sources and Acknowledgements for this chapter appear on pages 79-81.

Transport and Travel
Part 2: Public Transport

Peter Swan

Tonbridge Junction

The Station built in 1842 for the South Eastern Railway Company was on the opposite side of the main road from its present location; it was rebuilt 26 years later (1868) on the west side of the railway bridge, when the Sevenoaks line was constructed. Since that date Tonbridge has been the hub of four major railway routes – London via Sevenoaks, London by way of Redhill, the East Kent Coast, and down the line to Hastings. It might have been a very different story had Maidstone welcomed rather than rejected the railway prior to 1842. South Eastern had opened Redhill to Tonbridge as a main line in 1842. However, with the building of the new station here in 1868 and the availability of a quicker route to London, the Redhill line declined to almost local line status. Nonetheless, it carried a great deal of extra traffic during the First World War, taking soldiers to the Front and subsequently returning them on leave, wounded or finally demobbed. No lines were added during the period covered in this book, although at the turn of the century the eccentric Colonel Stephens, who had an office in Salford Terrace (now Quarry Hill Road), did propose a Hadlow Light Railway to bring in rural produce.

Both the town and its railway station underwent a change of name in the nineteenth century. The former was known as 'Tunbridge' until 1893, while the station name changed more than once. It became 'Tunbridge Junction' in 1852, then 'Tonbridge Junction' in 1893, only to be renamed simply 'Tonbridge' in 1929. Meanwhile, four large 'groupings' of numerous smaller railway companies took effect from 1 January1923, whereby Tonbridge became part of the Southern Railway. By the end of our period in 1939 the Southern had 600 miles of electrified track, but this displacement of steam did not reach Tonbridge until 1961.

Commuters and Complaints

Statistics for the volume of those commuting from Tonbridge to London by rail between the wars, and the original date when this trend began, have both proved difficult to find. In his early history of the town A. H. Neve wrote, 'From 1868 to 1914 many scores of commercial travellers, London professional and business men, and others to whom travelling facilities were a matter of importance made their homes in Tonbridge'. During the 1920s and 1930s employment in London became increasingly attractive to such residents.

The earliest firm figure I have discovered for commuters from Tonbridge Station is as recent as 1963. Then the statistic for all season ticket holders was given by H. P. White as '2300, a 44% increase over 1957'. This works out at around 1600 in 1957 and indicates rapid growth since the Second World War.

Although considerable numbers were commuting from Tonbridge to London between the wars, particularly after 1930, a figure of a few hundred is a best guess. The journey time to Charing Cross in 1930 was 55 minutes, and the timetable at peak periods still quite sparse. At any period the volume of commuters would depend on jobs available in London and their financial rewards. The cost of fares as a proportion of income is critical if the daily journey is to be economically viable.

The *Official Guide to Tonbridge* for 1935 (and advertisements in the *TFP* for the same year) give the cost of third class cheap day returns to London as 4s, with ordinary third class single fares at 3s 9d. Season ticket rates for commuters are not listed, but at a time when £5 was the average weekly wage for a skilled workman only the professional classes are likely to have commuted – a mere trickle compared with the tide of humanity now pouring into London daily by train from Tonbridge.

Whatever the true numbers, Tonbridge commuters had enjoyed the support of their own Season Ticket Holders' Association since the late 1920s. In the TUDC Minutes for January 1928 we read that the Clerk reported correspondence from Messrs G. W. Colyer and R. S. Children regarding the price of season tickets, and that an association was being formed. The previous year a letter had been received from the local Ratepayers' Association seeking the Council's help in obtaining a better train service to and from London. A Minute of February 1930 records that the Railway Company was to be asked 'to grant cheap daily tickets to London'.

The entrance to Tonbridge Station, prior to the 1934 refacing.

The Southern continued to come under fire from both the Tonbridge
Season Ticket Holders' Association and the Council for the state of its trains
and of Tonbridge Station. In 1933 the former group put on record its 'emphatic
and unanimous protest against the present train service between Tonbridge
and London; against the old gas-lit, uncomfortable and often dirty
compartments; against the many stops and the slow, unpunctual service'. If
that was not criticism enough for one year, Councillor Neve carried a motion
which condemned the station buildings as 'a disgrace to a progressive town
... and a serious menace to business'. In reply the Southern Railway expressed
its intention 'to proceed this year with the rebuilding of the station ...'.

Improvements at the Station

In the event, the word 'rebuilding' proved something of an exaggeration, at
least as far as the actual structure of the main station building was concerned.
In 1934 the Victorian brickwork was refaced, giving it a more modern but
less attractive look – a necessity, perhaps, but hardly an improvement. Most
of the mid-1930s alterations were to the rest of the complex, and represented
very positive gains.

At a meeting on 12 October 1933 the Southern Railway Board approved a scheme for remodelling Tonbridge Station at a cost of £95,000, to include new signalling, the re-alignment of the junction at the western end, and easing of the 'London' curve. This would allow the speed limit to be raised from 20 mph to 40 mph, and give Hastings trains a clear run through Tonbridge.

The station had two platforms and two through lines between them, with terminal bays on the outside. The up bay was lengthened eastwards to join the main line, while both platforms were extended and enhanced by better buildings and new roofs. Modern signal boxes were erected with electrically-operated levers, and a new marshalling yard was laid out. R. W. Kidner relates that on a single night in early June 1934, the whole layout was replaced at the up end of the station and the way in from Sevenoaks reconstructed.

The major works on the track at Tonbridge were not without incident. A Mills bomb was found on the site with its rusted pin intact, and handed over to the military authorities (*TFP*, 20 July 1930). Sadly the reconstruction did have its casualties, the local paper recording several fatalities among the workmen during 1934. In February an excavator driver was killed by a fall of earth, in March a labourer was crushed between the buffers of two trucks, and in June two platelayers were killed by a train when the ganger in charge failed to post a look-out man. Clearly a high price was paid for the improvements in human terms, as well as financial ones.

Social and Economic Impact of the Railway

During the early years of our period the South Eastern Railway at Tonbridge used horse-power to move wagons, several great shires being stabled at the nearby Angel Hotel. As the 1920s progressed, and the Southern Railway took over, so too did shunting engines. Although the railway's impact on the Medway as a working river was damaging, the iron horse brought its benefits. The railway made for speedier distribution of farm produce, brought hop pickers to west Kent in their thousands, and gave a boost to the taxi and hotel trades. According to *Kelly's Directory* for 1919 'cabs from the Rose & Crown ... meet nearly every train'.

On the debit side, pollution in the vicinity of the railway was a problem. The TUDC Minutes of August 1926 make reference to a petition presented to the Council (and passed on to the Southern) from residents of Vale Road.

They complained of excessive smoke and grit from the engines at the locomotive shed. Several years earlier, in June 1919, there had been a serious fire at the local railway wagon repair shop.

Without doubt the coming of the railway had been responsible for the growth of south Tonbridge, and for many years it was one of the largest employers in the town, with as many as 650 employees by 1932 (*TFP*, 3 June 1932). The provision of housing for those working here in the railway industry was a real concern. In February 1927, the Council wrote to the Southern for help with housing facilities for their employees who were being drafted to Tonbridge in numbers. Three years later the National Union of Railwaymen wrote to the local authority asking what plans it had for building council houses 'owing to the pressing need of so many railwaymen and others'. With the improvements at the station in the mid-thirties came partial relief for the town's unemployment problem.

Timetables and Publicity

Publicity was important to both the railway company and the town. In 1922 the former offered to place a Train Indicator on the wall near the Watergate Entrance to the Castle grounds, with panels for town notices. The Council accepted, charging a rent for the site of £5 per annum. The Urban District was not so responsive, a few years later, when the Southern suggested it take out an advertisement for the town in the company's 1926/7 edition of 'Hints for Holidays' – a missed opportunity in terms of tourism, perhaps?

The famous firm of Bradshaw still produced railway timetables in 1910, showing a slow train as early as 5.15 in the morning from Charing Cross via Tonbridge Junction eventually reaching Hastings at 8.57. The *Borough Guide to Tonbridge* of the same pre-war era advertised 'a late train down every night after theatres'.

While detailed timetables were published throughout the inter-war period (in 1935 the *Courier* produced a monthly one, priced 3d.) the local newspapers and guides carried advertisements for the railway, giving times, fares and special offers. Some idea of contemporary costs and frequency of service is therefore on record, in particular for the journey to London.

For example, the single fare from Tonbridge Junction to Waterloo in the early 1920s was 9s first class, 5s 8d second, and 4s 3d third. Return tickets cost 15s 9d, 11s 5d, or 8s 7d, there being no cheap day returns then. Weekday trains out of Tonbridge ran from 7 a.m. to around midnight, approximately every hour in the afternoon but more frequently in the morning peak period and early evening. The fast trains at this time took about 55 minutes to reach Waterloo.

After the station improvements in 1934 the London to Hastings line via Tonbridge and Tunbridge Wells became progressively faster and busier. By 1938 the weekday timetable offered 16 express journeys and 9 slow trains, with 15 on Sundays. Fares to London in the mid-thirties were 6s 3d (first class single) or 3s 9d (3rd) with cheap day return tickets at 6s or 4s. The express journey time was now under 50 minutes.

Redhill trains via Edenbridge were less frequent (some 14 each way in winter) and took between 45 minutes and one hour, depending on the number of stops. Sunday services were limited on this line.

The *TFP* regularly carried details of cheap day tickets to London and to the coastal resorts of Kent and Sussex in the 1930s. In 1934, for instance, the Southern Railway offered special 'penny-a-mile' tickets between all its principal stations for the Easter period. Cheap day tickets available from Tonbridge that year included Brighton (8s or 5s). On balance, therefore, passenger numbers grew despite competition from road transport.

Other services promoted by the Southern Railway through the columns of the local press at this time were in direct competition with existing road transport operators. Door to door furniture and family removals could be carried out using specially constructed road-rail vans. Under the heading of 'Railhead Distribution' the Southern also advertised a modern transport service for goods and farm produce.

Traditionally the railway transported an unruly multitude of seasonal hop-pickers from London to Kent every year. In 1910 the County Medical Officer had estimated that 10,200 'foreigners' came to the Tonbridge district alone. The annual influx continued throughout our period with 'Hoppers' Specials', and trains laid on for family and friends to visit the hop-pickers at weekends. The railway and the farmer were good for one another's business.

From contemporary *Kelly's Directories* we learn that the Superintendent at Tonbridge Station in 1919 was Mr B. Robbins, employed by the South Eastern and Chatham Railway. By 1929 E. F. Blackwell was Station Master for the Southern Railway, Eastern Section, and by 1939 Stanley Gordon Collard

The Southern Railway advertises its services in 1934 (Tonbridge Free Press, 14 September 1934).

was the man in charge. There may well have been other office holders in between. During the period under review train drivers earned an average of £4 per week, far more than other railwaymen, the wage being somewhat higher between 1920 and 1927. But what of the rolling stock for which they were responsible, back in the era of corridor carriages linked in sets of 3, 4, or 6?

The Trains

Numerous books and booklets have been published for enthusiasts on the locomotives, carriages and wagons of the railway companies, complete with photographs and technical data. Some of these expert sources are acknowledged in the bibliography at the end of this chapter. Such detail is outside the scope of a general survey, but a few facts may not be out of place here.

The names of Harry Wainwright (the South Eastern's Locomotive Superintendent from 1899 to 1913), his successor Richard Maunsell (in post 1913-37, with the South Eastern and Chatham Railway and then the Southern after 1923) and Oliver Bulleid are well known to railway buffs.

Locomotive 676 on the turntable at Tonbridge. It was in service from 1900 to 1926.

The practical considerations of the Great War brought about the South Eastern's decision to replace the green Wainwright livery on their locomotives with a dull grey colour by 1917. Despite the demands of war, however, Maunsell did produce new engine designs, notably the Mogul Class N locomotive. The prototype was built at Ashford in 1917. Like their inventor, the Moguls had great staying power, for they ran on the main line through Tonbridge until the last one was scrapped in 1966.

Maunsell subsequently produced, for the Southern, his highly efficient Class N15 'King Arthurs' in 1925 and the more powerful 'Lord Nelson' Class a year later. There followed the Class V 'Schools' in 1930, particularly suited to the steep gradients, demanding curves and tight tunnels of the Hastings line. These were destined to perform there until the end of the steam era from London down to the Sussex coast.

On the Buses – Autocar

Until the motor bus arrived on the streets of our country at the turn of the last century, horses were employed to pull public road transport for the most part. Around 1900 small family firms like Castle's and Ashdown's linked Tonbridge by omnibus with Hadlow, Hildenborough and East Peckham via Golden Green. Horse-buses were still in use between Southborough and Tonbridge in 1912, the year in which Autocar ran the first regular, through service from Tunbridge Wells to Hadlow.

Autocar Services Ltd. started trading in 1909, the brain-child of its three founder directors, Colonel John Eggington (an officer with the Kent Cyclist Battalion who was sent to the Western Front when war broke out), a younger Eggington and William Oscar Pritchard. The last-named rose rapidly from chief mechanic and co-director to Managing Director. Arthur Eaton joined Autocar as Manager under Pritchard in 1926, bringing valuable experience of the bus industry with Morecambe Corporation Transport.

Autocar quickly established itself in Tunbridge Wells, opening an office at the Opera House and building a garage in Woodbury Park Road. By 1914 it operated with Leyland saloons on the Tonbridge route every two hours, nine buses a day, and had a booking office here at Medway Wharf Road. After war began in 1914 Autocar was forced to run reduced services, since the War Department commandeered all but its oldest vehicles.

Maidstone and District (M & D, eventually to dominate the local bus scene) had been formed in 1911, but made little impact around Tonbridge until after the First World War. Back in 1904 Maidstone Corporation's new trams reached the municipal boundary at Barming, as its trolleybuses were to do in 1928, but neither mode of passenger transport was seen on the streets of our town.

By 1919 the population of Tonbridge was nearing 16,000, a gallon of petrol cost the equivalent of 8 pence, and Autocar paid its drivers £1 10s and its conductors 18s for a basic 56 hour week.

For many years (until as late as 1935) there was no through service from Tunbridge Wells to Maidstone via Tonbridge. Passengers had to change from Autocar to M & D vehicles at Hadlow, against a background of considerable suspicion between the crews and their respective companies.

Across the nation small firms of bus operators mushroomed after the Great War. The first truly local competition for Autocar on its Tonbridge routes came from Ashby's (a family concern of which more to follow) who opened a garage at the foot of Quarry Hill in 1921. Ashby's original fleet consisted of five Garfords in brown livery, each seating 14 people, which were affectionately known as 'Ashby's Rattlers'.

Redcar and the Bus Wars

Contrasting with the original green of Autocar, Redcar first appeared on the streets of Tunbridge Wells in early 1923. It was registered as a limited company in September of the same year. The founder was James Bogue Elliott, the son of a well known local doctor. Two of his brothers were also involved in the firm, which first operated from a yard in Albion Road, then from premises in Upper Grosvenor Road where a purpose-built garage was opened in 1925. Soon Redcar set up its headquarters in Monson Road, complete with booking and enquiry offices, waiting rooms, cloakrooms and a café.

By 1927 Redcar Services had a second depot in Avebury Avenue, Tonbridge, which employed over one hundred men. The well-equipped workshop enabled each vehicle to be overhauled and resprayed every nine months. A former employee recalls Dennis buses, with high chassis, being used to ferry people through the floods at the Station end of the High Street for a penny a time.

From 1924 Redcar competed on most of the Autocar routes with a fleet

One of Autocar's Leyland single-deckers in the High Street, c1929.

of small, speedy Talbot saloons. These had pneumatic tyres, and made for a more comfortable ride than their rivals could offer at the time. The resulting skirmishes developed by 1927/8 into an all out war on the buses, already covered in some detail by my article in *Bygone Kent* (1993) listed at the end of this chapter.

Apart from Ashby's (who sold a controlling interest to Autocar in November, 1923) other local bus concerns between the wars were Victor, who operated in the late 1920s from Pembury to Tonbridge with brown Chevrolets, and West Kent Motor Services. The latter ran for a short while around 1928 from Westerham to Tonbridge via Edenbridge.

The rivalry became very petty in 1927 when Redcar ensured that Autocar was fined for operating a vehicle marginally wider than the legal maximum. In January 1928 they fought over fares, undercutting one another until passengers (the only winners financially) could travel from Tonbridge to the Wells for just 'a penny all the way'. Each had its loyal band of supporters among the travelling public, and local magistrates were kept busy considering counter-accusations of reckless driving and the like. Eventually a working agreement was reached and a joint network and combined timetables introduced on 1 May 1928, with pooled revenue going 45 per cent to Redcar and 55 per cent to Autocar.

Kelly's Directory for 1929 indicates frequent Autocar journeys between Tonbridge Station and Tunbridge Wells: every 10 minutes in the morning, every five minutes after noon, with links to satellite villages also well established. By 1934 Redcar was running five buses a day to Hadlow, but only the following year was a through service from Tunbridge Wells to Maidstone begun by M & D.

Both the smaller rival companies had a good safety record, despite fierce competition for passengers which may have contributed to a collision between Autocar and Redcar vehicles on the dangerous Bidborough Corner in the late 1920s. Another unfortunate accident took place in Tonbridge High Street on 24 May 1930. Two brand new AEC Regents were on their way from Ransomes at Ipswich to the Autocar depot at Tunbridge Wells when a woman stepped off the pavement. The driver of the front vehicle had to brake suddenly, which the one following behind failed to do. It is to be hoped the driver did not have to pay for repairs out of the current wage of some £3 per week.

The Role of the Local Authority

Minutes of Committee and full Council meetings between the wars abound with details of licence applications considered and complaints received, some more serious than others. Open-top double-decker buses had been used on the Tonbridge to Tunbridge Wells route in the early 1920s, but it was the closed-top variety which caused local councillors some concern around 1930. These 'juggernauts of the road' were AEC Regents, which Tonbridge Urban District Council was reluctant to allow Autocar to employ on Quarry Hill, doubting their stability. A more realistic worry might have been possible damage to overhanging shop signs and blinds, or to lamp standards, but by the mid 1930s double-deckers had proved their case.

TUDC were often involved in decisions over the location of bus stops and other matters of detail. For example in April 1929, the Misses Pattisson of 'Graylings' successfully requested that a bus stop sign be moved from outside their house in the High Street. Another complaint was brought by members of the Angling Society in 1934. They blamed the nearby Redcar bus depot for oil pollution in the water at Buley's Weir, which had caused the loss of fish stocks. Nothing could be proven beyond reasonable doubt, so the Council declined to support the anglers' claim for £10 compensation.

Problems arising from speeding, overcrowding, dangerous turning, wear and tear on road surfaces and the leaving of litter all figure in the official records. The Clerk had to take issue with the bus operators from time to time, who in turn addressed genuine complaints with vigour. Extracts from the Autocar Assistant Manager's instructions to staff in late 1927 condemn the 'expensive swank' of drivers who roared and over-revved their Daimler engines. Conductors and drivers were also warned against 'skylarking and fooling about whilst on duty' and allowing 'girl passengers to sit beside the driver'.

From 1925 TUDC insisted on the registration of drivers as well as vehicles. Licence applications frequently came up for consideration; if agreed they were granted for six months or a year at a time, often with a proviso. In 1925, for instance, Autocar and Redcar were obliged to operate only with vehicles having both front and rear exits. Periodically the companies were bound to contribute to the cost of road repairs. In 1934 the provision of bus shelters was discussed by the Council. The local authority sometimes took the initiative by proposing new bus routes in the public interest. In 1938, for example, TUDC approached Maidstone & District and the Traffic Commissioners for a service linking Barden with the High Street.

Coach Travel and Outings by Bus

Since the mid-eighteenth century the market town of Tunbridge had been a regular stopping place on stage-coach routes from London to the Wells, Hastings and Rye. In the period under review the local Council Minutes are dotted with references to firms applying to run motor-coach services through Tonbridge. Timpsons of Plumstead were allowed to pick up and set down in Tonbridge on their way from London to the coast at Hastings. A few years later, in 1927, Redcar started a long distance coach service with Leyland Tigers from Tunbridge Wells to London. In the early thirties the return fare from Tonbridge to the capital was 5s, later reduced to 3s 10d. In June 1930 Autocar followed Redcar on the London route, using AEC Regals. These services were popular with Londoners visiting their relatives down in Kent for the hop-picking season.

Green Line was formed in 1930 as a subsidiary of the London General Omnibus Company, and by 1931 ran several journeys into Kent. After 1933 the newly established London Passenger Transport Board took control of Green Line and, two years later, Redcar's journeys passed to London Transport. By 1935 the *Official Guide to Tonbridge* announced that 'the Green Line service to London via Sevenoaks is run hourly' and that 'cheap motor-coach trips to seaside resorts and places of historic interest are made daily during the summer months'.

A further link with the big city might have been forged in 1932, when London General Country Services Ltd. seriously thought of opening a bus station at the foot of Quarry Hill, but failed to find a suitable site. By then the town's cinemas already attracted patrons from miles around, some of whom were carried by Sevenoaks Motor Services' 14-seater Chevrolet on private hire. In the mid-thirties the Chamber of Trade's free paper *The Month in Tonbridge* highlighted frequent buses to and from outlying districts for village dwellers to visit 'Kent's Economic Shopping Centre', and there was a regular advertisement in the *TFP* inviting local clubs to hire Maidstone & District coaches to ensure a successful outing.

The Supremacy of M & D

The founder of Maidstone & District, Walter Flexman French, had begun his career in transport around 1880 as a bicycle manufacturer, before becoming a pioneer of the bus industry in Kent and beyond. He ran the small enterprises from which M & D developed as a limited company in 1911. A local landowner, Colonel H. I. Robinson, joined French and his son in this venture, which had an initial share capital of £4000.

After 1922 the Maidstone firm outstationed one vehicle at Hadlow to work Service 7 to and from the county town. After 1928 Autocar was controlled by the East Surrey Traction Company Limited, only to be taken over on 1 July 1933 by Maidstone & District. It continued to run as Autocar until 1935, when M & D took over Redcar too and dropped both names, so winding up their Autocar subsidiary. The Maidstone giant had grown from operating a fleet of 119 vehicles in 1922 to one of 465 by 1933, and was to prove more than a match for its smaller rivals. The era of competition was soon to end.

By 1937 Maidstone & District had no fewer than 73 bus stop signs within our Urban District boundaries. In the late 1930s there was an M & D Enquiry Office at 15 Quarry Hill Road, to go with the former Redcar garage in Avebury Avenue acquired in February 1935. When the Second World War came M & D was the only bus company listed in the local *Kelly's Directory*.

The Ashby Family

A prime example of business enterprise in twentieth century Tonbridge was surely Arthur J. Ashby. He was born in the year 1900, the son of J. W. Ashby, an engineer who owned the busy Quarry Hill Garage. Educated at the Judd School, young Arthur was the envy of the school when arriving for lessons on a motor-cycle. As a fifteen-year-old in wartime he was granted a special licence to drive the essential ambulances (which also covered use of his father's car) and was a keen volunteer with the Castle firewatch.

When his father died in 1926 a well-trained and experienced young man took over, proceeding to develop the family firm. Mention has already been made of Ashby's fleet of Garfords, but at one time or another the business covered garage facilities (petrol pumps, tyres and repairs), school buses and excursion coaches, taxis, hire cars, even hearses and horseboxes. It was a partnership with Captain Peter Cazalet (trainer of royal horses) which led to Fairlawne Transport Limited.

The pages of the local press carried regular advertisements for the various services offered by Quarry Hill Garage. We learn that J. W. Ashby was an agent for Ford cars and parts in 1915-16, an official AA and MU (Motorcycle Union) repairer, had touring cars for hire and gave driving lessons. He even boasted 'the largest and most up to date stock of gramophones and war records' (*TFP*, 23 January 1915). Although they sold out to Autocar in 1923, Ashby's were back in the local bus industry by 1932, with a licence to operate between Tonbridge and Underriver. As well as running Ashby Commercial Vehicles Ltd. in the mid thirties, Arthur ran coaches under the fleet name of 'Ashline' which only passed to Maidstone and District in 1948.

For much of this section I am indebted to Arthur's widow, Mrs Peggy Ashby, and to Mr F. R. (Ron) Ashby, of Bidborough. The former was most generous with personal information and the loan of important documents. She confirmed my strong impression of a man who was devoted to his life's work, which doubled as his hobby. He was featured in a glossy Michelin magazine as one of 'four men and their companies whose forebears, or they themselves, have known the early pioneering days of the motor-car'. The article quoted Arthur Ashby thus: 'my work is my pleasure'. It went on to mention

his love of American cars, as the proud owner of a Ford Mustang and a Lincoln Continental, 'both shod with Michelin tyres'. The Ashby's Garford buses had American chassis and Michelin high pressure tyres, so why did locals nickname them 'Ashby's Rattlers'? Ironically, Arthur himself was inclined to describe the British Rolls-Royce in the same terms.

One of 'Ashby's rattlers', early 1920s (author's photograph).

This remarkable local businessman became Chief Transport Officer for the south-east during the Second World War, responsible for commandeering vehicles, organising emergency transport and the distribution of petrol coupons. Arthur Ashby never really retired, and died in old age while still hard at work.

Taxi Cabs

Horse-drawn cabs were still a familiar sight outside Tonbridge Station when the 1920s began, but competition from the motor taxi was to drive them off the streets over the next decade. Three of the last 'cabbies' were Mr C. Chivers, Mr A. Morley and Mr W. Church. William Church took over the horse bus between Hadlow and Tonbridge when Charlie Castle retired, moving house to Tonbridge around 1910 to run a cab service until the early 1930s. His horses were stabled first at the Bull Hotel and later at the Prince Albert in Vale Road.

Tonbridge Urban District Council's Minutes are a fruitful source of information. There we read of six hackney carriage licences being granted in mid-1919, three to Tonbridge Taxi Cabs Ltd. and three to Chas. Baker & Co., under the Police Clauses Act of 1847. The Ashby family were among several other taxi operators licensed between the wars. The Public Health Act of 1925 gave local authorities the effective means to make bye-laws regarding the regulation and licensing of hackney carriages, and the Ministry of Health produced model bye-laws. In June 1926, the Council requested its General Purposes Sub-Committee to make recommendations.

The Heskett family have run a taxi business in Tonbridge for decades now, from the era of the big, old 1932 Morris Oxfords. At that period the only taxi rank in the town was in Barden Road, and licensing was much stricter than in these days of deregulation.

Conclusion: the Impact on Tonbridge

In these two chapters we have considered the road system and the various modes of transport in and around Tonbridge from about 1910 to 1939. It would be an exaggeration on both counts to suggest that in 30 short years a transport revolution led to a social revolution. Nonetheless, the changes were not small.

What, then, was the social and economic impact of progress in transport and travel on our small market town? Were the effects favourable? Did they improve the quality of life enjoyed by the local residents?

On balance the changes did enhance people's lives in and around Tonbridge, most of all for those from the surrounding villages. For the many small communities not on a railway line, links to town were developed and mobility thereby increased. From the late nineteenth century local carriers' wagons with passenger benches added had served countrywide as rural bus services. After 1900 motor-buses began to offer villagers regular services to the nearest town; they also brought out parcels and post. Significantly, census figures show that the population of Tonbridge Rural District Council area, standing at 17,387 in 1921, grew by several thousand to 22,284 in 1951.

The freedom of movement referred to above opened up new opportunities for employment, shopping and leisure, both for rural residents 'commuting' to Tonbridge and for an increasing number of town dwellers who could now reach London within the hour by train.

Tonbridge supported numerous carriers, garages and car dealers, shoe and cycle shops. Transport was clearly good for trade, which was stimulated by visitors with time and money to spend in the town. Places of refreshment and entertainment thrived, while public transport afforded those in Tonbridge without a car (a decreasing majority) the opportunity to sample the countryside and the coast by bus, coach or rail.

The inter-war period was too early for specialist High Street travel agents, but successive bus companies had their Enquiry Offices in the town, while outings by coach and rail (including foreign trips) were well publicised in the local press. For drivers nationally the pneumatic tyre and the use of tarmacadam led to better maintenance of major roads. The Second World War came to a country well and widely served by public road transport, in contrast to the 'scattered routes and pioneer vehicles of 1914.' (John Hibbs)

With small, mass-produced cars available for nearer £100 than £200, private motoring spread rapidly. Although there was no crying need to curb the car between the wars, early manifestations of its modern side-effects were felt in Tonbridge, as elsewhere. Traffic jams, petrol fumes, noise, motoring accidents and wear and tear on road surfaces are nothing new, as already recounted. After a century of the motor-car we now face far more acute problems, but theirs were very real at the time.

Unemployment in Tonbridge exceeded one thousand only briefly during the Great Depression of the early 1930s, but it was a serious social problem to be addressed. The Southern and Redcar were major local employers, while railway improvements, road schemes, and the construction of Woodland Walk and other paths provided temporary jobs. The size and balance of the town was stable between the wars and its essential character remained largely unchanged. The 1921 population figure of 15,947 grew by a couple of thousand only by 1939, nothing like the expansion which was to follow when north Tonbridge was developed after 1950. Growth had been more rapid during the second half of the nineteenth century, following the arrival of the railway. In no way did our small market town become a dormitory for the capital, a description which even now would be unfair.

River, Road and Rail

So what can be concluded about the role of the 3Rs in the expansion of Tonbridge? Is it appropriate to ask which was the most important artery of trade and communication? Or did they complement one another, combining to make our town what it is? In some ways it was a joint effort.

The railway is the upstart, a mere one hundred and fifty years old. The first loaded barge reached Tonbridge in 1741, but for centuries a rudimentary road has given access to the town. Ironically, the transport of raw materials required for the construction of the Reading-Tonbridge line (opened in 1842) boosted traffic on the Medway for a while, but in the long run the railway was to undermine the economy of the river. The coming of the railway encouraged the growth of south Tonbridge through the later decades of the nineteenth century and into the present one. In turn, the railway lost considerable passenger traffic to public road transport between the wars, largely due to greater flexibility of both routes and fare charges.

We have traced the story of transport and travel in the Tonbridge area from the days of horses and the hiss of steam to those of traffic jams and diesel fumes. Along the way we have met some of the personalities and the controversies which influenced the course of the inter-war period. It is the old road from London to the coast, via the Medway bridge and our much altered High Street, which above all has shaped the town of Tonbridge. The river had its day, and the railway its decades after 1842, but historically this road governed the town's location. In our own century it has (together with its branches into nearby villages and other towns) remained our increasingly congested lifeline.

Sources

A select bibliography follows. Much of the material consulted forms part of the local studies and archives collection at Tonbridge Library.

General

Minutes of Tonbridge Urban District Council, 1910-39

Tonbridge Free Press, 1910-39

Kelly's Commercial Directories for the period

Various local guides and yearbooks

Aldcroft, D. H., *British Transport since 1914, an Economic History* (David & Charles, 1975)

Baldock, E., *Transport in Kent, 1900-1938, a selection of historic postcards* (Meresborough Books, 1991)

Barker, T. and Gerhold, D., *The Rise and Rise of Road Transport, 1700-1990* (Cambridge University Press, 1995)

Chapman, F., *The Book of Tonbridge* (Barracuda Books, 1976). Also his 'Warwick' columns in the *Kent & Sussex Courier*

Jessup, F. W., *Kent History Illustrated* (Kent County Council, 1966)

Joyce, J., *The Story of Passenger Transport in Britain* (Ian Allan, 1967)

Neve, A. H., *The Tonbridge of Yesterday* (Tonbridge Free Press, 1934)

Swan, P., 'From Turnpikes to Trains – two centuries of transport through Tonbridge (1700-1900)', *Journal of Kent History*, **49**, September 1999

The River Medway

Chivers, T., 'A Short History of the Medway Locks between Tonbridge and Twyford', *Bygone Kent*, **16**, 1, January 1995

Dumbreck, W. V., *Medway Navigation*, unpublished and undated typescript in Tonbridge Library local collection

Vine, P. A. L., *Kent and East Sussex Waterways* (Middleton Press, 1989)

The Railway

Course, E., *The Railways of Southern England : the Main Lines* (Batsford, 1973)

Jewell, B., *Down the Line to Hastings* (Baton Press, 1984)

Kidner, R. W., *The Reading to Tonbridge Line* (Oakwood Press, 1974)

Mitchell, V. and Smith, K., *Tonbridge to Hastings* (Middleton Press, 1987)

Morgan, J. S., *The Colonel Stephens Railways* (David & Charles, 1978)

White, H. P., *Regional History of the Railways of Great Britain, vol.2, Southern England* (David & Charles, 4th ed., 1982)

Bus Services

Baldock, E., *The Motor Bus Services of Kent and East Sussex* (Meresborough Books, 1985)

Hibbs, J., *The History of British Bus Services* (David & Charles, 1967)

Morris, C., *History of British Bus Services, vol.1, South-East England* (Transport Publishing Company, 1980)

Swan, P., 'War on the Buses', *Bygone Kent*, **14**, 3, March 1993

Turnbull, R. S., *My Tunbridge Wells Story, 1909-33* (publ. by the author, 1988)

Motor Cars

Ray, J., *A History of the Motor Car* (Pergamon Press, 1966)

Worthington-Williams, M., 'The Storey Brothers of Tonbridge', *Kent Life*, January 1968

Acknowledgements

The gleaning of material for a lengthy essay involves consulting the work of many others, and seeking the advice of numerous helpful contacts. I am particularly grateful to Dr. Christopher Chalklin (editor), Sydney Simmons (roads), John Hilton and M. J. Whitson (railways), the late Dick Turnbull, Eric Baldock and the Maidstone & District and East Kent Bus Club (bus services), Frank Chapman, Don Skinner and the Ashby family. Any errors remain my own responsibility.

The Butcher family (see page 85). Upper left, *their home in Lawn Road;* upper right, *Florence Butcher;* lower left, *her boys George, Harold and William at Sussex Road School;* lower right, *her daughter Elsie – the author's mother (author's photographs).*

Tonbridge Families Remembered: a Study of Life in South-West Tonbridge, 1918-39

Part 1: Home and School

Dr P. L. Humphries

Introduction

Anyone who can remember Tonbridge as it was even as recently as the early 1960s, or who has browsed through files of photographs taken at this date, can fairly claim an acquaintance with the streets and principal buildings of a town of a considerably earlier vintage. Though names on a few shop fascias might have changed in the interim, and the demolition of the Bull Hotel had swept away a well-loved landmark, this later Tonbridge was in most essentials the Tonbridge that had emerged from the High Street widening of the 1890s and 1900s, had seen its sons sacrificed in the mud of Flanders, and, barely two decades later, had stiffened its sinews once again, now to defy the onslaught of the Luftwaffe. But if progress sometimes marches slowly in bricks and mortar, styles of life, working practices, people themselves and their expectations seldom mark time for very long. To know the world behind the sleepy facade thus challenges the historian to muster afresh his traditional resources and to be alert to the potential of new recruits.

Contemporary newspapers and directories can tell us much about social and economic conditions in a town such as Tonbridge, where, in the generation between the world wars, the inhabitants tasted the nation's bitter-sweet cup of unemployment and rising prosperity. But other, more intriguing stores of knowledge are close at hand. Was this Tonbridge of the 1920s and 1930s not the Tonbridge of our parents, our grandparents, and perhaps our great grandparents, in whose vivid recollections, the events, the characters, and often the very spirit of that bygone society live on? Their testimony is a priceless inheritance, which, if caught like the proverbial fly in amber, helps illustrate and animate the annals of our town. History, too, is alive and waiting to be discovered within our own thresholds, in our lofts and our sheds, in dusty drawers, where long-forgotten diaries and scrap-books, a letter or two, or a box of faded photographs reveal glimpses of our forefathers at home, at school, at work, and in moments of leisure. In short, inter-war Tonbridge is the Tonbridge of my family and your family; its story is my story and your story.

But merely to offer a series of family reminiscences in the present volume would be unforgivable self-indulgence. The lives of the Butcher family of Meadow Lawn and the Humphries family of Barden Park Road may be fascinating on a personal level, whereas on the broader canvas of history they will be accounted of little moment, unless, like figures in the foreground of some old master, they serve principally to fix our attention, before drawing us into contemplation of the broader perspective and vitality of their landscape. If successful, the result of this juxtaposing of the specific and the general is a most fruitful synthesis. The town assumes a fresh aspect as soon as we start to view its institutions and traditions as the civic embodiment of the popular psyche, imbued with the ideals of local men and women, their prejudices, and their aspirations for bread today and cake tomorrow. Likewise, we see the denizens of old Tonbridge gradually become flesh and blood when once we begin to explore inside the schools they attended, the jobs they chose or had thrust upon them, the shops they patronised, and how they entertained themselves and their families at home and in their neighbourhoods.

What follows is an attempt to trace a number of themes in the history of Tonbridge between the wars, using as a primary source the experience of a particular family group as recalled in the memories of contemporaries. The focus throughout is upon those remarkably self-contained communities of south-west Tonbridge, built on either side of the railway, and stretching from the spire of St Stephen's Church to the white facade of Barden Park House. Wherever possible, the more traditional local records are supplemented with material gleaned from notebooks, newspaper cuttings, and items that lend a uniquely personal flavour to the narrative. Such an approach has its dangers, for the memory can play us false, thus placing a special onus upon the historian to weigh his evidence with care. On the other hand, the rewards are great, since first-hand accounts bring a splash of colour and a depth of conviction to the past life of our town that mere dates and facts and statistics can never hope to convey.

When Clarence and Florence Butcher settled in Tonbridge in the autumn of 1918, it was as occupants of the house in Lawn Road that was to be home to their children Vera, Harold, Bill, George, and Elsie during part or all of the next 12 years (see photographs on page 82). In many respects, the Meadow Lawn suburb of that date differed little from what we know today; the bare bones of its road map having been laid out in the 1890s and 1900s, to accommodate a steadily growing population for whom the railway or local industry offered secure employment. It is, however, worthwhile trying to draw a brief sketch of the neighbourhood at about the time of the Armistice, both to serve as a backdrop to the ensuing discussion, and because, in keeping with national trends, the 1920s and 1930s were to witness a renewal of house building that substantially fleshed out the original skeleton.

Approaching Meadow Lawn from the direction of the High Street, the pedestrian of 1918 would descend Station Hill and turn left into Waterloo Road at the Good Intent public house. Then as now, the first street running off on the right was Albert Road, a mixed development of small and larger houses, with those along its entire north side abutting the railway. At the farther end of Albert Road, in a sizeable plot of fenced land, stood the large, detached house known as 'Nightingales', while the gardens of the houses on its south side extended back either to Wincliff Road, or to the long lane that ran westwards from the end of Wincliff Road, past the boundary of 'Nightingales', and onwards beside the railway until it reached the bottom of Sussex Road at the extremity of the built-up area.

The Wincliff Road of 1918 differed from its present-day counterpart in that the area now given over to garages and workshops on the south side was then all fields. A shop and a few houses stood at the Waterloo Road end of the street, and at the other, beyond the expanse of grassland, two detached houses – one occupied by Mr Atherton (a foreman on the railway) and the other by the Waters family of hauliers – were separated by an archway that led into the yard and premises of Waters and Son.

The main artery of Meadow Lawn was Douglas Road, the third and final right-hand turning off Waterloo Road. In the early 1920s, there were still fields to left and right as Douglas Road ascended the hill as far as the entrance to Lawn Road. From this point onwards, houses, shops, and a small church had been constructed along both sides of the way, and also in a succession of five parallel streets, which, like ribs from a spine, ran northwards to the lane and the gardens of Albert Road, and southwards to the playing-fields of the Judd School.

The street-plan thus looked much as we know it in the 1990s, except that both Lawn Road and Lionel Road were incomplete at their northern ends – the former, for example, numbered four pairs of houses on its west side and only two pairs on its east. Meadow Road and the top half of Lionel Road formed a crescent, which began opposite Lawn Road and re-joined Douglas Road further to the west. Thereafter, the northern and southern halves of Mabledon Road, Chichester Road, and Sussex Road ran away on either side of Douglas Road, which itself terminated just beyond Sussex Road at the gates of Truscott's Dowgate Works.

In addition to some houses and cottages, the southern portion of Sussex Road contained a number of school buildings, and by way of the 'bird-cage' path, afforded access to Hayesden Lane and the agricultural land where the Brook Street estate would one day be laid out. Several other footpaths branched off from Sussex Road: one crossing the meadows to Jimmy Roger's farm; another running away beside the boys' school into the much-beloved Jimmy's Field, and thence through gates and a stile to the Jubilee Bridge over the Redhill line, and beyond this to the Onwards Field and the river, or away to the allotments and the London line that formed the border with old Barden.

In contrast to Meadow Lawn, Barden – and especially its more distant purlieus – remained essentially residential, perhaps even a touch rural in character, down to the outbreak of war in 1939. The commercial and social hub of the Barden area had long been centred in the vicinity of the railway station – in Holford Street, Danvers Road, and Avebury Avenue – where the community educated its younger children, and a variety of retailers and tradesmen, a dairy, a post office, and several public houses satisfied local demand for basic foodstuffs, services, and recreation.

The later nineteenth century saw houses erected along the Barden Road corridor that begins at the rear of the station, passes what around 1900 became the junction with Avebury Avenue, runs along beside the Medway as far as Nelson Avenue, and takes in the series of short side-streets – Northcote Road, Gladstone Road, Preston Road, Norfolk Road, Cromer Street, and Caistor Road – that link its south side and the railway cutting. Private building on a limited scale did take place in Barden Park Road from about 1895, but until 1918 the main thoroughfare, having once crossed the railway, wandered gently

The Humphries family. Left, *Leslie Humphries;* right, *his wife Ellen with their son Leslie Jack (the author's father – left), nephew Jack (centre) and son Robert (right) (author's photographs).*

through fields and an avenue of spreading chestnuts as far as Barden Park House and the adjacent dairy farm.

Exactly when Leslie and Ellen Humphries, and their sons Leslie Jack and Robert, arrived in Barden Park Road is unclear, though a date soon after 1920 is likely, since the majority of the post-war council properties were completed there by 1922. Once established in their new home, the couple doubtless watched as several hundred more houses and scores of new families transformed an area which, not so many years earlier, had known little more traffic than tipsy Farmer Betts rolling home from market, or a dilatory child made heedless of his tea-time errand by autumn's conker harvest or the delights of a wayside ditch.

Even in the 1930s, when local authority building had swept away the trees and the cows, all the land on the north side of Audley Avenue beyond the junction with Ives Road (now Chestnut Walk and Alders Meadow) lay out of bounds behind the iron gates and railings of the 'White House', except for a small cottage (possibly once a lodge) inhabited by a Mr Denton, from whom the locals bought eggs. Miss Leaf, who occupied Barden Park House with her companion throughout these years, seems to have lived a most secluded life, perhaps guarding the secret of the mysterious passage said to link the house to Tonbridge Castle, and never attracting to her door the streams of carriages and pleasure-parties that must have frequented the house's wide staircase, capacious cellars, and river-skirted lawns in more prosperous times. Though its mistress found herself interned during the war, the house was not demolished until after 1945; and as late as the early 1960s, the plan of rose-beds and many of the original shrubs and damson trees betrayed the touch of a vanished hand in the overgrown garden.

Such were the Tonbridge communities into which the Humphries and Butcher families moved at about the time the Great War ended. In common with many of their new neighbours, neither couple had any discernible connection with the town, whereas both, like countless newcomers to Tonbridge since the late seventeenth century, had roots in the great metropolis just 30 miles distant. Though born in Buckinghamshire, Ellen Humphries' birth certificate identifies Edmonton (possibly the home of her mother's parents) as place of registration. She seems to have spent her childhood at various country houses where Jesse Lammas worked as head-gardener, but was married at St Paul's Church, Rusthall, by which date her father is named as the proprietor of a local laundry. Thomas Russ raised his daughter Florence and five other children in Balham, and retired after fifty years in the postal service, having attained the not-inconsiderable rank of postmaster.

Family tradition identifies Philadelphia as Clarence Butcher's place of birth, though in the decade before 1914, Edwardian London was very definitely his adopted milieu. Leslie Humphries, by contrast, was as thoroughly a Londoner as Sam Weller. Born in Brompton the son of a coachman, at the time of his marriage in August 1915 he was living at Ponder's End, and is described as a 'munition worker', probably at the nearby Ordnance Factory in Enfield. Both men had been trained to a craft – Butcher as a silversmith and Humphries as a watch maker – which, again in keeping with past generations of metropolitan migrants, elevated them at least to the status of the skilled artisan, and doubtless fostered in each, some traits of the semi-professional, shopkeeping, modestly cultured, politically literate, self-help ethos so characteristic of Orwell's lower lower-middle classes, among whom their respective wives had been brought up.

Now Tonbridge had drawn together the threads of these four lives. Let us begin to explore the town, as, perhaps, they too explored its byways and amenities in the first months after they arrived.

At Home

Both Meadow Lawn and those parts of Barden lying south of the railway to London underwent extensive building programmes during the inter-war period. Interestingly, these attempts to redeem in the streets of south-west Tonbridge, Lloyd George's wartime promise of 'homes fit for heroes,' reflect the ideological dichotomy that existed on the housing question among his political successors. Chamberlain's Housing Act of 1923, for instance, advocated the building of properties for sale to the lower-middle classes, whereas an act passed by the Labour Government in the following year switched emphasis towards new houses for rent, and introduced subsidies to encourage the compliance of local authorities.

Hence, just as parallel housing developments by Tonbridge Urban District Council (TUDC) and Mr Thorpe of Southborough took place to the east of the Shipbourne Road in the 1920s and 1930s, in Meadow Lawn we find construction work being carried out by private, speculative builders like Alan Standen, while on the nearby Barden Park estate, the new houses were financed and erected by the local council. By 1930, most of the grassy spaces in Douglas Road and at the north ends of Lawn Road and Lionel Road had been built upon; and by a similar date, both Nelson Avenue and Barden Park Road had been extended, and the Audley Avenue, Pembroke Road, Ives Road, Clare Avenue suburb had assumed its present-day lineaments and topography on a green-field site.

Most of the council properties built at this date conformed to a standard plan of rooms and facilities. Downstairs comprised a kitchen, a sizeable larder, a bathroom, an inside lavatory and a coal-cellar – both accessible from an enclosed back porch – and a single living-room with a fireplace. The front door opened into a small, square hallway, from which the stairs gave access to three bedrooms, the two larger rooms each having a fireplace. Houses were either semi-detached, or else erected in blocks of four with a central passageway giving admittance to the gardens at the rear. Most streets also contained two or three pairs of the so-called 'parlour-type' houses, which differed from the basic pattern in that there were three rooms on the ground-floor: a kitchen, a living-room, and a sitting-room.

The Butchers' home in Lawn Road was built around an L-shaped interior passage that began at the kitchen on the right-hand side and ended at the front-door. The windows of both the kitchen and the dining-room afforded views of the back garden, while the bay-windowed parlour occupied most of the front of the house facing the street. Also accessible from the passage were a large larder, a cloakroom, and the stairs down to the cellar. Upstairs the house numbered three bedrooms (that in the front with a bay window), a box-room that doubled as an additional bedroom, and an inside toilet. The dining-room and the parlour each had a fireplace, as did the main bedrooms, though fires were never lit upstairs, and the parlour fire tended only to be kindled on Sundays.

Being several decades older than the council developments beyond the railway, the original houses in Meadow Lawn had no provision for a bathroom. In terms of sanitation and plumbing, however, the Butchers were more fortunate than many neighbours, the majority of whom possessed only an outside lavatory. At the better-appointed houses in Meadow Lawn, the coalman tipped coal direct to the cellar by way of a chute beneath a manhole near the front door. Elsewhere, he might carry his sacks to a shed behind the house, or sometimes even into the house itself, to a coal cupboard in the kitchen or scullery.

Properties in both areas incorporated gardens of a useful size. At the rear of their home in Barden Park Road, Leslie and Ellen Humphries found space for three apple trees and a cherry, large gooseberry and currant bushes, an ample vegetable plot, a patch of rhubarb, a wooden shed, and areas of rough grass where the ground began to slope away to the river. The front and side borders betrayed Ellen Humphries' upbringing as the daughter of a country-house gardener. She cultivated lilacs and laburnum, narcissi and daffodils in spring, hedges of privet and forsythia, honeysuckle, roses, clumps of phlox and Michaelmas daisy, and a vine and a rambler on either side of the tiny front porch.

Florence Butcher also took some pride in her garden. Outside the kitchen window was a bed where she nurtured stocks and short-stemmed sunflowers, and from which a Virginia creeper spread its autumnal glory across the rear of the house. There was a vegetable patch, a codling apple tree, a gooseberry bush, blackcurrants, raspberry canes, and loganberries. Also in the garden stood a loft for George's pigeons, an outside privy, and a brick wash-house; the latter having a space beneath its slate roof where the children kept their pet guinea-pigs.

Few of the householders in Meadow Lawn would have owned the property they occupied. Instead, groups of houses were in the hands of private landlords, many of whom doubled as their own rent collector. The Butchers in Lawn Road had a succession of such landlords, the last of whom was Mr Jell of Ashburnham Road. Whether landlords ever undertook repairs is unclear – the Butchers certainly seem to have taken responsibility for their own improvements and internal decoration. In 1931 Mr Jell offered to sell the pair of houses known as 'Hope Villas' to the Butchers for £250, but, as will be seen later, the time was not propitious for such a transaction.

In 1918 the Meadow Lawn area relied exclusively upon gas for its lighting. The lamp-lighter was still a familiar figure, pursuing his round on a bicycle each morning and evening with a pole to help him extinguish or turn on the street-lamps. The schools in Sussex Road were lit in this way during the 1920s, as was the neighbourhood's printing works at the start of the next decade. All the rooms in the Butcher household were lit by gas, though candles normally sufficed when retiring upstairs to bed.

During the later 1920s the Butchers arranged to have electric lighting installed in their hallway and principal downstairs rooms, paying for the work in monthly instalments until just before they left the town in 1931. By this date, the house in Lawn Road was among that third of all homes in the country using electricity, a figure that would rise to two-thirds by the outbreak of war.[1]

From the outset, the new local authority properties of the 1920s were connected to mains electricity for lighting purposes. Ellen Humphries used gas to cook her family's meals, and heated water for washing clothes in a gas-fired kitchen copper. Though Mrs Butcher did enjoy the luxury of a gas cooker, her stone copper burned solid fuel, and a coal-fired range in her kitchen remained the preferred place to boil saucepans and roast the Sunday joint. Both houses had only cold water at the kitchen sink. Hot water for personal toilette, shaving, and occasionally for a bath, had to be heated in kettles or the copper, and if needed upstairs, would be carried up in a jug and poured into a basin on a metal wash-stand.

Monday was traditionally 'washing day', and in an age without mechanical assistance, involved considerable physical effort. Having placed a galvanised basin in her sink and added soda to the water, the housewife would soap and scrub the clothes and other items on a ridged washing-board. Cotton garments, sheets, and pillowcases would then be boiled in the copper, while woollen and more delicate clothes were rubbed out by hand. Florence Butcher kept a mangle outside in the brick wash-house, which she used to wring the excess water from the washing prior to pegging it on the line to dry.

The only items not tackled by Mrs Butcher in her weekly wash were her husband's stiff collars. These she put into a round collar box and left at a shop in Waterloo Road for collection by the Baltic Road laundry. Everything else had to be pressed and smoothed with one of a pair of flat irons which were alternately placed on the gas cooker for re-heating.

If outside laundries were rarely used, except for the most specialised items, the practice of dry-cleaning was almost unknown during the inter-war decades. Shops like Flinn and Son, Scott and Son, and Achille Serre that offered this service developed only gradually before 1939, having begun as dyers. Dyeing was a regular household occurrence. A shop such as Norman's in Douglas Road sold 'dolly dyes', to which commodity Mrs Butcher often had recourse to freshen up fading curtains.

To keep the home clean and tidy represented a labour-intensive chore for every conscientious housewife. The linoleumed floors in Lawn Road had to be swept or scrubbed, stairs given the once-over with dust-pan and a small, hard broom, mats and rugs taken outside to be brushed or beaten, and the ornamental glass and rainbow-coloured china vases above the fireplace carefully dusted. Ashes were removed from the grate every morning, the kitchen range black-leaded with 'Zebra' polish, and the doorstep washed off and then whitened with a chalky hearth stone. Management of a domestic budget of something between £3 and £4 per week required Florence Butcher to combine all the self help of her Victorian upbringing with the socialistic virtues of mutuality and co-operation current in the society to which she and her husband now belonged. Though Mr and Mrs Butcher had no use for an account at one of Tonbridge's five banks, or even at Webber's post office, one cannot fail to be impressed by the care and prudence with which the weekly income seems to have been apportioned – a sixpence here and a shilling there, laid out to ensure funds existed when school uniforms or shoes had to be bought, or the Co-op had its sale. The family occasionally took in a lodger to augment father's wages and a small army pension, and, on the evidence of an admittedly very small sample, Mrs Butcher kept back some two-thirds to three-quarters of any money earned by her children as they entered the labour market.

Mending and darning occupied many an hour at the evening fireside. Florence Butcher possessed a black Singer sewing-machine on an ornate cast-iron stand. Working this by means of a treadle, she made many of her own clothes. Checked gingham at sixpence three-farthings a yard could quickly be hemmed and pleated into a summer frock for her daughter, curtains run up out of netting or patterned cotton, and extra bed linen fashioned out of cotton sheeting from a manufacturer like Horrocks or Dorcas.

But if money was tight, and labour-saving appliances powered by electricity almost non-existent, we should not imagine life in or about the typical home of the inter-war period was necessarily comfortless or devoid of amenities. The Butchers had a piano, and both the skill and the inclination to enjoy it, and sufficient discernment to pay to keep it in tune. Florence Butcher played well, and had apparently studied 'vocal music' at an Evening Continuation School in London in the mid 1890s. Her sister, Beatrice, was an accomplished pianist, and the Butcher children were encouraged to develop an aptitude for music. The Butchers also owned an HMV gramophone, with a handle to crank up the turntable mechanism, and a stock of soft, medium, or hard needles to help modulate the sound. Among the records they bought at this time may be mentioned Schubert's 'Unfinished Symphony', Sousa Marches played by brass and silver bands, a rendition of the 'Laughing Policeman', and a waltz or two by Strauss.

The acquisition of a crystal radio set by the family's neighbour Mr Richards caused quite a stir in the later 1920s. Enthusiasts graduated rapidly from the cat's-whisker models to the valve sets of the 1930s, when the programmes of music, comedy, and sport broadcast by the BBC became as much part of daily life as the need to take the large accumulator to be re-charged. With sets selling for between £1 and £3 by the late 1930s, probably as many as nine out of 10 households heard the Christmas message in 1939, when George VI counselled the nation to step out into the night and put its hand in the hand of God.

Once it became affordable, photography enjoyed a great vogue during the inter-war years, producing keepsake snaps of varying size and clarity.

Children, animals, moments of triumph, and scenes of celebration and excursion make up the greater part of the photographic archive; all timeless subjects, but to the historian of manners or costume, a priceless social tableau. From the early 1920s, for example, we glimpse the Lawn Road family at the wedding of eldest daughter Vera to Albert Holman: the women in lace collars and broad hats trimmed with flowers or ostrich feathers, brothers George and Bill in suits and Sussex Road ties, a fox-fur stole draped about Aunt Beatrice's neck. Family albums reveal the Butchers and friends at Margate and Sheerness in the 1930s, Ellen Humphries' sister Jessie amid the snows of her adopted Canada, and like the ghosts of Edwardian Christmases past, a pair of walrus-moustached and bushy-bearded grandfathers. Tonbridge also sustained two professional photographers at this date: Pickett (later Bert Flemons) near the old Baptist Church, and J. L. Allwork towards the top of the High Street. Studio portraits abound; a quaintly formal genre, that has captured George and William Butcher – young men eager to strike a modern pose – dressed in suits and hats that murmur something of fashions aped from the silver screen.

The Humphries' home lacked a piano, but had a mandolin and a wind-up gramophone, and both the boys played the violin. The family's library typified the late-Victorian and Edwardian tastes of the parents: collected verses by Tennyson, Longfellow, Mrs Hemans, and Rupert Brooke. The home also boasted a Bible, assorted volumes of plays and sonnets by Shakespeare, several dozen issues of the journal of the Royal Geographical Society, and a copy of H. G. Wells' *Outline of History*, published in 1920 with those evocative black-and-white drawings of dinosaurs and Neanderthal man.

The parlour furnishings in Barden Park Road included a grandmother clock, another ornate timepiece on the mantel-shelf, a three-cornered chair with tortoiseshell inlay, a settee and two armchairs, a dining table, a large barometer, a revolving bookcase, odds and ends of silver, porcelain and green glass, a sideboard, two tiers of a whatnot, a pair of Sheffield-plate candlesticks, and a framed print of one of those rustic idylls by John Henry Yeend King.

The 1911 system of state health insurance in effect between the wars extended a degree of sickness benefit to the wage-earner, but made no provision for wife or children. Illness or confinement therefore placed huge extra strain on a family's resources. The doctor's five-shilling fee and the cost of his prescriptions, the midwife, and a mother's-help like Mrs Shoebridge, all had to be paid. Wishing to supplement his cover, Clarence Butcher made weekly contributions to a railway 'slate club' at the South Eastern in Barden Road. Members received small sums if they fell ill, with the balance of the fund being distributed at the end of the year. The Butchers began a 'Whole Life Infantile Policy' with the Royal London Mutual Insurance Company within a fortnight of the birth of their younger daughter, which, for a premium of one penny per week, guaranteed half of the £15 sum assured should death occur within six months.

Visits to the surgery in Pembury Road were infrequent, and the horse and trap of Dr Watts of Salford Terrace called but rarely in Lawn Road, and then only to attend the bread-winner. The Cottage Hospital on the corner of Baltic Road had the facilities to undertake hernia operations on Butcher and one of his sons, while the inconsolable cries of a woman in the agonising throes of cancer announced to all who heard her from the street that medical science held out no relief for the terminally ill.

Families had mostly to rely upon proprietary nostrums from the chemist, and on a variety of homespun remedies such as onion broth for colds and sore throats, yellow liquorice powder for constipation, coal-tar ointment for skin complaints, tincture of iodine to cauterise cuts, warts, and pimples, and a bread poultice to treat an abscess.

Children had received free medical and dental inspections at school since 1907, and might be prescribed a tonic such as Parish's Chemical Food if thought to be under-nourished. Rickets was not uncommon among youngsters, while for a child to contract scarlet fever, scabies, or diphtheria meant six weeks in the Isolation Hospital in Vauxhall Lane and the compulsory fumigation of the patient's home. The whooping-cough sufferer, on the other hand, might expect frequent perambulations of the town's Gas Works, or perhaps a protracted banishment to the seaside.

Measles, mumps, rubella, and chicken-pox were accepted as part of the lottery of juvenile life. Tuberculosis could, and regularly did, decimate entire households in inter-war Tonbridge, and condemned many sufferers (among them one of the Butchers' lodgers) to spells of recuperation at Lenham sanatorium. An outbreak of polio reduced some of its victims to a life of disability, and prompted parents to seek vaccination for their offspring, which painful act was signified to the world by the wearing of a scarlet ribbon on the upper sleeve.

Hygiene and diet have always been prime constituents of a family's health and well-being. The very considerable effort needed to heat sufficient water ensured baths were taken far less regularly than nowadays. Washing with carbolic soap had to suffice in many households, but here again it is evident schools actively encouraged parents and children to practise personal cleanliness. The brushing of teeth with pink, peppermint-flavoured tooth powder is indicative of the growing consciousness of the need for improved dental health. Deodorants for either men or women were wholly unknown, and perfume or scent was not generally worn. Mrs Butcher permitted herself no more cosmetics than a dab of face powder, whereas foundation and vanishing creams, rouge, lipstick, and 'Amami' nail-varnish came to be widely used by younger women in the 1930s. The difficulty involved in drying long hair led generations of women to prefer constant brushing as the best form of conditioning, with the meticulous use of a steel 'flea comb' as the most effective means of detecting and removing infestations of the scalp. For those women who chose to wear their hair short, the shilling-a-week visit to a hairdresser purchased a 'Marcel wave' carried out with heated curling-tongs, until, that is, salons like that over the fishmonger's by the Little Bridge introduced the 'permanent wave' at a cost of £1.

Though undoubtedly wholesome, the meals eaten by our forebears of this period may strike the modern palate as somewhat stodgy and lacking in variety. Fruit and vegetables from the garden or allotment were strictly seasonal, unless, like Ellen Humphries, the housewife made jam, bottled summer currants and raspberries in Kilner jars, or laid up apples in a cool store. The packaging, tinning, and processing of foodstuffs was in its infancy in the 1920s and even the 1930s. Custard cream and Nice biscuits and the early breakfast cereals were sold loose at a shop like Sanders Brothers, a corn merchants in the lower High Street; butter, margarine, cheese, and preserves crossed the counter almost as they had left the dairy or commercial pantry.

The Butchers' Sunday lunch normally consisted of a joint of pork, lamb, or beef. Chicken is not remembered as having graced the family board. Monday – perhaps partly because the washing required so much of mother's attention – saw many families eating cold meat with mashed potatoes and pickles. Thereafter, the midday meal might consist of steak and kidney pie or pudding, shin of beef, mutton or rabbit stew, brawn made from pigs' trotters, cod in parsley sauce, or bacon and onion in a steamed suet pudding, followed by a rice-pudding, an apple pie, suet pudding with treacle, jam roly-poly, or maybe a Yorkshire pudding mixture with sultanas. Florence Butcher maintained strong objections to sausages, and offal seems rarely to have been consumed.

The family breakfasted on bacon, scrambled eggs with fried potato, and fried bread. Porridge made from rolled oats had to be boiled in a 'double saucepan' for half an hour, while shredded-wheat (dismissed by Florence Butcher as 'just a load of straw'), grape nuts, or Force's early cereal flakes were eaten with milk and sugar. Tea-time in Lawn Road saw parents eating boiled eggs, kippers, or fillets of golden haddock, and children satisfied with bread and jam, and perhaps a penny or halfpenny cake from Mr Oliver's bakery, or one of mother's rock buns.

Tea was drunk with most meals. Florence Butcher occasionally made herself a drink from a liquid essence known as 'Camp' coffee with chicory, while a mug of cocoa brewed with boiling water and a spoonful of condensed milk usually accompanied a late-evening supper of beef sandwiches or bread and cheese.

At the Shops

Talk of diets and household economy leads logically towards a discussion of shops and shopping. The absence of refrigeration, the general tightness of family budgets, and the lack of the sort of public or private transport taken for granted by most modern shoppers, meant that housewives tended to visit the shops on an almost daily basis, buying only what they could afford, what they could conveniently carry, and what they needed to prepare the next meal, or knew might be stored in a cool larder or down in the cellar. Many tradesmen sold or delivered from street to street; and when necessary, children ran errands for their mothers, often being sent out for a bunch of carrots, with a jug to the dairy or the Good Intent, or for a bag of iced buns to complete the tea table.

Analysing the experience of Meadow Lawn residents in the 1920s and that of their Barden counterparts in the 1930s, it is possible to identify four principal categories of retailer or service-provider: neighbours with a skill or a commodity to sell, door-to-door tradesmen, small, back-street shopkeepers and craftsmen, and the larger or more specialised businesses of the High Street. Each had its peculiar niche in the domestic economy of the typical family. The former offered a convenient supply of a few staples; the neighbourhood shops carried greater variety, and were close enough to cater for emergencies; while the housewife might resort to the High Street stores for luxuries, treats, and speciality or branded items.

Among the neighbours whose services the Butchers customarily purchased, mention should be made of Mrs Colyer, who sold bunches of cut flowers from her garden in Albert Road, a dressmaker from St. Mary's Road, and, when the chimney needed sweeping or the kitchen fire flared out of control, Mr Beavis of Wincliff Road.

Those who traded their wares at the doorstep were of several distinct types. Most ephemeral of all were the itinerants and hawkers – the gypsies who appeared from time to time, clutching baskets of ribbons, wooden clothes pegs, and posies of primroses or wild daffodils. The man who occasionally sold Mrs Butcher a dead rabbit also falls into this group. He charged about a shilling for each carcass, but would willingly skin the animal and pay a penny for the pelt.

Both fish and vegetables could be purchased from barrows, the former including half-pints of shrimps, golden haddock, and pieces of cod on the bone. These were the traders for whom a cart was their sole outlet and the street-corner their only market-place. The coalman had an established round, and the 'rag and bone' man worked the streets with his cart and a cry that set the younger children running and the dogs barking.

Most numerous were the local retailers who delivered from house to house as an extension of an established business. Several laundries fetched and returned clothing and linen. The Co-op delivered bread to houses in Meadow Lawn, as did the Douglas Road baker, who, on Good Fridays, would additionally bring warm hot-cross buns to the doorsteps of his regulars. Another familiar daily visitor was the Co-op milkman, carrying a galvanised pail and his pint and half-pint measures. And, of course, the newsagent supplied Clarence Butcher's *Daily Herald*, his three-halfpenny copy of the *Tonbridge Free Press* each Friday, both the *Evening News* and the *Evening Standard*, and on Sundays *The People* and the *News of the World*.

Nearly all the Meadow Lawn shopkeepers had their premises in Douglas Road. At the corner of Lionel Road stood the general store of Mr Norman, a biggish, rather dark shop selling groceries, paraffin, all sorts of hardware, brooms, mats, ironmongery, and commodities such as vinegar. Next came the tobacconist and sweetshop run by Mr Kelly, and a little further along towards Mabledon Road, the drapers of Mrs Pierce, where for many years the locals bought from a range of fabrics, wool, cottons, and silks, as well as women's and children's clothes, including swimming costumes.

A second cluster of shops on the south side of Douglas Road between Mabledon Road and Chichester Road, contained the dairy of Mr Baker, and close by, the bakery owned in the early 1920s by the Fagg family, and later sold to his chief assistant, Mr Oliver, who moved from his house in Lawn Road to live over the business. The bakehouse at the rear of the premises supplied bread and cakes for the shop, and it was common practice for neighbours to pay a few pence to bake their own Christmas or birthday cakes in the oven. Dough buns cost a halfpenny each or seven for threepence; a bag of yesterday's cakes or broken biscuits might be purchased for a halfpenny or so.

Fred Markwick had a butcher's shop on the other side of Douglas Road, near to the church and roughly opposite Kelly's tobacconists. Elsewhere, there was a shop at the corner of Wincliff Road where groceries, greengrocery, biscuits, and confectionery might be purchased on tick. Sweets were always on display here; the halfpenny liquorice and sherbet dabs being an irresistible temptation to children running errands for their mothers. Another little shop at the bottom of Station Hill sold sweets, and was later taken over by a watch-repairer.

As one would expect, Meadow Lawn numbered several shoemakers among its resident craftsmen. Mr Emerson of Albert Road kept a shop in Wincliff Road, while the tiny Tudor building next to the Good Intent in Waterloo Road was successively occupied as a cobbler's by Mr Cash, Alf Ollerenshaw, and Arthur Gurr in this period.[2] Not far away, in the basement of one of the houses at the top of Priory Road, Mr Cunningham had his umbrella-repair business, patronised by Florence Butcher whenever her brolly had a broken stave. Even in the 1930s, the Barden estate was less well-endowed with retailers and street traders than Meadow Lawn a decade earlier, although technology and probably choice had moved on apace. A Barden Road greengrocer sold his fruit and vegetables from door to door, Mr Edwards the baker had his round, and the milkman – now with his milk in bottles rather than a pail – delivered not on foot but in a motor van. Best remembered of all, however, were the Nices, father and chatterbox daughter Irene, whose horse-drawn cart and its motorised successor kept customers supplied with groceries that bore the unmistakable trademark taste of paraffin.

All Barden's outlying shops fell into the category of small general store, each serving a small local clientele with a limited range of day-to-day necessities. Orridge's lock-up shop on the corner where Barden Road curves sharply towards Nelson Avenue was one such. Mr and Mrs Barker sold sweets, tobacco, and groceries from the converted front room of their cottage on the railway side of Nelson Avenue, and Fermors at the bottom of Cromer Street purveyed a roughly similar stock-in-trade. A butcher's shop next to the farther entrance into River Walk was run for many years by Mr Bramley.

Nearer still to the railway station, Frederick Nice had his grocery, oil, and hardware store on the north side of Barden Road, and close by were a dairy and Edwards, the well-known Tonbridge baker. Opposite the Barden Road entrance to the station stood more shops, including another baker, Avery the grocer, a greengrocer, the barber's run by Mr Walder, and the post office on the corner of Danvers Road also kept by Mr Walder.

Slightly further afield, on a parcel of land opposite St Stephen's between the main road and Alexandra Road, were the greenhouses and plantations of Webber's nursery. The Webbers had more greenhouses on the north side of Skinners Terrace, and sold seeds – a pint of peas or a twist of parsnips perhaps – in an adjacent shop, later combined with a sub post office. The Malpass family ran a cooked-meat shop on the other side of Skinners Terrace, Mr Norman of Douglas Road kept a furniture store hereabouts, and by the 1930s, additional shop premises had resulted from the re-development of the Webbers' land and Salford Terrace. The row of little lock-up shops on the Station Approach supported more local traders; men like Mr Scorey of Waterloo Road the greengrocer, and Mr Williams of Barden Road who sold miscellaneous hardware.

Almost without exception, therefore, the shops of Meadow Lawn and Barden Road in the inter-war decades were small, devoted solely to the sale of staple commodities, or the provision of basic services such as hairdressing or shoe repairs. Some were situated in purpose-built premises, but many had been set up in the converted living-rooms of houses or cottages. Most were family businesses, with the shopkeeper and his family living above and behind the shop or in one of the adjoining streets. Producer-retailers such as bakers, dairymen, and cobblers could still make a living, though as a class their star would soon be totally eclipsed by greater mobility and enhanced purchasing power on the part of their erstwhile customers, for whom the High Street (or even Tunbridge Wells or London) possessed attractions undreamed of and unattainable a generation earlier.

It remains to render some account of the shops and retailers of the inter-war High Street, a diverse community comprehending the emporium, the producer-retailer, and the pitch on the corner of Botany where chestnuts roasted on a brazier in autumn and thirsty children bought summer ice-creams from the boot of a tricycle.[3] This is not the place for an exhaustive study of a fascinating subject. Rather, the memories of contemporaries must be allowed to highlight what was important to a particular family or a particular social grouping, for in the end, have not shopping patterns as much to do with loyalty and custom and personal prejudice as with considerations based purely upon quality or price or variety? Personal and printed sources make it clear the inter-war decades saw the steady consolidation of earlier trends in retailing and consumerism in ways that profoundly affected Tonbridge people. Never had the sole trader felt himself so much an endangered species as in 1918; never had competition been keener; never had so many shopkeepers and store managers offered so much choice to local householders. Though many of the old fascias survived to 1939, yet the nature of both shops and shopping altered radically in the interim.

By the 1920s, the multiple store had become an accepted feature of most small provincial towns. Entrepreneurs like Thomas Lipton, Joseph Hepworth, Jesse Boot, and Sir George Watson had pioneered this form of mass retailing in the three decades before 1900, when, first brewing, Singer sewing-machines, and the grocery sector, and later tailoring and the shoe trade, took up the challenge of supplying low-cost goods at the point of working-class demand.[4] Urbanisation and steadily rising wages created the conditions necessary for retailing on a national scale, helped further, in the case of the provisions and grocery trade, by the removal of import duties and the availability of raw materials from overseas: eggs, cheese, and butter from Ireland, grain and sugar from the Americas, bacon from Europe, and tea from the Empire.

In about 1918, Pearks Dairies, the Maypole Dairy Company, Home and Colonial Stores, and Lipton had shops on the west side of the High Street below the Little Bridge. Roughly opposite stood a branch of the International Stores, while in the 1920s Sainsbury built a large shop next to the town's Post Office, on land formerly occupied by Bartram's brewery.

Choice of multiple remained a matter of fierce loyalty, though the selection of groceries on offer was fairly uniform. Lipton and the International were the largest of the Tonbridge stores, selling everything from soap to bacon and breakfast cereals. The Home and Colonial built its national reputation in the 1890s on the sale of blended teas. Butter, margarine, and sugar were quickly added to its list of staples, and the 1920s saw diversification into coffee, cocoa, custard, blancmange, tinned milk, treacle, self-raising flour, baking powder, jams, and jelly.

Even before its amalgamation with Home and Colonial in 1924, Maypole Dairies had begun to enhance its traditional range of eggs, cask butter, bacon, and condensed milk (much of it imported from Denmark) with lines such as lard, sugar, dried milk, marmalade, tinned fruit, slab cake, 'Mikado' tea, and beef suet, but was best known as market leader in the margarine war of that time, when products from its Erith refinery regularly out-sold 'Blue Band' and 'Pheasant' brands from the Dutch giants Van den Berghs and Jurgens respectively. Mrs Butcher always visited Maypole for her half pound of 'Mayco' margarine (launched in 1921 at a shilling a pound), and also perhaps for a quarter of butter. One of the assistants would break a piece of margarine from the large block on the counter, knock it into shape with wooden implements – 'like little cricket bats' – and hand her the weighed purchase wrapped in greaseproof paper.

Another important phenomenon of the inter-war period was the emergence of the so-called variety chain store, run on the 'penny bazaar' model made famous in the 1890s by Marks and Spencer. Situated between Medway Wharf Road and Botany, Woolworth championed the 'nothing over sixpence' sector in Tonbridge, being remembered in particular for sweets, its glassware and crockery, jewellery, cosmetics, gramophone records, and its selection of spectacles. Domestic Bazaars Ltd (just north of Frank East) also fell into this category of bazaar-type outlet. The wooden-floored shop sold every imaginable item of cleaning and cooking ironmongery, and stocked an Aladdin's cave of cheap trinkets, rings, necklaces, little knives, sweets, and celluloid dolls to tempt children eager to spend the halfpenny held back from the missionary box at Sunday School.

The first department stores had evolved in the 1870s and 1880s, chiefly from among the largest of London's drapers, and by 1918, Debenhams, the John Lewis Partnership, and their competitors were poised to make inroads into the provincial market. Inter-war Tonbridge boasted two sizeable drapers:

Gunner and Son on the corner of Lyons Crescent and Frank East in Manchester House next to the old Congregational Church. Though neither quite rivalled even a medium-sized store like Chiesman's of Maidstone, they both exemplified the principal of many specialist departments collected under the roof of a single emporium. One's image of both shops is of establishments run along old-fashioned lines that will be familiar to readers of H. G. Wells or Arnold Bennett's *The Old Wives' Tale*. Of the two, Frank East catered for a more well-to-do, middle-class clientele; its various departments offering a wide variety of off-the-peg garments for men, women, and children, while its haberdashery counters displayed cottons, buttons, pins, and ribbons to suit every need of fashion or utility. Gunner's also sold made-up clothes, woollen, lisle cotten, and silk stockings, etc., but like the more traditional drapers of a generation earlier, the shop stocked materials by the bale and the roll – ginghams, huckaback, and bombazine, cottons, calico, and corduroys – to be bought by the yard and run-up at home into curtains, trousers, dresses, towels, shirts, and blouses. Rayon was widely purchased to make tablecloths and children's clothes.

The store that exercised the greatest influence over the lives of families in South Tonbridge during the inter-war period was the Co-op.[5] As one historian of shopping has observed, the success of the Co-operative movement owed much to 'communal feeling and solidarity.'[6] Co-ops throve best in built-up areas, where the loyalty of a close-knit neighbourhood restricted competition. Co-ops added an important social dimension to the community they existed to serve, and there can be no doubt the ideals cherished by the Victorian pioneers of co-operation were sympathetically maintained in many of the working-class households of Meadow Lawn and Barden. At bottom, however, the Co-op continued to draw its strength from Rochdale's revolutionary concept of 'vertical integration' – the harnessing of wholesale and retail practices and co-ordinated channels of distribution – which enabled its branches to sell simple, wholesome commodities, as well as small luxuries like newspapers and cigarettes, at the lowest possible prices.

Post-war generations will recall the semi-derelict, boarded-up front of the Co-op building in Quarry Hill Road (Priory Terrace) opposite the entrance to Priory Road, as a sorry spectacle of commercial decay. But in its heyday the Co-op was as much a scene of bustle and endeavour as any modern supermarket. When approaching from Waterloo Road, the pedestrian first passed the Co-op shoe shop. Next came the street-door of the grocery department, and a few yards further along the pavement one reached the door of the clothing and hosiery department. The grocery section consisted of counters down either side of a long hall: one selling greengrocery, loose biscuits, and the like; the other given over to staple provisions such as butter, margarine, and bacon. The clothing department might be entered through an archway at the far end of the grocery hall. A flight of stairs led up to additional rooms set aside for the sale of hats and the trying-on of clothes.

In the mid 1930s, the *Tonbridge Free Press* carried advertisements for the Co-operative Wholesale Society's 'Wheatsheaf' range of children's clothing and footwear.[7] Boys' flannel suits were on sale from 5s 6d and boys' tweed knicker suits from 10s 6d. Girls' school coats sold from 6s 11d and school frocks from 4s 11d. When paying for these goods, the customer saw her money and a price ticket placed in a small box-like container, which was conveyed by means of a network of overhead wires to the office at the bottom of the shop, whence it returned duly receipted, and with the appropriate quantity of change.

Florence Butcher obtained by far the greatest proportion of her weekly shopping at the Co-op. She did so, one assumes, partly because the store was close at hand and formed an intrinsic part of the Meadow Lawn community. The Co-op accepted written orders and made deliveries. Goods might be taken home on approval, and it was common practice for housewives to pay into one of the society's savings clubs to accumulate funds for children's clothes or the proverbial rainy day. In the main, however, the Co-op found favour with Mrs Butcher because low prices still represented value for money, and because, as an enrolled member of the local co-operative society, she was entitled to a 'dividend' based upon the value of purchases made throughout the year. Every member of the Co-op had a dividend book. For each transaction made, the purchaser received a dividend slip, details from which were transferred to the dividend book at the branch office. The format of the dividend differed from society to society. When the Butchers moved to Plumstead in the early 1930s, for example, the Royal Arsenal Co-operative Society gave metal tokens that might be spent in its branches. In Tonbridge, however, the annual dividend was paid out in shillings and pence. It clearly played an important part in the family budget, and ensured that whenever practicable, the Butcher household was fed, shod, and clothed from the Co-op.

Multiple stores of all types and across all sectors of retailing operated a regimen founded on competitive pricing, quick sales, cash over the counter, no orders, and strictly no credit. Throughout the inter-war decades their marketing strategy continued to target the working-class consumer, with the result that the High Street in a town like Tonbridge retained many specialist shopkeepers capable of attracting custom by dint of their professional skills, the variety or quality of their goods, or the additional services they offered. Hence, for example, while a branch of Freeman Hardy and Willis had sold shoes in the town since the 1890s, its presence did not stifle the trade of Nelson Gale by the Little Bridge or of Dolcis a little lower down. Small dress shops and corset-makers like that of Gladys Lark near St Stephen's, or Hersey's in the High Street, or Fisher's close to the corner of Avebury Avenue – where Florence Butcher purchased her mid-brown hair nets for a penny three farthings – steadfastly resisted the superior resources of the town's principal drapers. And in this age of Montague Burton's fifty-shilling suits, Tonbridge could support Tom Coles among several resident tailors, and also the outfitting establishments of Bailes Ltd and E. W. Parsons.

While Woolworth, the Co-op, and most of the back-street shops of Meadow Lawn and Barden sold sweets and tobacco, the High Street sustained a number of more specialised tobacconists. Mr Chielman's shop just south of Botany was one such, and Jupp's is fondly remembered for its coconut chips and the annual chance to guess the weight of a huge Easter egg. The West family had a double shop just below the Bull Hotel that one fancies retained something of the neatness and profusion of Dickens at his most expansive. The left-hand entrance opened upon the tobacco, cigarette, and pipe counters, while the bell that jingled above the right-hand door announced the arrival of customers among the shelves of multi-coloured sweets in large, stoppered jars. Locust beans, tiger nuts, sherbet suckers, gob-stoppers, clove balls, and aniseed drops all attracted the attention of the Butcher children. George nurtured a penchant for things liquorice, and Clarence Butcher went off to work each morning sucking a bull's-eye to 'keep out the cold'.

MacFisheries (founded as late as 1919 by Lord Leverhulme) sold fish, poultry, and sometimes game in its Tonbridge branches, while in the meat trade, the multiples had always stocked ham and bacon, and certainly from the 1930s the Co-op employed its own butcher. Florence Butcher, however, tended to buy her meat from Mr Dawes just above Avebury Avenue, whereas, if a pound of Mr Bramley's scrag or a shilling parcel of his steak and kidney failed to please the eye, her eldest daughter, Vera Holman of Audley Avenue, would switch her custom to Malpass's sawdust-floored shop at the corner of Church Lane. If the housewife wanted fish, the choice invariably lay between Thompson's on the Station Approach (perhaps for some of those bloaters smoked in the lower part of the premises that opened into Barden Road) or Reading's beside the Little Bridge – a site used by fishmongers like the Bewleys almost from time immemorial – where one of the Butcher children would be sent for a three-halfpenny pair of kippers and a halfpenny cod's-head for the cat. House specialities and the personal touch thus continued to add an indefinable value that kept the customer loyal.

With the exception of the Co-op and maybe the Kent Wallpaper Company, Tonbridge traders like Bonner the upholsterer, Peters the china dealer, and Coates and Son, suppliers of quality leather goods, encountered little competition in the household furnishing market. Local ironmongers such as Woodman and Son and Seale, Austen and Barnes coexisted with Timothy White's hardware business, as did Clarke and Coleman and O. M. Wisdom successfully counter the West Kent Drug Store's inroads into the pharmaceutical and patent medicines market.

The example of Ernest Upton the chemist helps explain just why such local traders stayed in business so tenaciously. With the traditional coloured carboys proudly in its window, Upton's shop next to the Loggerheads at the top of Waterloo Road stocked an astonishing diversity of pills, potions, and ointments on its shelves, backed up by a readiness on the part of the proprietor to perform all kinds of semi-professional services, including eyesight tests, basic veterinary skills, and later the developing of films. The Butchers bought their supply of Beecham's regulatory pills at Upton's, as well as dog powders, 'Melrose' and 'Snowfire' preparations for chilblains, and a mysterious concoction necessary for the fermentation of ginger wine; and it was to Mr Upton that the family paid a shilling to put to sleep an ailing pet dog in a special gas chamber. What multiple store could aspire to so catholic a trade?

Many provincial grocers survived the high-street tussle with the multiples because large manufacturers moved to preserve a variety of outlets for their products by enforcing a system of 'retail price maintenance' that prevented the wealthier stores cutting prices below levels viable for the sole trader. Other grocers were saved from oblivion by concentrating their appeal on middle-class tastes, or by adopting the blending, marketing, and advertising techniques of their more illustrious competitors. Fifield's tea, for example, is described in the *Tonbridge Free Press* as having been 'blended on the premises to suit the local water'.[8] Tommy Vane of 71 High Street (between Botany and the Bull Hotel) used the same newspaper to laud the merits of his 'home-made' marmalade, which retailed at 2s 9d for a 7 lb jar.

The 1930s witnessed the development of nationally recognisable brands based on packaging and press and other advertisements. We see aspects of this marketing culture at work in such novels as Orwell's *Keep the Aspidistra Flying* and Dorothy Sayers' *Murder Must Advertise*. Devotees of Force breakfast flakes might, for example, save labels and acquire thereby a rag-doll replica of the cereal's Sonny Jim mascot, complete with cutely turned-up hat. But the multiples had no monopoly over the commodities so promoted. Packaged margarine could now be sold with convenience at corner-shops, while the wrapping of bread and meat products brought the standard sliced loaf and the pound of Richmond sausages into most outlets, along with Smith's crisps and the quarter of 'Mazawattee' tea.

At School

An Elementary School was established in the upper portion of Sussex Road in 1907 with a staff of five and an initial intake of sixty. By the 1920s, the infants' school alone had more than 270 children on its roll; and the original foundation had expanded and diversified into four separate components: the infants' and girls' schools along the east pavement, the boys' school and the 'special' school on the west side. Pupils were attracted from the St Mary's Road and Judd Road area, from Barden Park, and from Meadow Lawn itself. The Butcher children, the Humphries boys, and later Eric and Kenneth Holman of Audley Avenue all attended the 'mixed infants'' school between the ages of five and eight, after which the sexes went their separate ways through the junior and secondary phases of the educational structure.

Miss Eaton and Miss Price of The Drive were headmistresses of the infants' and girls' schools respectively in the 1920s, while across the road, Mr MacFarlane and Mr Cook served as headmaster and deputy-head at the boys' school. Discipline was strict. Mr Cook administered the cane with some severity, and on one occasion felt moved to chastise Eric Holman when the unfortunate boy arrived late, having been ducked in a nearby pond where he had gone to investigate the drowning of some puppies. Neither was the caning of wayward or delinquent girls unknown. Classes were conducted in silence, preserved when necessary by the judicious application of ruler to knuckles, and one fidgeting girl found herself tied by the leg to a desk.

By the 1920s, most schools operated an internal 'house' system. Miss Price, for example, divided her 'big girls' into six houses: Aphrodite, Athena, Muse, Hygieia, Demeter, and Atalanta – each denoted by its own colour: blue, white, mauve, red, green, and orange. Each girl wore a badge of the appropriate colour as part of her school uniform, which otherwise consisted of a brown tunic over a white blouse, brown socks or stockings, and brown shoes. House loyalties and rivalries counted for much in the daily round of games and competitions, and the school maintained a hierarchy of merits and demerits awarded for good work or bad behaviour.

All the teachers at the infants' and girls' schools were women, most – like Miss Witt, Mrs Pullen, Miss Stacey, Miss Pelham, and Miss Humphrey – being responsible for a single class or 'standard'. Subjects taught included reading, writing, composition, recitation, geography, arithmetic, spelling, and scripture. Girls went to Miss Bullock for cookery, to Miss Laskey for music, and to Miss Cherry for needlework and knitting. Drill and country dancing took place in the assembly hall, with netball and rounders being organised in the playground, often against other Tonbridge schools, when the boys would line the railings to cheer on their sisters and neighbours. Jimmy's Field, where the school had a long-jump pit, was the venue for the girls' annual sports day. Most classes paid a weekly visit to the Tonbridge swimming-baths during the summer term.

All classrooms were furnished with a blackboard on an easel, derived warmth from a coal fire, and were illuminated by gas-jets. Pupils sat in pairs, with each double desk slightly separated from the next. Everyone faced the front. Where a boy or girl sat in class signified his or her age and achievement. Standing erect before the hearth, 'Miss' found herself free to strike her best Sarah Bernhardt pose and delight her eager audience with popular verses from the pen of A. E. Housman, a patriotic Kipling ballad, or maybe one of Mr Masefield's nautical ditties. Rhymes heard in this simple theatre dwelt long in the memory.

The infants initially used chalk on slates, and for a considerable time the juniors wrote their lessons in printed script, before finally graduating to the dipping of nibs into ink-wells and 'joined-up writing'. Painting was always an enjoyable lesson, as was model-making with plasticine. Toys were provided for the youngest infants. Parents attended open days to inspect displays of work; and the annual festival of music, singing, and drama at the Opera House in Tunbridge Wells usually saw both girls' and boys' schools carry off prizes or a banner.

The schools in Sussex Road kept a stock-room of uniforms, and encouraged parents to pay sums of a shilling per week into a bank to ease the purchase of necessary items. Next to the boys' school was the health clinic, where pupils received medical inspections by a doctor and a dentist. Dr Tucker is recalled as having 'a fleshy wart on his bald head', while the school dentist – regarded by his victims as a 'butcher' – would fill or extract teeth, and often advised sceptical parents on additional treatment. Girls had to wear long hair in plaits, and all heads were regularly checked for lice by a visiting 'nit nurse'. Parents were also given medicines or tonics to improve the nutrition of sickly children.

During the 1920s, the children at Sussex Road began to receive milk, at first in the form of Horlicks, and later in the more traditional small bottles. Neither scheme was free, but cost parents a halfpenny a day. However, the innovation came to be regarded as sufficiently beneficial for a group of girls to be dispatched to the Market Room at the Rose & Crown to meet the local press and sing a little promotional ditty of their own:

Milko, milko, penny to pay,
To ride on the top of the world today.
Milko, milko, at work or at play.
Milko, milko, hip hip hurray.

It soon became a mark of a teacher's benignity that he or she pulled the daily crate of bottles close to the classroom blaze, an act much appreciated by pupils on frosty winter mornings.

School dinners were not provided. Most children lived nearby and hence went home for their midday meal, though some did bring sandwiches to be eaten in a large shed in the playground. The left-overs from an 'old girls' reunion were occasionally sold round the school, as were the unwanted creations of cookery classes. The boys' school taught gardening, the fruits of which useful tuition George Butcher brought proudly home to his mother's kitchen.[9]

One can speculate that the existence of the Tonbridge Special School (set up in 1914 and not closed until 1938) may have been a factor influencing the Butchers' move to Tonbridge, since their son Harold attended the school for several years after 1918.

Fisher's Education Act of 1918 set the school-leaving age at fourteen, and instituted national testing and the School Certificate. Thereafter, though the inter-war years heard frequent lamentations about the wasted talents of the nation's youth, no Government found it possible or expedient to alter the provisions of this statute prior to the outbreak of war in 1939. By the late 1920s, however, most children sat some kind of examination at the age of eleven, and were sometimes re-examined two years later, in order to determine how best they might pass the remainder of their school days. The influential Hadow Report of 1926 had advocated the establishment of 'modern schools', and urged that a change of school environment after the age of 11 would pay dividends in educational terms. Here Tonbridge made some real progress. In the late 1920s, most girls transferred from Sussex Road to the Technical Institute in Avebury Avenue, and in the 1930s to the new school in Brionne Gardens. Boys like Jack Humphries, on the other hand, completed both primary and secondary phases of their schooling at Sussex Road, though during the 1930s, some Sussex Road boys were moved to Slade School as juniors.

Sent to the Technical Institute at the age of eleven, young Elsie Butcher found the classrooms lit by electricity, and perhaps realised with a passing regret that a building heated by radiators rather than coal fires meant cold milk on chill mornings. These differences apart, however, the curriculum and internal organisation at the 'Tech' were very similar to those prevailing at the elementary level in Sussex Road. Sapphire, Ruby, Emerald, and Topaz were the four houses (allegiance to which was indicated by a blue, red, green, or orange belt) around which Miss Goddard, the headmistress, and her staff operated a system of 'honours', prefects, and captains. Class teachers like Miss Tully and Miss Simms taught the whole spectrum of subjects, except for singing and music, and also cookery, the latter being the preserve of Mrs Lemmon. Pupils left at 14 with a personal testimonial and maybe one of the Queen Victoria Memorial Scripture prizes.

Grammar school places were open to all those whose parents could afford them. Scholarships won at the age of 11 or 13 took care of fees for the less well-off, but still it was by no means uncommon for a bright child to triumph

The Drill Team in the playground of the Technical Institute in Avebury Avenue (now the Adult Education Centre) in 1930. (Author's photograph)

in the examination hall, only to be held back because family resources could not stretch to uniforms, tennis rackets, hockey sticks, and all the paraphernalia of a grammar-school education, or because parents like Florence Butcher valued an extra wage more highly than 'book learning'. For a fortunate few, however, the 'eleven-plus' opened a path to the Judd School or the County School for Girls in Deakin Leas. Hence, when their younger son Robert won a 'free place' at Judd in 1929, one assumes Leslie and Ellen Humphries resolved, as did many other parents on modest incomes, to make whatever sacrifices were necessary to forward his prospects, since to have attended such a school counted for much in inter-war Tonbridge.

Following an act of 1919, the fees for day boys at Judd had been set at £3 10s per term or 10 guineas a year, not including, of course, the additional cost of clothing, games, clubs, and trips. Throughout the next 20 years, the school attracted pupils from the lower-middle and better-off artisan classes of the town and its surrounding villages and parishes, while Tonbridge School remained the preserve and the preference of local professional families. In 1928 the boys on the roll numbered 314, a figure that stood at 355 in 1939, having been as high as 376 in 1935.[10]

The inter-war decades saw Judd adapting to its own use the traditions and practices of the public schools, many of them centred upon the four school houses: Alpha (mauve), Beta (green), Gamma (red), and Delta (yellow). Buildings and playing-fields were extended in the 1930s, and the period witnessed the popularisation of soccer, cricket, athletics, boxing, debating, drama, music, and foreign travel. The programme published on Sports Day in May 1933 lists throwing the cricket ball and tug-of-war alongside the usual running and jumping events, and evidences keen inter-house rivalry and a reverence for past and present achievements. Robert Humphries represented his House in swimming relays, played for the school's First Rugby XV, and in 1934 took second place in the Angell Cup for Life Saving.

By 1930, the academic curriculum of Judd had evolved markedly from the Commercial School of William Bryant's day, when the prevailing ethos demanded the provision of basic reading, writing, and grammar to the sons of local farmers and tradesmen. Bryant retired in 1908 after 20 years service, to be succeeded first by John Evans, and then after 1928 by William John Lloyd Morgan until 1946. Instead of book-keeping, shorthand, and composition, a boy like Robert Humphries might now expect to study English, history, biology, and current affairs, and perhaps also French, German, woodwork, and art. Standards had climbed on to an altogether higher plane. The infectious enthusiasm of a master like the celebrated amateur astronomer A. P. Norton (from 1914 until he retired in 1936) gave an added fillip to the study of mathematics, physics, and geography. Robert Humphries left Judd at the age of 16 having passed his General School Certificate. For the brightest pupils, on the other hand, Matriculation represented the pinnacle of scholarly achievement, that for a handful could even open the gates of an Oxbridge college.

The schools of inter-war Tonbridge could not hope to broach every subject or hone every skill. Private tuition thus found no shortage of willing students eager to pay for additional accomplishments or some knowledge likely to advance a career. Florence Butcher sent her younger daughter for piano lessons to a Miss Bushel in Barden Road, and later to one of the Miss Nortons in the family home on the corner of Norfolk Road; and in the 1930s, Kenneth Holman studied the same instrument (lessons cost half-a-crown and sheets of music a shilling) at the Lyons Crescent home of Mr Miller, organist at the Parish Church. Jack Humphries attended evening classes at Constable's Commercial College in St Mary's Road, where he acquired proficiency in typing, shorthand, and book-keeping. Correspondence courses also assisted those with an appetite for 'self help'. The School of Accountancy, for instance, ran company secretarial courses from its Glasgow headquarters.

In an address delivered in August 1936 at the annual prize giving at Tonbridge Senior Boys' School in Sussex Road, Mr S. A. Fletcher sought to assess the weaknesses and strengths of the school where he was in his second year as headmaster. In a sense, what he had to say summed up the fortunes of popular education at the close of the inter-war period. His most pressing concern was clearly the shortage of facilities for art and science; and he made no secret of his desire to see the boys of South Tonbridge given a new building like that recently opened for the senior girls of the area.[11]

These reservations aside, Mr Fletcher was anxious to be positive, and proceeded to catalogue an impressive list of events organised over the past year, including a concert that had raised £14, an open day, a sports day, swimming, cricket and football matches, athletics, and a trip to Windsor. Boys had made metal models for an exhibition in London, had contributed to a school magazine, had entered the Kent produce show, and had gone on visits to a demonstration of bee keeping, and also to the farms of Mr Vizard and Mr Large. The school had participated in the Tunbridge Wells music festival, and currently found itself in a fertile period of hymn and other musical composition. All pupils were soon to be involved in gardening courses; and the headmaster looked forward to using the school's recently-installed radio receiver to pick up the BBC's new educational broadcasts. A junior branch of the League of Nations had been established at the school, which, amid the crises of Mussolini's Abyssinian adventure and Hitler's invasion of the Rhineland, Mr Fletcher hoped would 'help, even if only in a very small way, to foster a spirit of friendliness and balance at a time which is proving to be one of so much disquiet and unrest among the nations'.

We hear little of the school's academic prowess, except that, at the close of his speech, a proud headmaster congratulated one boy on winning a Smythe exhibition to the Judd School and another on his engineering exhibition to the Technical Institute in Tunbridge Wells. Like English 'secondary school' education as a whole, it appears the essential content and direction of the curriculum as pursued at Sussex Road by the classes of Eric and Kenneth Holman (who completed their school days under Mr Fletcher and his successor, Mr Herman) remained much as it had been in the days of their uncles, George and William Butcher. Trips to Penshurst Place and Tonbridge Castle, music, and basic chemistry with bunsen burners, test tubes, and clouds of pungent gases may have stretched horizons at the corners, but foreign languages and other sciences were not taught. As had been the case two decades earlier, the teaching of English, arithmetic, team games, and the cultivation of plots near to the bird-cage path looked little further than the perennial equipping of fourteen-year-olds to make their way in the local employment market.

Sources

1   Stevenson, J., *British Society, 1914-45* (Penguin, 1984), p110

2   'Cobbling among the cobwebs' in Chapman, F., *Tales of Old Tonbridge* (Brasted, 1995), p27

3   Neve, A. H., *The Tonbridge of Yesterday* (Tonbridge, 1933), p378ff contains lists of High Street proprietors in 1932

4   Compare Mathias, P., *Retailing Revolution: a history of multiple retailing in the food trades based upon the Allied Suppliers Group of Companies* (London, 1967) and Jefferys, J. B., *Retail Trading in Britain 1850-1950: a study of trends in retailing with special reference to the development of Co-operative, multiple shop and department store methods of trading* (Cambridge, 1954)

5   See the sympathetic introduction to this subject in Cole, G. D. H., *A Century of Cooperation* (London,1944)

6   Davis, D., *A History of Shopping* (London, 1966), p279

7   *Tonbridge Free Press*, 28 August 1936

8   *Ibid*.

9   Compare the striking parallels in Flack, M., Hamilton, J., Hume, A., and Wood, S., (eds), *Hildenborough C of E Primary School 1847-1997* (Tonbridge, 1997)

10 Taylor, G., *The Judd School 1888-1988* (Tonbridge, 1988), p64

11 *Tonbridge Free Press*, 28 August 1936

Acknowledgements

Acknowledgements relating to this chapter are included in the list on pages 140-41.

Tonbridge Families Remembered: a Study of Life in South-West Tonbridge, 1918-39

Part 2: Work and Leisure

Dr P. L. Humphries

In the autumn of 1933, the author J. B. Priestley undertook a tour of England, determined, like Defoe and Cobbett in earlier centuries, to discover the economic and social condition of the people.[1] At its heart, Priestley's journey led him from the West Riding to Staffordshire, through Liverpool and Lancashire, as far north as Newcastle, and into the coalfields of East Durham; and at every stop he seemed to find working-class communities shackled and manacled in the chains of poverty, hopelessness, and unemployment. The weavers and merchants of Bradford and Blackburn, the potters of Stoke, and the shipyard hands and engineers of Wallsend and Hebburn had a common story to tell – a story of loafers and 'corner boys', of mean and dingy houses, of slatternly women, of dereliction and decay, and of urchins playing in grimy streets. Priestley describes Gateshead, to select one example from many, as a shapeless, sprawling town, devoid of character and amenity, which industrialisation had built, solely and soullessly, for men 'to work in and to sleep in', where only funerals temporarily dispelled public lethargy now that work had fled. Well might the novelist and playwright spill his ink in lamentation of the distress he encountered in such undisguised and unrelieved abundance, for the plight of millions was parlous and often past remedy.

But had Priestley chosen to include Tonbridge in his 1933 itinerary, and in consequence found himself putting up one late-autumnal evening at the Rose & Crown, what impressions might he have gathered of the town and its inhabitants as he strolled down the High Street to the Angel, stopping (as was his custom) to chat to a bookseller, a publican or two, and the knot of bystanders outside some brightly-illumined window? For every housewife, every shopkeeper, and every teacher and school-leaver, no subject in those depression-ravaged months depicted in *English Journey* attracted more concerned scrutiny than did the health and vigour of the local economy. Without a doubt, Priestley would have heard accounts of unemployment and hardship, maybe, too, of ruined businesses and near destitution. On the other hand, he would certainly have been gratified by reports of new industries, modest prosperity, and the evolution of an affordable popular culture. Nature had not been banished from Tonbridge in the same ruthless manner Priestley so deplored in Bennett's Five Towns or on the Tyneside where Catherine Cookson grew up. Community feeling ran strong and deep – there yet breathed a god in the machine of life.

In choosing to settle in Tonbridge in the early 1920s, one assumes both Clarence Butcher and Leslie Humphries were moved to do so because, with military service and war work at an end, the town held out the prospect of secure and gainful employment. Likewise, as their children grew up, they too cast about (latterly under the direction of the youth employment service on Quarry Hill) for ways of earning a living in their own neighbourhood. The opportunities for work, and also for play, Tonbridge afforded the families of its south-west suburbs, and some of the options selected by the Butcher and Humphries households, form the subject matter of the ensuing discussion, a discussion that leads us towards a final appraisal of the contradictions, the shortcomings, and the achievements of inter-war society.

At Work

Since its arrival in Tonbridge in the 1840s, the railway had acted as a powerful economic catalyst, drawing people to the town to work in a diversity of occupations, lending impetus to local building and retailing, and encouraging the establishment of other industries that needed easy access to a transport network for the movement of raw materials and finished goods. For much of the 1920s, Clarence Butcher (his craftsman's training long disregarded) worked as a checker in the goods-yard situated between the railway and Vale Road, booking-in and dispatching the apes, the ivory, and the peacocks of contemporary commerce. Entered through large iron gates on the corner of Vale Road opposite the Angel Hotel, this yard contained office and storage facilities, a rest and refreshment hut for the men, and a network of paths, concrete stacking bays, tracks, and sidings where trucks were loaded and unloaded. Among many other Meadow Lawn men to derive a livelihood from the yard may be instanced Butcher's foreman, Mr Atherton of Wincliff Road, and Mr Cripps of Chichester Road, who drove his horse and cart about the town delivering the parcels that came in by train.

For many Tonbridge families, service on the railway meant a way of life to be pursued as a matter of course by generation after generation. The Butcher's son-in-law, Albert Holman of Audley Avenue, came from one such family. His father had been a guard, his uncle a driver, and his brother was a signalman. He himself began life on the footplate as a fireman, stoking the engines of those incomparable steam locomotives, which, after many years of arduous apprenticeship, he would drive on shunting duties in the Jubilee sidings, then on freight movement, and finally on passenger service up and down the mainline.

Throughout the inter-war period, the focal point for the footplatemen of Tonbridge was the depot just beyond the railway bridge in Priory Road. Here the engines were housed in large sheds, and here, too, were the turntables and water-towers. Apprentices cleaned the engines and other rolling-stock, shift rotas were drawn up and posted, and teams of gangers mustered to ensure the integrity of rails, sleepers, signalling equipment, and points.

Tonbridge Junction in the 1920s and 1930s much resembled the station of the late twentieth century, except that in earlier days the booking-hall embraced one of W. H. Smith and Son's newspaper outlets, and there was access to the platforms from Waterloo Road as well as via Barden Road. Ticket-collectors on every gate, porters eager to carry heavy bags, booking-clerks, and a stationmaster with gold braid on his cap all earned a living from the passenger traffic, which, especially in the 1930s, included day-trippers and the first commuters. Taken together, the Southern Railway thus exercised a profound influence over the communities of south-west Tonbridge. The work it provided could be hard and dirty, but for the most part employment was secure, and promotion held out the prospect of wages among the best available to skilled workmen.

The shops of the High Street and the town's suburbs offered further important employment opportunities to Tonbridge men and women of all ages, as sole traders, managers, and behind-the-counter assistants. H. G. Wells, himself apprenticed to a draper, gives us an insight into the world of late-Victorian and Edwardian shopkeepers and shop workers, and one fancies a greengrocer like Mr Scorey would have acknowledged little change during the 20 years since the publication of *Kipps* in 1905 and *The History of Mr Polly* in 1910. Alfred Polly, for example, sets up his small outfitter's shop for something less than £300, while £500 is the sum named to the aspiring Kipps as being necessary to establish a drapery business. Quite by the late 1920s, Leslie Humphries of Barden Park Road had entered this milieu. He is identified in several sources as a 'clock maker', and in *Kelly's Directory of Kent* for 1934 is named as proprietor of the jewellers shop at the High Street end of the Station Approach.

Scores of similar small, independent shopkeepers formed the backbone of Tonbridge's retail community, responsible for every facet of their business, with wives and family helping out in the shop. Wells has left us his belief that the lot of the majority amounted to little more than a life-long struggle to eke out a dwindling capital, and an unwinnable battle to stave off insolvency in the face of competition from the 'tea stores' and the drapery bazaars. Nothing daunted, Mr Polly and his contemporaries evidently regarded themselves as belonging to the lower-middle class, and between the wars, Tonbridge's leading shopkeepers were men of consequence in local affairs. What united the provincial doges and 'village-Hampdens' of this shopocracy was a determination never to sink back into the subservient ranks from which they had painstakingly extricated themselves, though on a day-to-day level, they might find their enterprise stultified by boredom and apathy, and their ranks very frequently riven by petty jealousies, often the result of religious or masonic differences.

Much of what we learn about the conditions of service experienced by Kipps and Polly in their apprentice days is of less relevance to Tonbridge in the 1920s and 1930s, since its shops were generally too small, and in any case working-class acceptance of the old live-in regimen had markedly diminished. Moreover, conscription during the Great War had forced retailers like Home and Colonial to abandon the practice of employing only men as assistants. Women and girls quickly came to make up the great majority of shop workers, and almost exclusively so in the large grocery chains like Maypole, at the Co-op, and in the drapery and clothing sectors.

Nevertheless, the ethos – if not all the day-to-day practices – of the retail emporiums of the 1890s and 1900s undoubtedly persisted in shops as otherwise diverse as Gunner's, Frank East, the branches of the multiple grocers, the Co-op, and even those local businesses with two or three counter assistants. Men like Mr Richards of Lawn Road, who managed a corn chandlers in the High Street from the late 1920s, no less than Mr Bennett of Barden Road at the Home and Colonial before and during the Great War, expected high standards of conduct, politeness, punctuality, and sometimes religious observance from their employees. Systems of fines for trivial offences were not uncommon, and as a result, one gets the impression labour mobility – the 'crib hunting' and 'the key of the street' of Wells' day – was still widespread.

Long hours, poor wages, and time for leisure restricted to Wednesday 'early closing', Sundays, and occasional holidays were still the norm. As delivery-boy for Malpass the butcher in the mid 1920s, William Butcher pedalled many miles each day, often returning home soaked to the skin, while as a baker's roundsman, his younger brother probably fared little better. Nearly a decade later, a school-leaver of 14 could earn a meagre four shillings (increased by a further shilling after six months) for a six-day week in a shop, working from nine o'clock in the morning until six-thirty at night – eight o'clock on Saturdays. The fortunate teenager would be expected to run errands, sweep floors, and clean toilets and windows, in addition to serving customers.

The larger and more old-fashioned stores might still offer indentures, with satisfactory apprentices progressing to the status of 'improver' after five or seven years. Young Eric Holman became, for example, one of two apprentices working in Frank East's men's outfitting department in the late 1930s. Such shops also employed window-dressers, shop-walkers, departmental buyers, and delivery boys, alongside counter staff, packers and warehousemen, and ledger clerks in their counting-houses and offices.

No survey of the employment trends of the 1920s and 1930s can ignore the massive expansion of clerical work that took place during these decades. Known as 'black-coat' but increasingly as 'white-collar' posts, the acquisition of such a job in the office of a business like the Dowgate Press, or as a teller in the Westminster Bank, or perhaps in the employ of the gas company or the town's council, was a consummation devoutly wished by the parents of many a working-class or lower-middle-class family, for whom inky fingers represented progress if father habitually had grease under his nails or sawdust on his apron. Retailing, industry, and commerce all required clerical support, as did solicitors like Bailey and Cogger and Stenning, Knocker and Co, Pearl Insurance, estate agents like Isaac Race and Neve and Son, and W. Tibbits the auctioneer, whose businesses lay at the heart of Tonbridge's burgeoning professional sector.

Accordingly, we find that on leaving Judd School, Robert Humphries took up a situation with Messrs Creasey, Son and Wickenden, accountants of Tonbridge High Street.

Though more and more younger women began to choose clerical work in preference to the harsher duties of their mothers or their contemporaries in shops or manufacturing, typing and stenography in the offices of a company like South Eastern Tar Distillers Ltd of Vale Road remained a male preserve as late as 1939. Jack Humphries joined this firm as a school-leaver, working first as a laboratory assistant, but later, with the backing of his night-school qualifications, advancing to the accounts department. By the late 1930s, a 20-year-old clerk might earn £2 10s for a forty-hour week, with a week of paid holiday per annum.

The clerks and shop assistants of 1930 would doubtless have echoed – perhaps even more loudly given the liberating effects of war and the new political confidence of organised labour – the social superiority felt by their Wellsian counterparts over those engaged in manual work or domestic service. Yet both these latter remained important providers in the local employment market. Though probably on a more conservative scale than hitherto, the professional families of The Drive and Goldsmid Road, and farther afield in the Dry Hill, Yardley Park, and Bordyke areas, still required housemaids, cooks, charwomen, and old-fashioned nannies, as well as men to tend their flower-beds and maybe also to tinker with or drive the new gleaming motor car.

Throughout the inter-war period, many women found jobs in the washing, drying, and ironing rooms of the Baltic Road laundry. Agricultural work was also available, mostly on a casual and seasonal basis. Crops of soft fruit, cherries, apples, plums, and pears all had to be harvested. One tends to associate hop picking with migrant labourers from East London, but there were many in Tonbridge like Vera Holman who relished the opportunity to earn extra money in the hop-gardens on the outskirts of the town.

The construction industry and its allied suppliers like the Baltic Saw Mills of Lyons Crescent proved a generally reliable source of employment. Everyone in South Tonbridge knew the whistle that regulated shifts at the brickworks at the top of St. Mary's Road. Here, under the supervision of Mr Edward Thompson, men and boys quarried clay and prepared tiles and bricks for the kiln. Local builders and decorators such as Elkington's of Avebury Avenue, or Punnett's at its Quarry Hill or later its Vale Road premises, regularly took on craftsmen and apprentices; while maintenance of its ever-growing housing stock led the TUDC to recruit a sizeable body of labour to provide repair, decorating, and gardening services, much of whose work it co-ordinated from the materials store beside the railway bridge in Audley Avenue.

As elsewhere across the country, traditional manufacturing enterprises tended to decline between the wars. The Powdermills near Leigh continued trading only until 1934, and a blacksmith shop like the low, dark Waghorn's Forge in Avebury Avenue could not indefinitely supplement the dwindling profitability of shoeing horses with the small-scale manufacture of agricultural implements. The scattered cricket-ball manufactory, which in 1919 had employed 240 persons in workshops like those of Thomas Ives just off the Barden Road, though it survived throughout the inter-war decades, did so at reduced levels of output in the face of stiff foreign competition.[2]

By contrast, light industry, the service sector, and utilities grew apace. The Crystalate Gramophone Record Manufacturing Company, for example, employed between 400 and 500 persons at its factory in Cannon Lane, where records (destined for both the home and foreign markets) were pressed under labels such as Rex, Eclipse, and Imperial. British Flint and Cerium Manufacturers made cigarette lighters at its Vale Road plant, and a neighbouring factory processed sheepskins and sold such items as slippers and powder-puffs. The Gas Works in Medway Wharf Road, the electricity generating station in the Slade, and the Water Works on the edge of the Race Course all benefited as new houses were built and others improved.[3]

By the 1930s, the influence of private motor cars and commercial lorries, vans, and buses had made itself a power in the land, giving rise to work for young men in the rapidly-diversifying transport business, or as trainee mechanics or storekeepers in a garage like Speedway House at the corner of Priory Road or that of Chas Baker (later bought by Caffyns) in the upper High Street. At the end of this period, Kenneth Holman began work as an apprentice storeman at the latter dealership for five shillings a week, of which 13d was deducted for insurance and the washing of overalls. Weekly wages rose to 10 shillings and then 15 shillings in successive years.

Perhaps characteristic of the new inter-war industries was South Eastern Tar Distillers Ltd (SETAR), set up in 1924 to process crude tar on behalf of a collective of municipal gas companies across Kent, Sussex, and Surrey. The works in Vale Road had its own railway sidings to receive the raw tar, which it refined into pitch and into materials for road surfacing. In addition to invoicing and accounts functions and laboratory services, SETAR maintained garage and repair facilities for its fleet of tankers. Johnson Brothers of Aylesford (taken over in about 1927) acted as the contracting arm of the business; preparing tenders, and managing the resultant road-making contracts with county and town councils.

For many in Meadow Lawn and Barden, however, the best chance of work away from shops and the railway remained Tonbridge's sizeable printing industry, which, between 1890 and 1911, had been principally responsible for the marked growth in Tonbridge's population. Bradbury Agnew of London established a factory in Medway Wharf Road during the closing decades of the nineteenth century, to print among other things *Punch*. Under the innovative management of W. S. Minton of Lyons Crescent, this enterprise became the Whitefriars Press in 1916. Morning, noon, and evening, hurrying hands from the factory thronged the High Street, among them for a while William Butcher, who went to work at Whitefriars Press only weeks before the famous fire of June 1926, and like many of his fellows, found himself laid off for several weeks until production could be resumed.

In the very bosom of Meadow Lawn stood the Dowgate Works of James Truscott and Sons Ltd, opened in 1899 to accommodate an enterprise that had formerly employed 750 to 850 people in the City of London. While the firm remained in the hands of the Truscott family, visits by Sir George Truscott periodically set the factory in a fluster of preparations for what quickly assumed the trappings of a royal progress. Mr Anthony Brown became company supremo in the late 1930s, following the merger with printers Brown and Knight of Tooley Street near London Bridge, while throughout most of the 'thirties', day-to-day management was the responsibility of Mr Ford of Goldsmid Road and his secretary Miss Chalklin, the former remembered as the proud owner of a new Ford car each year.

The abiding impression of the Dowgate Press during the inter-war period is of a thriving business, providing employment for a large number of men, women, and teen-aged boys and girls in a wide variety of skilled, semi-skilled, and manual occupations. Among the best paid workers were the machine minders, men who set up the printing presses and other machinery prior to a particular job. Boys served a full apprenticeship for this, as for many allied trades, after which the majority were re-engaged as journeymen. The ritual of 'banging out' an apprentice on the day he completed his indentures indicates the importance attached by the entire working community to the attainment of skilled status. Everyone on the shop-floor participated in a noisy clattering of tools or rulers on machines and benches. Craftsmen really might look forward to 'a job for life', while failure to 'make the grade' meant for the printer, no less than for the shop assistant, a life of drifting in and out of poorly-paid jobs.

Truscotts' workforce included many women, though none of the occupations in which they were engaged required an apprenticeship. A new girl might begin as a feeder, perhaps in the ruling department, to assist in the production of cash-books for customers such as shipping lines, oil and insurance companies, and agricultural marketing boards. Once the minder had set up his machine to the correct specifications of a job, the novice operative would first feed sheets of paper into a mangel-like contraption that ruled the faint or horizontal lines. The minder then reset the machine, and the sheets were fed in once again, this time to rule the vertical columns. And woe betide the hasty or inattentive feeder who caused the paper to run crooked, especially if the checker in the department could not blot out the resulting discrepancy with an application of lime solution.

Machines were set up in the sewers' department to punch holes in paper or to draw lines of perforations to assist in tearing. Having obtained a job-sheet from Miss Eaton, the overseer, one of the more experienced women would prepare her machine to match the master diagram of the desired output. Once tested and agreed, work began to fulfil the order in the required quantity, with productivity being recorded on an official timesheet.

This sewers' department generally employed women to operate its rows of sewing-machines. The larger, more expensive books tended to be sewn by hand, while a row of noisy wire-stitching machines fastened cheaper volumes and magazines with metal staples. Prior to sewing, blocks of pages had sometimes to be interleaved – that is, double or single printed sheets were placed one inside the next to constitute the body of the publication. Most books were machine stitched, an operation involving great dexterity and the co-ordination of hands and feet to position the pages and work the treadle.

The paper-cutting, type-setting, and proof-reading departments were staffed almost exclusively by men. Men loaded and unloaded lorries, and performed all the heavy manual tasks in the warehouse and the packing-bay, where, however, women packed parcels for dispatch.

In the print-shop the machine minders set up the presses for jobs as diverse as books, Christmas cards, periodicals, and large posters, and were assisted by feeders, most of whom were women or girls. Colour printing took place in the lithography (litho) department, and the men's bindery dealt with some of the most classical work, often requiring the use of vellum and the finishing of volumes bound in leather. One very delicate task involved the positioning of gold-leaf to form the lettering on the spines and covers of books. Deft fingers and a keen eye were essential when transferring sheets of 22 carat gold – so fine that a hasty breath would cause it to crumple – from between protective leaves of tissue paper to the specified spot on the book, where the desired legend was cut out and affixed by the application of a red-hot stamp.

When Elsie Butcher went to work at Truscotts at the age of about fifteen, it was for the princely sum of 7s 6d per week. The working day began as employees clocked-in at seven-thirty – Monday to Friday – and was concluded by a hooter at six o'clock in the evening. Wages rose to 8s 6d, 9s 6d, 12s 6d, and 17s 6d at six-monthly intervals, and finally to a maximum figure of 32s 6d. All employees clocked in and out, and a system of fines operated to deter slack timekeeping. Many hands returned home for a midday meal during the hour-long lunch break; others ate sandwiches inside the factory. Additional work to fulfil special orders was often on offer on Saturday mornings at a flat rate of five shillings. Each department had an overseer and a deputy, both skilled operatives who knew their particular trade in all its minutiae. Sam Emery and Mr Hutchinson filled senior posts in the ruling and men's bindery departments respectively, where, from strategic offices of wood and glass, they kept an eagle eye on business. Women like Miss Steer and Daisy Stone (both of Meadow Road) acted as supervisors within smaller sections, maintaining standards of work and discipline. Miss Steer, for instance, checked the quality of all items before they left the sewers' department.

Trade unions had an important role to play in the daily life of the factory. Workers took it in turns to hold the posts of Father of Chapel and Mother of Chapel, one duty of whom was to collect the threepenny subs from members each Monday morning and hand the money to the local union Secretary, Mr Sam Bradbury, himself employed at Dowgate Press as a cutter. Disputes over working practices had also to be settled between union and management. During her term of office as Mother of Chapel, young Elsie Butcher found herself embroiled in the furore caused by the appointment of a new assistant overseer in the sewing department. Unaccustomed to prevailing norms, this newcomer stirred up a hornets' nest among the women, when she sought, among other things, to outlaw singing during working hours. Talks were held with the men; and later, as the dispute escalated, full-time officials from union headquarters attended a meeting in the Co-op Hall in Waterloo Road. It fell to Miss Butcher to liaise with Mr Brown, the local Trades Council, and union representatives, and at length to address the workforce assembled in the packing-bay, where, standing on bales of paper, she called a strike that lasted until the powers of the too-zealous overseer had been reviewed.

At Play

The enduring popularity of books by Flora Thompson and Laurie Lee attests the powerful fascination exercised by homely reminiscences and images of childhood and adolescence. Family excursions, the passage of the seasons, civic and religious festivals, the excitement of a fair, pastimes, and the cultures of the school playground, the cinema, and the dance-hall all emerge in guises as fluid as they are eternal, unchanging and yet subtly different from generation to generation. No other facet of Tonbridge life between the wars better reflects the power of the oral record to recapture the sparkle in what Wordsworth so memorably terms 'the light of setting suns'. The study of leisure also has real value as social history, serving, for instance, to document the striking correlation between increasing prosperity and the demand for recreational pursuits, which in the inter-war decades allowed the far wider commercialisation of sport, holidays, and travel, and transformed the provision of facilities by the public and voluntary sectors.[4]

The Butcher family's close connection with the railway made the train a more affordable means of recreational travel than might otherwise have been the case. Margate was invariably the venue for the family's annual holiday in the 1920s, usually passed at a bed-and-breakfast boarding-house in one of the little roads close to the clock tower. Games on the sand or out among the rocks made up the daily entertainment, spiced, perhaps, with a donkey-ride and a visit to the timeless melodrama of the Punch and Judy show. Florence Butcher took her youngest daughter for a fortnight of convalescence to Weymouth following a bout of whooping-cough, while father and daughter paid a visit to Portsmouth, where they looked over *HMS Victory*.

Florence and Clarence Butcher on holiday in Margate in 1937 (author's photograph).

Other seaside treats remembered from the 1920s include the annual charabanc outing to Hastings organised by the Baptist Sunday School, when the smart kids were those who kept close to 'Daddy' Taylor, famed alike for his avid distribution of tracts and his liberality with buckshee ice-creams.

Travel had expanded still further by the 1930s. Boys from Judd School enjoyed holidays on the Continent, and the Southern Railway advertised day trips to Boulogne at 14 shillings for adults and seven shillings for the under-fourteens. Special excursions to the Kent and Sussex coasts by train were available throughout the summer on Wednesdays and Sundays, when, for example, a cheap day ticket to Lewes cost 2s 6d. In 1936 the first-class return fare to London was six shillings and that in third class four shillings.[5] A party from Truscotts made a trip to Southend in the mid 1930s, the Humphries family spent at least one holiday in Sandwich, and jaunts to Hastings allowed Tonbridge folk to enjoy the annual carnival through a long summer afternoon and evening of fireworks and dancing on the seafront. Tonbridge Swimming Club arranged its end-of-season outing for 1935 to Westgate, Minnis Bay, and Margate, and a year later seniors and juniors visited Brighton.

Midsummer saw Tonbridge itself in a state of high excitement. Bunting criss-crossed the High Street to welcome celebrities like Don Bradman and other visitors to Cricket Week, when the players themselves lodged at the Angel and slaked their thirst at the nearby Prince Albert. The Angel Ground (once the home of the Kent Nursery) greeted with furious applause each new feat with bat or ball performed by the county's cricketing heroes. Frank Woolley (Tonbridge bred and reared) scored 108 in the Somerset match of 1929 and Les Ames plundered 210 from the Warwickshire bowlers in 1933. Though the county championship never came Kent's way in these decades, who could watch unmoved the tireless spin of 'Tich' Freeman or the elegant dash of Percy Chapman?

Youthful scholars suspended studies to taste the pert and nimble spirit of the season's mirth. Gaily lighted craft of every kind bobbed on the river. Canoes and punts vied for clear water with an aquatic cavalcade of decorated floats: some manned by the scouts or the police or fire-brigade; others sponsored by local businesses or the LAMPS, or one of the town's more eccentric inhabitants. And if the rain held off, fireworks and dancing on the night of the Venetian Fête made the Castle lawn a scene of civic merriment that echoed back and forth from Norman keep to Thomas Hooker's Georgian pile.

Autumn and winter have always delighted children with their succession of celebrations leading inexorably up to Christmas. Hallowe'en saw the school at Sussex Road decorated with pictures of witches and spooks and hung with lighted lanterns. The children brought food from home on the appointed day, and participated in traditional games of apple-bobbing and 'pennies in the bucket'. Dressed in witches' attire, Miss Stacey toured the classrooms, broomstick in hand, reciting the misfortunes of Little Orphan Annie with whoops of ghoulish glee.

Prior to Bonfire Night, the Butcher children collected blackberries in the hedgerows of Hayesden and cycled out to Penshurst to pick up chestnuts in the park, both which they sold on to neighbours or to Mr Scorey the greengrocer. In due course, the money so accumulated bought rockets, little demons, Roman candles, and other fireworks at Kelly's shop in Douglas Road. Come the big night, young George had his guy ready to sit astride the bonfire he and his mates had built on the grassy spaces at the end of Lawn Road. A decade later, the Holman family attended the firework carnival at Edenbridge to watch the parade and gather round the communal blaze.

The one sombre rite in this season of smoky dawns and russet hues was Armistice Day, when Tonbridge, in keeping with the whole nation, came to a standstill at 11 o'clock to remember the dead of the Great War. Poignant memories of young and hopeful lives cut short made observance of 11 November as universal as any religious festival. Children from the Sussex Road schools marched to the war memorial (then situated in the middle of the highway outside St Stephen's at the junction with Pembury Road) many carrying floral tributes like the chrysanthemums given by Mrs Butcher to her daughter. At the sound of a cannon from the Big School, the town fell silent;

traffic in the streets, pedestrians, workers at their machines in the Dowgate Works all motionless, united in a two-minute act of civic grief.

Preparations for Christmas at Sussex Road school included the making of more decorations, carols, and one year a playlet for an audience of admiring parents, in which the children were dressed as fairies in crinkly-paper costumes to represent such figures as Holly and Mistletoe. The Baptist Church gave a party and concert for the Sunday School classes in the hall adjacent to the vestry, and on a separate day held a tea for parents. The Whitefriars Press Club in Avebury Avenue organised its annual Christmas party at the Rink in Bradford Street. On these occasions, a tea was followed by the distribution of presents from a large tree by Father Christmas and his fairy helpers, and on departure each child took away an apple, an orange, and other goodies in a bag.

Door-to-door carol-singing around the Meadow Lawn streets could sometimes be rewarded with hot mince-pies and a few coppers, whereas for the more adventurous Butcher brothers, a sortie as far afield as The Drive meant appreciative sixpences and shillings, sometimes sent down from the drawing-room on a silver salver.

Workers at Truscotts saved money throughout the year in 'thrift boxes' to finance the celebrations held during company time on the last afternoon before Christmas. The ingenious accumulation of a 'rain box' cost each contributor in the sewers' department a penny for every day when the heavens opened. Everyone brought a store of cakes or drinks to work on the day of the party, when the contents of 'the boxes' bought something special at Prentis's (a vintner in the High Street), usually a quart bottle of ruby 'Taragona' wine and a bottle of 'Green Goddess' cocktail. Each section dispensed its own hospitality, usually with such liberality that evening engagements had to be cancelled.

The near approach of Christmas found Mrs Butcher seated with her children around the kitchen table to mix the pudding according to her own mother's recipe. Everyone had a task. Never in all the year was there such a washing and drying of currants and sultanas, such a grating of breadcrumbs, or such a fine-chopping of beef suet. Those large, sticky raisins had to be halved and their seeds removed, while nimble fingers divided pieces of candied peel from the fragments of sugar and diced them into tangy cubes of orange and cinnamon green. Ingredient after ingredient tumbled into the great bowl, there to be stirred with the flour, eggs, and glacé cherries, and moistened with a measure of 'old ale', until each cook had taken a turn with the wooden-spoon and made a wish. Finally, once the new-scrubbed silver threepenny bits had been added, the mixture was ready to be wrapped in a cloth, or placed in a basin beneath a protective layer of suet dough, and steamed in the copper.

Every family has its own way of marking Christmas Day, determined sometimes by the scarcity of money, but perhaps more frequently by the inclinations of parents. The Butcher household in Lawn Road was decorated with chains made out of coloured strips of gummed paper, but never had the sort of tree with real candles and a doll on top that so delighted young Elsie Butcher at a neighbour's home. A joint of pork or beef normally graced the dinner table, followed by the steaming plum pudding. Only once did the family eat turkey, and that was the year Clarence Butcher won the bird in a raffle. How his wife struggled to fit this imposter into the modest oven on her kitchen range! Oranges, large Blenheim apples, figs, nuts, and sweets were ritually placed on a side-table, along with bottles of home-made ginger wine. Everyone simply picked and nibbled at his or her favourite sweetmeat.

Some families kept open house at Christmas; others preferred the family circle in the flickering firelight. Evenings in Lawn Road passed unpretentiously: children playing games of ludo and snakes and ladders, trying out the mysteries of the magic lantern show, or reading the new paperback annual; parents listening to the gramophone or joining in a hand of snap. Clarence Butcher would pull at his Christmas cigar and sip his fiery ginger wine. By contrast, the parties attended by the Holmans and their friends in Audley Avenue in the 1930s were events of convivial good humour, singing round the piano, and refreshments till long after the chimes of midnight. Games popular at this date included grunt piggy grunt, poor Mary sits a weeping, pass the parcel for the children, and maybe a turn or two at charades.

Christmas aside, organised activities for the young people of south-west Tonbridge included the Sunday School at St Stephen's where Mrs Smith of 4 Lawn Road taught for many years, stoolball teams and Mr Jenner's 'Pleasant Sunday Afternoons' band at the Congregational Church, and a youth club run by a Mr Green at the Free Church in Douglas Road. Children celebrated Empire Day (24 May) with gymnastics, a May Queen, and dancing round a maypole on the stage in West's Empire Theatre in Avebury Avenue. In the 1930s, the Dowgate Press built tennis courts and a sports pavilion for its younger employees, and ran a social club for dances, table tennis, and board games. The Rink satisfied the roller-skating craze, the town's public library (opened on its Avebury Avenue site in 1900) attracted Clarence Butcher to its reading-room and his younger daughter to its lending department, while the Territorial Army offered to William Butcher the swagger of a uniform and the chance to play the drum in its band.

Eric Holman was a noted scout and rover in the days when Skipper Wright and Miss Winnie Hoath superintended the 1st Tonbridge pack at the Lamberts Yard hut. The Humphries boys belonged to the same troop in the later 1920s. One photograph shows Bob as leader of the Golden Plover patrol, and numerous snaps survive of Ellen Humphries helping at a camp at Worthing. George Butcher had also been in the cubs and scouts, while his younger sister was a guide in the 3rd Tonbridge group based at the YWCA hall in Lyons Crescent. Uniforms – which for girls included the traditional navy blue tunic, a distinguishing red scarf, a leather belt, a lanyard, and a broad, stiff hat – could be bought or borrowed. Monthly church parades saw the youth of the town marching down the High

Jack and Bob Humphries at Scout Camp (author's photograph).

Street to the war memorial. Both scouts and guides went off to camps and jamborees, played organised games, and learned the secrets of cooking, knots, morse code signalling with a blue-and-white flag, and first aid in the pursuit of badges and stars.

Tonbridge had possessed a municipal swimming-bath near the Race Course since about 1910. A collection of newspaper cuttings kept by Robert Humphries indicates that an earlier Swimming Club was re-founded in about 1934, its President being the town's MP, Lieut-Col Herbert Spender-Clay, and its Secretary, Mr A. R. Sweetman of The Drive. The club met on Tuesday and Thursday evenings after 7.30 p.m., when exclusive use of the pool allowed juniors and seniors of both sexes to practise their chosen stroke, try a spot of diving, or learn the art of life saving. Membership was buoyant in 1935, when the club began negotiations with the TUDC for a filtration plant costing £600,[6] and the committee talked longingly of erecting an indoor pool.[7] Subscription at this date was a half-crown for seniors and a shilling for juniors.

Robert Humphries is named as the winner of several three-length breaststroke races during the 1935 season. He played in the water polo team that lost to Bexhill by 10 goals to one in June, and may well have witnessed the further three-goal and six-goal defeats by Sevenoaks and Ashford respectively in July and August. The high-light of 1935 was undoubtedly the Jubilee Gala on 27 July. Having paid the entrance fee of a shilling or sixpence for adults and sixpence or threepence for juniors, the audience watched a programme of swimming demonstrations and races, and enjoyed a parade of swimming costumes in the old and the contemporary styles.

This gala proved something of a red-letter day in the Humphries household, as young Robert defeated F. V. Bournes to carry off the Spender-Clay Challenge Cup for life saving.[8] Not surprisingly, Robert became a 'popular captain of the club' in 1936, and at that summer's gala – described to the audience with the aid of a 'mike' – retained his trophy, on this occasion beating C. L. Cannon by a narrow margin.

As in every generation, the street and the school playground were places of kaleidoscopic activity, where games came in and out of vogue as fleetingly as fashions on a 'flapper'. For a season, boys and girls would hurry to school, sticks in hand, driving their steel or wooden hoops like sheep to market. A fortnight later, and the same children might be observed whipping one of the many spinning tops along the same street, or maybe practising one of those infinitely various skipping sequences. Games of ball were legion, and in winter the ice on the Sussex Road playground was worn so smooth that even Miss Price could not eschew a giddy slide. The approach of Boat Race Day made fervent partisans of infants who would never dip an oar in the Isis or the Cam. A badge or a bow, a doll, or a boat trimmed in the favoured blue, could be bought for a halfpenny or a penny, to be worn or displayed with as much pride as by any freshman at Balliol or Peterhouse. Boys had trouser pockets crammed with marbles, with prize conkers in autumn, or with a pack of cigarette cards – eager, as the fancy ran, to do battle or to swap Jack Hobbs for Fred Archer or a Rhode Island Red.

Not surprisingly, the proximity of the river and the countryside exercised a powerful attraction for Tonbridge children throughout the inter-war decades. Every boy had his egg collection, each speckled specimen the trophy of some high adventure – a hazardous climb to a sparrowhawk's nest or a close encounter with an indignant swan. The Humphries brothers and their friends spent countless hours on the riverbank or at the Ballast Pit, waiting for the bream or the perch or a tench to start biting, and for ever dreaming of a carp, huge and scaly at the end of the next cast. Jack tempted his best roach with hemp at Powdermill Point, his largest chub with cheese or wasp grubs. Most tackle was home-made: goose-quill floats, split-cane rods, wooden rests and winders, ledgers, lures, and a feathery fly to tempt the wiliest trout.

'Delight and liberty', enthuses Wordsworth, 'the simple creed of childhood'. A bag of maize from Mr Wendy in Butler's Yard (or in the 1930s from Tom Maylam, the High Street corn chandler) guaranteed for mother and toddlers a clamorous flock of mendicant pigeons in the lee of the Water Gate. There was swimming at the Weir, diving off Lucifer Bridge, and impromptu camping under the stars. A boat might be hired from Norton's yard in Barden Road, wherewith to beguile an afternoon paddling round Tinker's Island or downstream to the locks. Then, once a year, the fair brought its peculiar brand of dazzle and hurdy-gurdy to the town, erected its swings and roundabouts on Botany Field, and pitched the hoop-la booths, the rifle ranges, the coconut shy, and the tent where a gipsy fortune-teller discerned romance and prosperity in her misty crystal ball.

So many wild and mysterious landscapes to explore. The song of spring in the woods of Upper Hayesden; such a gay abundance of primroses, bluebells, and catkins to gather. The Shallows on summer evenings in its pomp, when sand martins dipped and skimmed for flies above the placid pools, and the cattle came snorting down to stoop and drink where the stream rippled across those smooth, flat stones you just had to make hop and skip to the farther bank. Autumn along the Straight Mile, a stretch more fruitful than the groves of Arcady; its hedges heavy with hips and haws and plump, purple sloes. The Medway in winter spate; skating on Somerhill lake; wide-skied afternoons tobogganing and tumbling down Lamb's Bank; the water-meadows all awash with January floods.

Sunday-evening walks took the Butcher and Holman families by way of Hayesden Lane to the Shallows, or round the Race Course and up to the Castle to hear the Epics in the bandstand, or maybe past the Gas Works and out to the Postern. Children rambled far and wide across meadow, grove, and stream at weekends or in their holidays, straying for miles up the Redhill line, or into Jimmy's Field to search for newts and frog spawn, or out to the Onwards Field to gather watercress in the clear streams and pick the knobbly 'toddling grass'. The tank and the howitzer outside the Castle Offices served as a rendezvous and the theatre of many a re-enacted battle; and later, perhaps, as twilight thickened and the curfew tolled, the braver spirits might dare a swing on the revolving chains of the Giant's-Strides on the nearby Outer Bailey, until put to flight by the fearsome keeper.

Cycling was another popular pastime, again usually on Sundays, often in Hayesden Lane or round the Frying Pan. Denton, Brooks, and Chatfield all supplied the town's cycling fraternity; but with a new machine costing from £3 to £5 in 1932, many younger boys had to piece together a frame and a pair of wheels salvaged at a local dump. Autocar and Redcar provided local bus services, useful for those who would shop or see a film in Tunbridge Wells. Private motoring and motor-cycling expanded steadily as prices fell and road surfaces improved. The number of cars registered nationally rose from 200,000 in 1918 to one million in 1930, and had doubled again by 1939. For those who could afford an Austin, a Morris, a Humber, or a Wolseley from Chas Baker, the Old Barn near Leigh became a favourite destination, to swim or to dance or to inspect Commander Tomlinson's zoo.[9]

Clarence Butcher's leisure-time interests included his allotment on land between the Jubilee Bridge and Clare Avenue, a flutter on the horses with Thompson the bookie, crossword puzzles, the radio, and, of course, his gramophone music. In addition, he was active in local politics, both as a member of the Tonbridge Trades Council, and as an unsuccessful candidate in one election for a seat on the TUDC. A caricature that hung for many years in the Medway Hall depicted the would-be councillor hammering on the door of the council chamber. Following some disagreement with his party, Butcher temporarily switched his allegiance to the Conservatives, a circumstance which helps explain why the *Daily Herald*'s Bobby Bear annual was superseded by the *Daily Express*'s Rupert Bear annual in his daughter's Christmas stocking.

Membership of the Co-op had both a political and a social dimension. Florence Butcher played the piano at meetings of the Women's Guild held in one of the halls behind the store. Before 1914 these guilds had been prominent campaigners on issues such as women's suffrage, while in the 1920s the Co-operative movement aligned itself more closely to the Labour Party and the trades unions. Youth work assumed a greater prominence between the wars with the establishment of junior guilds and bodies like the Woodcraft Folk. In Tonbridge the Society organised an annual fancy-dress parade for the children of co-operators. Costumes were made out of paper advertisements, and shown off in a procession up the High Street to a field beside Elm Lane, where Clarence Butcher took his turn organising egg-and-spoon races and similar competitions.

Among other Tonbridge societies patronised in these decades may be mentioned the Ancient Order of Druids, the Buffaloes who gathered upstairs at the Dorset Arms, the Brotherhood, the Rotary Club, the Association of Men of Kent and Kentish Men, and the Tonbridge Angling and Fish Preservation Society, as well as clubs that promoted the playing and watching of football, cricket, and rugby. Leslie Humphries had become a member of the United Grand Lodge of Ancient Free and Accepted Masons of England at a lodge in London on 6 November 1918. In Tonbridge he joined the Town of Tonbridge Masonic Lodge, founded back in 1877, which met regularly in its hall above the shops on the north-east approach to the Great Bridge. The British Legion held meetings in Avebury Avenue, the Congregational Church ran its Sisterhood, and the Theosophical Society organised a programme of lectures on social and spiritual topics.

Neither the Humphries nor the Butcher households attended church services on a regular basis. Perhaps they and the majority of their neighbours found Anglicanism remote and socially forbidding; and the dissenting community had lost the vigour and the vision that, for example, had prompted the secession of the Baptist congregation in the 1860s and 1870s, and had bolstered the Liberal interest before 1914. This is not to imply irreverence or even ignorance on religious matters. Families looked to the churches to perform the rites of christening, marriage, and burial; parents preserved the solemnity of Sunday and Good Friday. Florence Butcher possessed a thorough knowledge of the Bible, accompanied the hymn-singing at various women's meetings, and sent her children to Sunday School and to a club run by Sister Edith above Singer's near the Little Bridge. Kenneth Holman sang in the choir at the Parish Church.

Throughout the year, Mr and Mrs Butcher's principal place of relaxation was the Whitefriars Press club in Avebury Avenue: father playing cribbage, mother gossiping with her cronies in the children's room, daughter kept entertained with a glass of 'Vimto'. Also in Avebury Avenue was Swift's fish and chip shop, renowned for such delicacies as battered potato scallops and pieces of fried fish skin known as 'crackling'. Walks across the fields to sit in the inglenook at the Plough near Leigh won favour among the younger generation of the 1930s, while the Bull Hotel attracted anglers eager to yarn and reminisce, few of whom could long ignore the presiding genius of the giant pike, so mirthfully malign in his case behind the bar, with, or so it sometimes seemed, a fathomless store of riverbank lore in his glassy, glittering eye.

Above the Big Bridge, Tonbridge had two high-class cafés: Aplins on the west side of the High Street just above the Chequers, and the Carlton Café on the east side. Though open to sell bread and cakes on its ground floor, the Carlton Café dispensed morning coffee and afternoon teas in an upstairs room, and had a number of large function rooms which were let out for wedding receptions and events such as Truscotts' Christmas dinner and dance.

The cinema assumed greater and greater importance as a place of popular entertainment as the inter-war decades progressed. The Capitol opened in 1921 in the former Public Hall building near the entrance to Bank Street. Garbo, Valentino, and Mary Pickford quickly emerged as the heart-throbs of this early era of the silent movies, while at the Star in Bradford Street, Miss Skinner won local celebrity for her musical accompaniments to the frenetic antics of Buster Keaton and the Keystone Cops. Buster West owned two 'picture palaces' in Avebury Avenue: the Pavilion and the Empire Theatre. The latter, known familiarly as the 'Bug Hutch', showed cowboy films each Saturday morning, along with suspense serials like 'The Claw' which invariably climaxed with some cliff-hanging dilemma. Children who lacked the penny admission fee would often creep past the snoozing proprietor to watch the show under the benign eye of 'Old Dingle' who worked the projector.

The age of the talkies opened with Al Jolson's 1927 classic 'The Jazz Singer' at the Pavilion. Janet Gaynor and Charles Farrell won a following among devotees of the early romantic movies, and by the time the Ritz opened the doors of its plushest of Tonbridge auditoriums in Botany in 1935, the public clamoured for its twice-weekly fix of Hitchcock thrillers, the comedy of Charlie Chaplin, and swashbuckling adventures with Charles Lawton. All the cinemas changed their programme of entertainment in mid week, and charged from sixpence a sitting to watch two films and the latest newsreel.

By the outbreak of war, both the Medway Hall and Phil's Café – situated behind the line of the High Street at the river end of Bradford Street – offered dancing and live music throughout the week. Beginning with a tea-room next to Doust's boat-yard, Phil Mandel built up his sixpence-a-night dance-hall on the musical reputations of Jim Vesey on saxophone and Tom Berry on piano.

Young people were wild for the latest jazz standards and somewhere convivial to lead out a partner for the slow fox-trot, a waltz, or the quick-step. Dances were also held in the Territorial Hall in Avebury Avenue and at the Tonbridge Working Men's Club in Lyons Crescent. Revellers adjourned during the mid-evening interval to the Castle Hotel, or the Bull, or maybe to the Angel for a drink, a game of darts, or an amorous tête-à-tête.

Conclusions

Though few can have guessed it at the time, those few sombre words of Mr Chamberlain in the autumn of 1939 effectively tolled the knell of another parting phase in Tonbridge history. Six months passed and there were spitfires in the skies above the apple-blossomed gardens of Barden Park Road. Young men and young women like Robert Humphries and Elsie Butcher enlisted or were called up, no longer clerks or printers, but suddenly soldiers primed to fight on foreign soil; while for those brothers and sisters who remained in Tonbridge, wartime experiences gained in the Home Guard, the Red Cross, or the ARP transformed irreversibly the workaday current of their pre-war lives.

Later, with victory assured, the demobilising troops could scarcely doubt that the glimmering social and economic landscape their fathers had built – the society of their own formative years – had already begun to fade. Far from preserving the status quo, war had hastened its demise. Liberated at last from a Prussian POW camp, Lance-Corporal Humphries found his contemporaries alive with talk of secondary schooling, though few of them had studied beyond the age of fourteen; clamorous for National Insurance, where Clarence Butcher had once relied on his 'slate club'; and resolved upon a free Health Service that should banish Dr Watts' consultation fee. Meanwhile, as Staff Sergeant Butcher knew from her service with the British Army Staff in Washington DC – where telephones, refrigerators, nylons, dry-cleaning, and 'Arrid' deodorant creams were commonplace – a trans-Atlantic tide of technology stood poised to sweep a second revolution through every household in the land. In short, the war had set an ideological, cultural, and electronic girdle round about the national consciousness that divided 1945 from 1939 as effectively as the railway sundered Barden Road from Meadow Lawn.

But this is to anticipate themes still nascent in 1945. Our purpose here must be to look back rather than forward, to determine whether or not it is just the wistfulness of age that lends such fondness to memories of the inter-war Tonbridge of our parents' and grandparents' generations. For surely, does not every schoolboy know these 1920s and 1930s were the grey decades: the decades of unemployment; the decades of the hunger marches, of factories and mines and shipyards standing idle; the decades of life-and-death strikes, of class conflict, of political apostasy, and the heartless cutting of the dole? What says the testimony of our Tonbridge forefathers?

Throughout the 1920s, the occasional tramp or beggar en route to the doss-house in Botany had knocked at the Butcher's door in Lawn Road, asking, perhaps, for old clothes or if there were knives to be sharpened, and grateful for a jug of tea or a morsel of bread and cheese. Incidents involving thieving from gardens and washing-lines were not uncommon: for there were families in South Tonbridge who knew real poverty, first in the slump years of the early 1920s, when out-of-work men constructed the River Walk and the hard path round the Race Course, and again during 1932, when unemployment in Tonbridge rose from 837 (including 91 women) in February to more than 1000 the following winter.[10]

In 1929, Neville Chamberlain (then at the Ministry of Health) transferred responsibility for care of the distressed from the boards of guardians to Public Assistance Committees, which from 1931 administered 'assistance' and imposed a means test on those whose statutory benefit had been exhausted. Hence, when depression deepened, the provision of relief in Tonbridge fell to the Urban District Council, backed by wealthy individuals and public donations to such projects as the Unemployed Social Centre Fund. In the wake of the 1931 sterling crisis, the TUDC and the Trades Council used a grant of £2,000 to institute the Woodland Walk project, designed to landscape a pathway between Starvecrow Hill and Higham Lane across land donated by the Cage Farm estate.[11] Such measures, of course, could only palliate the harsher consequences of unemployment, which did not begin to diminish until trade cycles took a turn for the better during the mid 1930s.

The Butchers' son Bill had been no stranger to spells of unemployment during the 1920s. Then, in about 1930, Clarence Butcher himself lost his job in the Vale Road goods-yard. Trade was bad. Economists preached retrenchment, a balanced budget, and the shedding of labour.

Idle, aimless men loafed for hours on the pavement outside the public library, having tarried for as long as possible in the reading-room to absorb the warmth and scan the papers for situations vacant – George Orwell knew the routine and describes it so vividly in novels like *A Clergyman's Daughter*. Numerous households had recourse to the pawnbroker near to the Co-op; and, most chilling of all, at the end of the long slide into helpless destitution, the spectre of the workhouse at Pembury cast its grim and shameful shadow over the lives of the aged, the infirm, and the orphaned.

But if deprived of his livelihood as a checker, Clarence Butcher did find alternative work on the railway, first as a relief ticket-collector up and down the main line, and later in a permanent situation at Plumstead station. Within a year, the Butchers had packed up and left Tonbridge. Relocation, though it meant disruption to education and precious friendships, was a price many other unemployed families would have paid willingly for the security and dignity of a regular income.

The great paradox of the inter-war decades, however, is that for those in work, the period offered a standard of living and a level of consumer choice never before open to the population as a whole. As J. B. Priestley wrote at the beginning of his journey round England in 1933: 'If the proletariat has money in its pocket now, it can lead the life of a satrap'.[12] Thus, while no community escaped the cancer of unemployment, the worst effects of recession were suffered in the old industrial areas of Scotland and the north. Tonbridge, by contrast, fortified by its light industry and printing, its professional and commercial enterprises, and its retail interests and agricultural trade, found itself far better nourished to withstand the malaise.

Priestley believed he had discovered three Englands: the Old England of the cathedral and market towns, where F. M. Mayor's rectors and squires clung bravely to traditional values; Victorian England of the depressed industrial cities and *Love on the Dole*; and the New England of the fashion-hungry, consumer-conscious suburbs.[13] Tonbridge had elements of all three, and yet in essentials the integrity of the body was preserved. Perhaps neither the town's middle classes were so affluent or so exclusive, nor its working families so beset or dispirited, that they lived their lives oblivious to the needs and the virtues of the other, and immune, if one can be forgiven so bold a generalisation, to the new equalities, new freedoms, and new social common denominators inherent in the spirit of the contemporary age. The culture of the cinema and the dance-bands appealed to the middle and working classes alike: for, as Priestley noted while in Boston, Lincolnshire, girls all over England were made-up to resemble the same Hollywood stars, just as the picture-theatres he passed on the way to Southampton were showing the same films as their American counterparts.[14]

Cricket at the Angel Ground, the swimming-pool and the tennis-court, jaunts to the seaside by road and rail, the chance to dress cheaply but fashionably, newspaper advertisements, improved and improving diet, gramophones, radios, the multiple stores, studio photography, and the river lit up on Venetian night were for everyone, and as much part of the common Tonbridge experience of these decades, as were hunger and disillusion the bitter portion of Jarrow or Orwell's Wigan.[15] Commenting in January 1939 on attendance figures of between 8,000 and 9,000 for 'Snow White' at the Capitol, the *Tonbridge Free Press* observed significantly that no fewer than one in three of the local population had queued to share in Disney's latest masterpiece.[16]

Tonbridge, moreover, drew strength from its sense of community. The power and influence of the local shopocracy had never been so strong as in these inter-war decades. Councillors Norton of Audley Avenue, Gunner, Webber, John Angell, Tom Ives, and their ilk lived at the heart of the town whose economic prosperity they helped sustain, and no doubt instinctively read the pulse of the men and women whom they served in their shops and met daily as school managers or club presidents. Community also meant close-knit areas like Meadow Lawn and Barden Road, where, through two and three generations, mothers and daughters had married at the same altar, where father and son practised the same trade, tilled the same soil, and drank at the same public bar, and where, though families came and went, children garnered cowslips in the same hedgerows and sweethearts courted by moonlight in the same secluded lanes. Though pursued and persecuted by cyclical depression or personal tragedy, these Tonbridge folk were proof against destruction. The funeral of a notable railwayman – the memory is strong enough to have survived seven decades – saw his colleagues, his neighbours, indeed his whole community, unite in solemn procession, from street to street, silent but proudly marching, behind the horse-drawn hearse.

Every town and every family has its own tale to tell. Seldom, as the elegist reminds us, of 'the pomp of power', but rather of 'useful toil' and 'homely joys' among men and women of 'destiny obscure'. Though now we have but a jumble of memories to guide us, and a scrapbook or two of smiling, sepia faces to bid us trace 'the noiseless tenour of their way', the lives we encounter have a value and a virtue that transcend the personal and the universal, and help lighten the darkness of the past. Dust they may have become; names unknown on forgotten and untended graves. Yet, having read in this essay the story of the Butcher and Humphries families, perhaps you will say like Major-General Stanley in the Pirates of Penzance: 'I don't know whose ancestors they were, but I know whose ancestors they are'.

Sources

1   Priestley, J. B., *English Journey* (London, 1934, Jubilee edition reprinted 1984), chs 8-13

2   'Ball workers liked a "snob day" off', in Chapman, F., *Tales of Old Tonbridge* (Brasted, 1995), pp46-47

3   Neve, A. H., *The Tonbridge of Yesterday* (Tonbridge, 1933), pp101-102 and 145

4   See, for example, Jones, S. G., *Workers at Play: A Social and Economic History of Leisure 1918-1939* (London, 1986)

5   *Tonbridge Free Press*, 28 August 1936

6   *Courier*, 7 June 1935

7   *Tonbridge Free Press*, 24 and 31 May 1935

8   *The Advertiser*, 2 August 1935, *Courier*, 2 August 1935, and *Tonbridge Free Press*, 2 August 1935

9   'Great days at the Old Barn', in Chapman, F., *Tales of Old Tonbridge*, pp 42-43

10 *Tonbridge Free Press*, 26 February 1932

11 *Tonbridge Free Press*, 12 February 1932 and 6 January 1933. Cf. 'Work for the jobless in the Great Depression', in Chapman, F., *Tales of Old Tonbridge*, p106.

12 Priestley, *English Journey*, p9

13 *Ibid*, pp297-303

14 *Ibid*, pp281-282 and 24

15 Clark, P. and Murfin, L., *The History of Maidstone: The Making of a Modern County Town* (Stroud, 1995); ch. 9 describes a strikingly similar contemporary experience

16 *Tonbridge Free Press*, 13 January 1939

Acknowledgements

I am grateful to Mrs Phyllis Gilham, Mr Eric Francis, Mr Kenneth Holman, the Secretary of the Judd School, and in particular Mrs Elsie Humphries, without whose keen memory and patient advice these chapters could not have been written.

Tonbridge Ladies' College.

Recommended by the REV. DR. WOOD

(Head Master of Tonbridge School), and other eminent authorities.

Head Mistress: MADAME VETTERLI KING.

Teacher's Diploma (First Class: 14 Subjects), Zurich;
(First Class: 13 Subjects), France.

SYSTEM OF TEACHING.—Thorough education for the daughters of gentlemen. High School system, combined with methods acquired by the Head Mistress during eight years' studentship in Zurich, six years in France, and nearly twenty years' teaching experience in England.

FRENCH AND GERMAN LANGUAGES.—Unusual advantages offered for the study of Languages, which are taught by the Head Mistress and resident Foreign Governesses. Pupils have every opportunity for learning to speak French and German fluently.

PIANOFORTE, VIOLIN, AND SINGING.—Taught entirely by Masters. The Virgil-Clavier method used for Pianoforte Technique. Clavier's and Technique Tables provided. Classes for sight reading and accompanying. An Orchestral Class held weekly.

HOUSE AND GARDEN.—The House is commodious, and has every accommodation for the comfort and care of Boarders. Seven large rooms are available for teaching purposes, and for Swedish Drill and Calisthenics (daily). Nearly three acres of picturesque grounds for games and recreation.

EXAMINATIONS.—University and Musical Examinations if desired. Five successes last Oxford Local (six entered). An Annual Examination held by the Royal Academy and Royal College of Music (Associated Board).

PARENTS' REFERENCES. — References and recommendations from a large number of parents, including : The Rev. Dr. T. A. Blyth, D.D. (Oxon.), F.G.S., The Vicarage, Stoke, Coventry ; Mrs. Trevor, Bordyke House, Tonbridge ; Mrs. Stuart Smith, Brooklyn, Southsea ; Mrs. Tawney, Hanover House, Tonbridge ; Dr. Lynes, J.P., Priory Road, Coventry ; Mrs. Reeves, Wateringbury Hall, Maidstone ; J. B. Henson, Esq., Hilden Grange, Tonbridge ; Dr. Eyre Ievers, Bayham House, Tonbridge.

PROSPECTUS ON APPLICATION.

Advertisement for Tonbridge Ladies' College (later Fosse Bank School) in the Tonbridge and District Guide, *c1900 (see page 155).*

Private Schools

Alison Williams

This is a study of preparatory schools and secondary schools for girls. It excludes Tonbridge School because of its size, exceptional facilities and the fact that it is described in several other books. The schools discussed were new foundations with one to six teachers and up to about 120 pupils.

By 1909 the system of state elementary schools initiated by the 1870 Education Act had been developed and refined to the point where small private schools for the working classes had virtually disappeared. The advantages of the flexibility of the small Dame school, where attendance and payment could vary from week to week depending on home circumstances and the availability of cash, had largely disappeared with Acts which compelled attendance and gave free places to all. By 1909 private schools, large and small were the preserve of the middle and upper classes.

Certainly at the beginning of the period governesses were still in demand. There were advertisements in the *Tonbridge Free Press (TFP)* most weeks asking for suitable teachers for single or families of children. In the issue of 14 January 1910 a governess was advertising for daily or part daily work, while the following week someone was advertising for a nursery governess at a salary of £25 p.a.. By the 1920s and 1930s, however, the son of the founder of Hilden Oaks, Alan Keith-Lucas, gave as the reason for expanding numbers in the school the fact that middle class families could no longer afford private governesses for their children.[1] Attitudes also changed as parents came to value the companionship and competition which other children provided, some specialisation in subject teaching, and better sports facilities.

Over the period 1909-1939 several private schools opened and several closed but there were between 12 and 15 schools operating in Tonbridge at any one time. An analysis of census statistics of 1881 yields the information that of the total school population, 1370 were in public elementary schools and 450 in private education.[2] By 1909 a report, 'Education in Kent 1911-1912', shows the average roll of children at public elementary and voluntary elementary schools in Tonbridge was 2723. Unfortunately it has not been possible to obtain a comparable figure for 1939 but the population of Tonbridge grew quite slowly at this time, from 14,697 in 1907[3] to 16,332 in 1931[4].

How many attended private schools? Accurate figures for individual schools are very difficult to obtain and must have varied considerably over the period. With few exceptions they can only be estimated from pupils' memories of class sizes and the number of classes in the school, or calculated from one of the few extant school photos. If we are trying to estimate the proportion of Tonbridge children attending private schools the picture is further confused by the fact that, at the larger schools which took boarders, many came from outside the area or even from a foreign country. At the same time some Tonbridge children must have left the town to board at schools elsewhere, a fact suggested by an advertisement in the *TFP* (8 March 1929) for a boarding school in Berkshire. It would be reasonable to estimate that during the period the total number of Tonbridge children attending private schools in Tonbridge seldom exceeded nine hundred, even when the 350-450 boys at Tonbridge School are taken into account.

To what extent did these schools provide an efficient education? Obviously some were better than others and their functions varied. In its report fifty years before, the Newcastle Commission had commented that parents continued to favour private schools because 'the children were more respectable and the teachers more inclined to fall in with the wishes of the parents'. This was probably still true in 1909. There is little evidence that the rudimentary inspection procedures which were in place by 1909 were actually enforced. The 1899 Board of Education Act gave the Board powers of inspection but even after these were augmented in 1902 it was only by a very circuitous route that a bad school could be closed. After 1918 the Board was meant to be notified of the name and address of any 'school' with more than five pupils.[5] After 1921 it was no longer a defence against proceedings brought by the school attendance officer to say that your child was attending a private school, unless that school was open to inspection and proper registers kept. In the report 'Education in Kent, 1933-38' the authority admitted that, while there were more than 300 'privately conducted schools' which were open to inspection in compliance with section 147 of the 1921 Education Act, they had not carried out any, except at the request of the proprietors.

Anecdotal evidence suggests that attendance could be very lax. Mrs Gordin remembers being shocked when her friend, the well-known Miss Bull, was kept off school by her mother to go to the cinema. As late as the 1960s, Mrs Brenda Bentall asked the school attendance officer whether he concerned himself with pupils at private schools. He replied that he would, if requested by the schools, but never remembered this having happened. Nevertheless, most old pupils are adamant that they were at least proficient in the 3Rs before they left.

Some of the schools were very small indeed and, apart from the fact that they were located in the more respectable residential areas, differed very little from the traditional Dame school of the previous century. A former pupil of one describes how his teacher, duster in hand, would drift in to set a few more sums, then out again to put on the dinner. Few of the teachers in these small schools were qualified but some were no doubt excellent. Often there was only one teacher, at most three or four, but they were assisted by visiting specialists. Miss Ella Sutton, a dancing teacher, features in the accounts of several schools; there were men who taught the boys games at Brooklands, and a former Fosse Bank pupil remembers 'a visiting artist – complete with beard'. They prepared girls to go on to the county school or to the larger private schools, such as Fosse Bank or the Convent, and boys for the Judd, or occasionally Yardley Court and Tonbridge School. Most of their pupils were under 12 though a few, weaker either in health or wealth or mental abilities, remained until they completed their schooling.

About some of the schools nothing is known except the fact of their existence. They are mentioned in *Kelly's Directory* or the *TFP* but no one now remembers them. For example *Lavinia Cooper*, of 73 Quarry Hill Road. Her 'school for boys and children' is in *Kelly's* for 1909 but is not mentioned in the 1919 edition. Mrs E. W. Handcock's *Portland Villa* preparatory school at 32 Quarry Hill is advertised in the *TFP* in 1904, but by 1909 the address is that of a doctor of medicine. *Lechford, Harry*, is listed as having a school at 42 Hadlow Road in 1909 and 1911 but by 1913 a Miss Topham has replaced him at that address. In the *TFP* in January 1929 there is an advertisement for *The Chestnuts*, 'a school for children needing open air education. Apply E. M. Muldoon'.

Some, although remembered, had a very brief existence. *Mrs Elizabeth Fricker* kept a small school at 89 Lavender Hill. She is listed in *Kelly's* for 1909 and 1911 at that address, with the word 'school' following, but by 1913, although she still lives at that address, the word 'school' no longer appears.

Ridge House School appears in *Kelly's* for 1937 but by 1939 has disappeared both as a school and as a private address. Mrs Brenda Bentall remembers this school as being a small, purpose built, pre-preparatory school, taking both boys and girls. The head was a Mr Carter who had been a master at Yardley Court. An advertisement in the *TFP* on 22 March 1935 announced 'Ridge House School (Mr and Mrs W. Carter). Pre-preparatory for boys 4-10.' By 1937 however it was advertising for 'boys and girls 4-10' and continued: 'Modern methods, experienced teachers, physical training, games taught, percussion band, nature study, country walks. Very young children taken one hour daily. Close to good bus service to all parts.' Whether this fuller advertisement indicates success or increasing desperation is difficult to decide. Mrs Bentall believes that it may have closed because Mr Carter was called up.

Two other schools have been mentioned by an informant, Mr King of Tenterden. *The Castle School* he remembers being run by a Major Le Fleming, whose father was a master at Tonbridge School, and a tutor at Eton House, London Road. Major Le Fleming specialised in cramming for the army and navy. The *TFP* of 25 March 1910 mentions pupils from this school gaining scholarships to Rossall School. He also remembers a school called *Clare House*, kept by a Mr Darling, formerly a master at Tonbridge School. No other information on these schools has come to light up to this time.

The schools are difficult to trace as they open and close and change. Some are persistent in location but change their name, for instance Brickwood Lodge which became Pinewood Lodge, and was then replaced on the same site, at the Bordyke end of Hadlow Road, by The Mona School. Others, like Newlands and Ravenswood, change location but keep their names. Most peripatetic of all was Miss Thompson's which constantly adapted to circumstances.

Miss Thompson's school was probably one of the smallest schools and nearest in character to the traditional Dame school. It does not appear in any of the directories until 1934 but is still remembered by several people well before that date. It was located at one period in an upstairs room in the house of the two Miss Thompsons, at 19 St Mary's Road, one of whom did the teaching, the other the house keeping. At another time it was in The Drive, at 'Martenscroft', now No. 49. Whether this was also the home of the invalid boy, who, in effect, had the school come to him, or whether his house was yet another location, no one is now sure.

Mr J. K. Bentall, who attended the school in 1913-16, remembers there were at least four different houses involved. He says there were about a dozen children, boys and girls under eight, but another former pupil, who attended in the 1920s, never remembers there being more than about eight children. Mr Bentall describes how the day began with a Bible story, after which the pupils wrote out tables on slates. Arithmetic was also done on slates, up to long division and money sums. Copy books were only used for practising copper plate writing in ink. Children were called out one by one to read. In later years there were French exercises and drawing if other work was finished in time. There was a not very strenuous physical exercise class, which at one period at least, used dumbbells. Mrs Linnet, who attended the school in the 1920s, doubts if Miss Thompson had any qualifications but thought her an efficient teacher and felt well prepared when she went to the County School Junior Department at the age of eight.

Brickwood Lodge, a well established Tonbridge school which often featured in the *TFP*, had opened in 1881. The advertisements appeared regularly: 'Boarding and day, girls and little boys. Pupils prepared for examinations, fees moderate'. Unusually a description of the town in 1908 gives more details of these fees: eight guineas a term for boarders over 12 and seven for those under twelve; day pupils were charged 25s over twelve, 20s under 12 and 15s under seven. Piano lessons were 10s 6d per term and advanced drawing 15s per term. Callisthenics, dancing and painting were also offered. A picture of 1908 in *Who's Who and Where: the Illustrated Year Book of Tunbridge Wells and District*, shows four teachers and 49 pupils. The headmistress was a Miss Pledger and she was, according to another advertisement in 1910, running a school and kindergarten at 24 Hadlow Road, 'assisted by a qualified mistress and certificated teacher'. Each term notices were placed to announce when school would recommence and there are other mentions, for instance in 1910 pupils donated 10s to the Cottage Hospital and in 1903 there was a long and detailed account of a 'breaking-up concert' held at the Public Hall. The Revd C. G. Baskerville, who gave away the prizes, commented on Miss Pledger's 'good work for education', the children's success in gaining certificates from such institutions as the Kensington Local Examinations Board and the London College of Music, and the parents' satisfaction 'that their children were being well grounded in all that would be useful to them in after life'.

In 1916 Miss Pledger was still the headmistress of Brickwood Lodge, but in 1919 *Pinewood Lodge* appears at 3 Hadlow Road, still with Miss Pledger in

BRICKWOOD LODGE
—— SCHOOL AND KINDERGARTEN. ——

I N the Hadlow Road is the old-eatablished School and Kindergarten—established twenty-seven years ago—of which the principal is Miss Louisa Pledger, '' Brickwood Lodge,'' for boarders and day pupils—girls and little boys.

BRICKWOOD LODGE SCHOOL.

Miss Pledger is assisted by a qualified staff who prepare pupils for the various examinations (if their parents so desire), including Music examinations.

The school is pleasantly situated within easy distance of the favourite walk across the river to the Postern.

Advertisement for Brickwood Lodge in the 'Borough' *Guide to Tonbridge, c1912.*

charge. By 1922 the school was no longer listed and in 1931 Miss Pledger is no longer in the Directory. In 1927 *The Mona School* appears at 3A Hadlow Road, probably on the site of a building marked 'Mona Cottages' on an 1866 Ordnance Survey map[6].Why there was a change of name, whether this implies a change in location, whether The Mona School was yet another name for Pinewood/Brickwood Lodge or whether they co-existed for a time, or whether there was a gap when there was no school on the site, remains a mystery.

The Mona School was first listed in the Directory in 1927. In 1924 Miss Lane was at 9 Hadlow Road and in 1927 at 3A Hadlow Road, as headmistress of The Mona School but in 1937 the address was No. 7 Hadlow Road although the Headmistress was still given as Miss Alice Lane. Miss Lane and her sister lived in part of the house. A pupil from 1935, Eileen Burley, says it was then still on the Bordyke side of Goodlands garage, and in 1936 or 1937 it moved to the other side where it remained until its closure in 1939 on the death of Miss Lane. An advertisement of 1937 mentions 'bright sunny class rooms and a nice garden' so presumably the new site was an improvement. Spelling and tables were taken very seriously. Girls and small boys attended and girls could stay till leaving age. 'Swedish Drill' was held in a room in The Mitre pub, opposite the school, and PE and dance at the YWCA in Lyons Crescent. Concerts were held there too. Mothers were expected to make elaborate costumes, sometimes for several appearances.

The *TFP* (19 December 1930) reports the annual Christmas concert in the Medway Hall, with over 200 people present. Miss Lane reported on progress; Forms I and II had done good work and shown greater keenness; the arithmetic standard was higher, the improvement in English maintained, and drawing and painting improved. Form III had done steady work with nature study and geography lessons under Miss Sawyer being appreciated. Form IV was satisfactory, the little ones improving and the older boys progressing. The needlework class was on two afternoons a week and the little ones enjoyed handicraft and clay modelling. In summer there was tennis on the Sports Ground and cricket for the boys. Miss Smyth taught older girls in the morning, Miss Flemons the little ones, Mrs Coulting singing lessons. Miss Ella Sutton, who advertised as an associate of the Imperial Society of Teachers of Dancing, visited to teach drill and dancing, as she did in several other schools. The school had the reputation of giving pupils a very good grounding in the basic subjects and many went on to larger schools like the Convent or County school, although others stayed until they were fifteen.

Probably slightly larger was *Newlands School*. In 1909 a Miss Caroline Wilson had a 'Ladies' school, preparatory for boys', called Newlands at 1 Woodfield Road, on the corner with St Mary's Road. The school was listed in *Kelly's* and regular announcements appeared in the *TFP*: 'School commences Tuesday, April 26th, Miss Wilson at home Monday 4-8, to see parents', appeared in an April edition in 1917. By 1920 however, the school at 1 Woodfield Road was still called Newlands but the principal was a Mrs Parkinson. Mrs Holms says that when she attended the school in the 1920s Mrs Parkinson was assisted by a pupil-teacher, Miss Burt and other qualified teachers. She remembers Mrs Hyle, Miss Rogers and Miss Crispin. The age range was between five and 15 for girls, and there were also small boys. There were three classes of about 10 to 12 pupils, taught in one main room, with special lessons taught on the platform. The boys mostly went on to the Judd school. Basic subjects were taught though there was little science teaching. There were games and exercise classes in the garden. By 1931 Miss Burt had taken over as head and moved the school, literally physically, in that a great part of the school consisted of a large hut, to a plot of land at 43 St Mary's Road. Mrs Holms has the impression that the school was not quite so large or prestigious after the move. In an advertisement in the TFP (1 January 1937) Miss Burt, the principal, announced the commencement of term and gives details: 'Kindergarten class for infants 3½ -5 years. Junior classes for pupils 6-9 years. Backward or delicate children treated individually. Good ground work. Organised games. FEES MODERATE. NO EXTRAS. Modern methods'. When the school finally closed in 1954 the hut moved yet again to become the church hall at Cage Green, and Miss Burt became a scripture teacher at Fosse Bank.

Brooklands Prep School was opened by a Miss Ronald in a big house on the corner of Brook Street in the mid twenties. She later married and became Mrs Sunderland. In 1929 a former pupil remembers there were three classes, kindergarten, transition and preparatory and four teachers, Mrs Sunderland, Miss Jones, Miss Hewer and Miss Church who taught art and craft. There were about 25 children, boys and girls but most were under eight years old. The school grew in size and status during the thirties and by 1939 numbered about 120. It still took girls and boys, though most boys left by eight to go on to prep school. There were seven classes by this time and several teachers, one of whom wore a gown and one was Fröbel trained. Visiting men teachers took the boys for games and Miss Sutton came in to take dancing. As well as the 3Rs, arts and crafts, French and nature study were taught. By this time Miss May Jones had become head and a former member of staff remembers it as a happy school with good teachers and a sensible attitude to uniform. This was a cheerful red and grey, and only the blazer had to be purchased from a specialist school shop. Many people have mentioned Brooklands as having a good reputation, but after moving to Southborough it finally closed in the 1950s.

Malvern House, at 72 Quarry Hill Road, was run by the wife of a master at the Judd school and at one time acted, informally, as a prep school for it. Malvern House is first mentioned in *Kelly's* in 1924 as a school for boys under the direction of Mrs Clapham and B. R. Clapham, her son. It seems to have fluctuated in size. At one time it was comparatively large and at least one pupil was removed from Miss Thompson's and sent there because it was thought to be a better school. An advertisement in the *TFP* (6 September 1929) announces a 'Common Entrance class now forming' and 'boarders received'. There was a uniform with a grey cap and boys had to have cricket whites for the summer term. Sports lessons were at the recreation grounds. In 1934 it is listed in *Kelly's* under the direction of Mr and Mrs B. R. Clapham. In later years, just before the war, it was very small with only 10 to a dozen pupils aged between five and 11 years. Except when Brian Clapham appeared and gave stimulating lessons it was very informal, with the 3Rs and spelling occupying most of the time. One informant who went on to Sussex Road found that school a complete contrast, much bigger, of course, with pupils up to 14 years, and with efficient well qualified staff and a much wider curriculum.

A school which must have been of a similar size in the 1920s and 1930s was *Ravenswood*, which in 1942 moved to Dry Hill Park Road and, under the Gracey family has continued to grow and develop as *Hilden Grange*. There seems to have been a school of that name at least as early as 1903 when a prize giving there is mentioned in the *TFP*. The headmistress was a Miss Du Pré and she boasted that numbers had risen from 54 in the previous autumn to 67. There were three permanent teachers and some visiting. Oxford local examinations were taken. In 1904 there is simply an announcement that 'Miss Janson is in residence at Ravenswood to see parents'. The large house was obviously divided and many of its occupants had some connection with education.

By 1924 *Kelly's* is listing F. H. Spicer, tutor, Ravenswood, and he is still listed in the 1926 and 1927 directories. In the 1929 Directory, however, there is more precise information. No. 1 London Road, Flat A, is occupied by A. T. Morris BA (Oxon), and is described as a preparatory school. The school was advertised in the TFP on 10 January: 'Pupils prepared for Common Entrance and other examinations ... A few vacancies for January 20th'. The advertisement in the paper on 31 January added the inducement: 'Individual teaching with very successful results'. A. T. Morris had been a master at Tonbridge School and lived at Hadlow Stair where he was well known for breeding Airedales. Possibly a little out of his depth with older boys he made a success of his prep school, and in 1934 he was joined by F. G. Morgan MA (Cantab). Mr M. Warriner, a pupil at that time, remembers Mr Morgan, who was also at one time a master at Tonbridge School, as a lively and stimulating teacher, especially in his main subject, French. There was a younger teacher assisting, first a Mr W. H. Stroude, replaced by a Mr Clarke, and then Mr Stevens. A school photograph of 1935 shows Mr Morris, flanked by Mr Morgan and another, younger looking teacher, Mr Stevens, and 26 boys. The three masters between them taught Latin, French, English and Maths to boys who arrived, aged eight, from pre-prep schools such as Newlands, already grounded in the 3Rs. They were prepared for Common Entrance at 13 and most went on to Tonbridge School or Sevenoaks.

The original Ravenswood occupied part of the large house at 1 London Road, a basement flat on the left and to the rear of the house, but in 1933 it moved further down London Road, to a house now used as a veterinary surgery by Mr R. J. Noble. The whole house and garden were used for the school. There were three classrooms and a common room for the boys. Three or four boarders were accommodated upstairs in the charge of Matron, who was sometimes helped by Mr Morgan's wife. A field on the opposite side of the road, near to the Langley Hotel, was used for games, soccer in winter and cricket in summer. The Ravenswood uniform was navy blue, including a cap with a green Maltese cross. Although the teachers were well qualified the school was small and did not have the prestige of Yardley Court. A former pupil thinks the fees were lower and seems to remember 'fifteen guineas per term, plus extras' being mentioned. In 1939 Mr Morris was involved in an accident and shortly afterwards the school was taken over by Mr P. P. Mallam, who in 1942 moved the school to Dry Hill Park Road.

A school which caused a slight stir when it first opened was *Our Lady's Convent*. The new Catholic church in Lyons Crescent was dedicated in 1903.

In the same year an order of nuns arrived and took over a large house at 6 Charlton Terrace, in Mill Crescent, called 'Shrublands'.[6] On 9 January 1904 the first advertisement appeared in the *TFP*: 'Our Lady's Convent, Under the direction of the Sisters of Charity and of Christian instruction, of Nevers, France. Lessons to Private Pupils will be given in the following subjects:– French, German, Spanish, Music, Drawing, Painting, and Fancy Needlework. Apply to the Lady Superior'. There does not seem to be any report in the paper of its opening but there was a background of some anxiety on the part of the Protestant Union. The Revd Westmore S. Smith, reported in the *TFP* in 1904, urged parents 'never to send their children to be educated by nuns and priests, selling their child's soul for the sake of a good education'. Nevertheless the school seems to have been suc-

OUR LADY'S CONVENT,
SHRUBLANDS, HADLOW ROAD, TONBRIDGE.
UNDER the direction of the Sisters of Charity and of Christian Instruction, of Nevers, France.
Lessons to Private Pupils will be given in the following subjects :—
FRENCH, GERMAN, SPANISH, MUSIC, DRAWING, PAINTING, AND FANCY NEEDLEWORK.
Apply to the Lady Superior

Advertisement for Our Lady's Convent in the Tonbridge Free Press, *29 January 1904.*

cessful from the beginning, attracting Protestants as well as Catholics. The atmosphere was certainly religious. The Reverend Mother had known St Bernadette of Lourdes when she was young, 'consequently we felt the saint was part of our lives'. There was a life sized statue of Our Lady in a grotto in the garden and a small chapel was built where twice daily attendance was compulsory for Catholics, as was Sunday attendance at Corpus Christi church. There were retreats, penances in Lent, and fêtes on Saints' days, but Protestant pupils felt under no pressure to join in, although most did. The order, which also had a convent at Brighton, came from Nevers and in the early days most of the nuns were French or Belgian. French was therefore a strong subject, but English was also well taught and by 1918 there was an English nun who taught Maths.

One former pupil, Beryl Gordin (née Hucks), who was at the convent from 1918 to 1926, considers that examinations were taken seriously. Oxford and Cambridge Local, Associated Board, and Royal College of Music examinations were taken, and Mrs Gordin has the impression the results were quite good. She herself gained honours in history and literature and just scraped maths. Mrs Bear, a pupil between 1926 and 1934, took her school certificate in all the normal subjects. Classes were small, even in 1934 – about 30 to a class with two age groups in each. The nun would set work for one group while teaching the other. Mrs Bear always found it easy to get attention and the nuns seemed kind and caring. In September 1939 a commercial course was introduced. Sewing was mainly making garments for the poor. Mrs Gordin remembers only plain sewing, striped winceyette night-dresses. Mrs Bear remembers shapeless brown dresses, with knickers to match instead of the night-dresses, but also remembers doing embroidery and making lace. In the early days there was little by way of games, only walking in the large and well kept grounds. Later, according to Mrs Bear, there was more activity. Netball and lacrosse were played on Tonbridge sports ground and there were matches against Fosse Bank and Kent College. Tennis was played on a court in the grounds, although according to Mrs Gordin there was no net! Each week Miss Sutton and her pianist appeared for a dancing lesson, chaperoned by one of the nuns. Gymnastics were not too demanding: 'We marched into the hall and spaced ourselves out. We only did very gentle exercises, and finished by lying on the floor and doing leg exercises, no mean task in a thick serge tunic reaching to the knee and long black stockings'. These stockings, made of wool, were a torture in summer and day girls longed to get home and take them off.

Weekday uniform was white blouses and navy tunics, though for a time, until laundry bills proved too costly, the boarders wore white tunics on Sundays. The dress code was strictly enforced after the first years, during which there was no uniform, and one informant remembers being punished for carrying rather than wearing her hat in the town. Punishments were not very severe and mostly consisted of writing lines and loss of privileges: loss of play time, not being part of religious processions, early bedtime. One boarder, however, was expelled for passing a note to a Tonbridge schoolboy in church. There were small boys as well as girls, boarders as well as day pupils. A school photo of 1925 shows 78, which implies a full complement of 80-85. Many of the boarders came from abroad and some were Indian. Another group were the French and Belgian students who came to learn English. Obviously the school evolved over the years and would have appeared differently to different pupils. To Beryl Hucks, arriving as a boarder in 1918 aged seven, the first impression was of 'bare boards and no curtains'. She was shorn of her ringlets and dressed in a plaid skirt and button boots. The cook at that time was a Mère Clotilde, an economical Breton who served bread and margarine for breakfast and a soup made from two tablespoons of marmite and two gallons of water. This was accompanied by 'dog' biscuits and followed by a terrible rice pudding known as 'grit pudding'. On Friday there was fried fish and on Saturday evenings cocoa and castor oil. By 1926 the advent of an Irish nun had much improved the food and there was even some choice at breakfast between tea and coffee and brown and white bread. Boarders were allowed one bath a fortnight and made do with foot baths in between. All the French and Belgian pupils bathed wearing a cotton shift, out of modesty. Many boarders remained at school during the holidays. Walks, always in a crocodile, and the occasional visit to another convent, did little to relieve the monotony. At the beginning of the Second World War the Convent was still a thriving school, and it was not until after it had moved to Hildenborough that the school closed in the 1970s.

Another successful girls' private school during this period was *Fosse Bank School*. Its first headmistress, Madame Vetterli King, had met Dr Joseph Wood while she was teaching at Coventry High School. She must have impressed him because when he later became headmaster of Tonbridge School he urged her to open a school for girls which would provide a worthwhile education for the sisters of his pupils. The school opened in 1892. First announced as a High School, it was no doubt intended to be in the same mould as others founded at this time. For her day, Madame Vetterli was well qualified to be headmistress. Born and educated in a German speaking part of Switzerland she continued her education in France coming to England in 1872, at the age of 20, to attend a 'young ladies' seminary'. There followed years of teaching in England, including the period at Coventry High School. Perhaps one of the reasons why the school never achieved a comparable academic standing with other similar girls' schools founded at about that time (such as Ashford School) was that Madame Vetterli had recently married and had a daughter. From the beginning the school had to support a family rather than merely provide a salary for a headmistress. Her husband, formerly a choirmaster at Kings College, Cambridge, taught singing and dealt with the business side of the school. He is remembered as being much milder and more approachable than Madame, who, especially in later years, commanded more respect than affection.

Fosse Bank School in the 1920s, showing the founder and headmistress, Madame Vetterli King, in the centre, with her daughter Dorothea on her left, and on her right Miss Ragetti, both of whom were later headmistress (author's photograph).

The first school, which soon became known as Tonbridge Ladies College, was at the north end of the High Street, on the corner with Lansdowne Road. It was in a pleasant Georgian house with a coach house and stables, orchard and kitchen gardens, and a croquet lawn where an early photo shows young ladies in long skirts at play.[7] By 1903 the original 'handful' of girls had increased to about 50 day girls and boarders. The new School House with classrooms, large hall and stage was therefore built in the grounds. It was here that Madame staged the dramatic productions which seem to have been popular with the girls and well attended by the public. The *TFP* in December 1911 carried a highly complimentary account of the 'Breaking-up concert' in the 'beautiful schoolroom' which 'clearly showed the abilities of teachers and pupils'. The First World War saw a temporary halt to expansion, but new building continued during the twenties and thirties, culminating in a large gymnasium with a tennis court on top. From this time sport was taken more seriously and matches were played against the Our Lady's Convent and Kent College. Two existing buildings were also purchased. It was planned to make a finishing school or college of Ormonde Lodge in Southborough but the idea was eventually dropped because of the economic depression in the thirties which affected private schools as well as other small businesses. Quarry Hill House, rented in 1924 and later purchased in 1952, was first a boarding house for the school in the High Street and later the nucleus of the school when it moved to Quarry Hill. As a boarding house it seems to have been popular with the girls who welcomed the chance to leave school at the end of the day. The school magazine, published regularly in the twenties and thirties, shows that the school was home to many boarders whose parents lived abroad. Madame wrote long letters to their parents, detailing their progress. Those who had to remain at school during the holidays saw a softer side of her character as she did her best to make a real holiday with treats and later breakfast and bed times.

In spite of a serious attitude to work and Oxford Board examinations taken at 12, 13 and 16 years of age, the emphasis was still on the more ladylike pursuits. Languages, literature, 'physical culture', dancing, harmony, manners and religious knowledge were more stressed than mathematics or the sciences. There is some evidence that this was not Madame's idea, but the parents'. At a prize-giving ceremony in 1904 she deplored the fact that 'parents did not appear to desire their girls to undertake the work necessary to pass [public] examinations'. Languages were studied seriously, especially after Madame's daughter Dorothea returned to the school as a teacher. She had been one of the school's most successful pupils, coming top of the country in the Oxford Board Senior Honours in German, and fourth in the kingdom for French (*TFP,* December 1911). She later obtained first class honours in German from King's College, London, and taught at Bedales before returning to Fosse Bank School. At the school's fortieth anniversary celebrations she spoke of her mother's struggle to gain her pupils a reputation for 'hard work and successful examination results in a generation when hard thinking was still considered an unladylike occupation, tending to be destructive of female beauty'.

Although close links were maintained with the Parish church, Madame was never bigoted in religious matters. An old girl remembers her exclaiming in a scripture class: 'If you all think you have your own little special gates into Heaven you are mistaken, so get used to the idea early in life. Heaven is a state – not, as some hymns imply, an overcrowded jeweller's shop!'

For its first 25 years the school had no uniform, but in 1918 pleated navy dresses with a gold FBS embroidered on the pocket were introduced, worn with black stockings in winter. In summer white dresses were substituted. Later the distinctive berets, with their gold cross and tassel were added – at one time a source of pride but in the hatless seventies they became a torment to the unfortunate girls who had to wear them. One old pupil remarks of the food 'perhaps it was not very imaginative but it was certainly plentiful. I wonder how many remember "Rock of Ages Pudding"!' An extra shilling a week could purchase fruit. Another pupil however remembers 'lunch was appalling and to be dreaded'.

By 1932 the school was large enough to be divided into houses, first three and later four. After this there was a more competitive spirit. In 1937 Madame died. Although in her last years she was an alarmingly severe figure, on her death the school magazine was flooded with letters from old girls remembering acts of kindness and happy times at 'Madame's Annual Dance', and above all recording the influence of her teaching and example. The next years were to form a watershed in the history of the school. When Madame died her designated successor, her daughter Miss D. V. King, became headmistress. In the following year the old Fosse Bank in the High Street was sold and the whole school was transferred to Quarry Hill. The house, which had previously just accommodated boarders, was extended by wooden buildings which held school rooms and a gym. Although the buildings were not of such a high standard as those relinquished in the High Street, the grounds were much larger and pleasantly sited on the edge of town. However much she was missed, Madame had been 84 at her death and her daughter was well qualified by experience and training to take over. By the end of the year, however, Miss D. V. King had married the retired vicar of Tonbridge and left the school. Her father had married a former pupil and also left the school. As it had been in effect a family business, these two events must have had financial implications for the school. Worst of all, the removal to the new school was overshadowed by the knowledge that the outbreak of war could not be long. In the circumstances the school was fortunate to survive the next few years.[7]

Hilden Oaks, a very different school, which still flourishes today, was opened in 1919. Mrs Alys Keith-Lucas with her friend Muriel Boldero decided after considerable research that the best opening for the sort of school they planned would be in Tonbridge. The school was intended for girls up to 13 or 14 and boys up to nine, who would then be ready for a prep school and then Tonbridge School. Kenford School, as it was first called, opened with three pupils, one Alys' youngest son. It soon grew, however, and within four years there were 50 pupils. This meant a move from 'Kenford' to a large three-storey, semi-detached house and the renaming of the school Hilden Oaks. By 1920 there were several members of staff, a Miss Henson, Miss Hodgson (later Mrs Rucker), Miss Clapin (later Mrs Dawson), and Miss Franks (later Mrs Herman). These were later joined by Mrs Bickmore of Yardley Court, Mrs Bottle, Miss Dickinson and Miss Clay, as house keeper to Mrs Keith-Lucas. These teachers were paid from £30-£40 a term which did not compare very favourably with that of teachers in state elementary schools, although it is possible that the teachers worked only part time. The fees were five guineas a term.

The school was known as 'progressive'. Mrs Bottle, the music teacher, pioneered having children make and play their own pipes and Alys' methods of discipline were very gentle for that time. Her son says of her that 'she was quite unconventional in her teaching but loved to help [her pupils] find their own solutions to their problems. She once said she hoped to help them not to have "so demanding a conscience".' Indeed unusual for a teacher of the time. A former pupil comments on the happy and relaxed atmosphere of the school. By 1931 there were 101 pupils in the school, partly, Alan-Keith Lucas believes,[8] because during the depression people could no longer afford governesses. As the depression bit deeper however, the school was severely affected as were many others, and the numbers declined to 70. Alys had always been delicate since an illness in 1919, and after an operation in 1932 she decided she must retire although she was only 44. As she had already parted company with her former associate, Miss Boldero, she asked her son Alan, who was now teaching at the school, to take over.

Alan Keith-Lucas continued the school and its progressive traditions, being very proud that he never had to punish a child. He took Miss Nancy Dickinson as a salaried co-principal, and built on a wing for her to avoid the scandal of living under the same roof. Later, when he went to America, Miss Dickinson took over, and the school became known locally as 'Miss Dickies". The school survived not only the depression but also the war years and still flourishes today.[8]

Yardley Court, founded in 1898, always had the closest of connections with Tonbridge School. A. J. Bickmore, its first headmaster, had been head of the Junior School at Tonbridge school. When he set up his own prep school in a large house off Yardley Park Road all the junior boys from the school were transferred there. Financially there was also a close connection. Neither A. J. Bickmore or his wife had the capital to buy such a large house so the money was borrowed, partly from the Skinners' Company. It is possible that the approval of the then head of Tonbridge School had similarly helped Madame Vetterli King when she set up Fosse Bank School six years before. By 1902 there were 60 boys at Yardley Court, and by 1911, 80. In 1901 a wing was added to the original house and further additions were made in 1902 and 1923, for which another £10,000 was borrowed. There were five class rooms, dormitories for the boarders and other communal rooms and playing fields adjacent to the buildings. By 1938 there were 60 boarders and 60 day boys.

Yardley Court continued to be owned and run by the Bickmore family with the help of assistant masters. It always had the reputation of being the most formal and prestigious of the prep schools in Tonbridge, because of its size, facilities and close connections with Tonbridge School. It was also the most expensive. Yardley Court stayed on its original site until it moved to Somerhill in 1990.

Considering that in the 1920s the fees per term even in the smaller private schools were more than the average manual worker earned in a week, it is understandable that most Tonbridge boys and girls went to the free state schools. However, numbers in private schools in Tonbridge were growing. By 1939 a few children of middle class families were being sent to state elementary schools, and some attended private schools in other areas, but the growth of the local population and the disappearance of governesses and private tutors boosted fee paying schools in the town. Children whose parents paid for private education had small classes and sometimes individual teaching and the company of children from a similar social background. Of girls over 14 still attending school perhaps half went to the County School with its rather more academic education, but half were in private schools such as the Convent or Fosse Bank.

In 1939 most of the private schools in Tonbridge were still in a healthy state. However some of the changes which would lead to the closure of several were already becoming apparent. Although seldom enforced, there was a framework in place which would enable the education authority to inspect and insist on adequate standards in private schools. It has been difficult to find out the salaries paid to teachers in private schools in the period but in the smaller private schools after the 1939-45 war it was certainly customary to pay less than Burnham scale. If the example quoted for Hilden Oaks is typical, £90-£120 p.a.[9] compared to the elementary school teacher's average of £285 in 1921,[10] it would do little to encourage the best qualified teachers to work in private schools. At the same time parents were beginning to expect more specialised teaching and better facilities for their children. Pressure for middle class children, even female, to succeed academically and fit themselves for a career, was increasing. Even in 1929 the Reverend Mother of Our Lady's Convent felt it necessary to stress in an advertisement in the *TFP* that 'parents are reminded that girls educated at the convent are fully equipped for the battle of life as is proved by the fact that many old pupils fill important posts in banks and commercial firms'. Before 1914 the majority of girls in middle class families did not expect to work when they left school. By 1939 most of them received further education for teaching, nursing, or secretarial work and even most of the professions were open to them. For middle class boys and girls a good education was of increasing importance and those schools which survived the dislocation of the war years had to change to compete with an improved free state system.

Sources

1   Keith-Lucas, Alan (compiler), *A History of Hilden Oaks School* (unpublished)

2   Chalklin, C. (ed.), *Late Victorian and Edwardian Tonbridge* (Kent County Library, 1988)

3   *Kelly's Directory*, 1909

4   *Kelly's Directory*, 1934

5   Curtis, S. T., and Boultwood, M. E. A., *A History of English Education Since 1800*. Also, Barnard, H. C., *A History of English Education since 1760*.

6   Ordnance Survey Map, 25 inches to the mile, 1866

7   Williams, A., *Fosse Bank School*

8   Keith-Lucas, Alan (compiler), *A History of Hilden Oaks School* (unpublished)

9   Bacon, Mrs H. J., *A History of Hilden Oaks* (unpublished)

10   *TFP*, 3 March 1921

Acknowledgements

I am extremely grateful to the following for information, both oral and written: Mr King (Castle School, Clare House), Mr J K Bentall and Mrs Linnet (Miss Thompson's), Eileen Burley (Mona School), Mrs Holms (Newlands), Mr M Warriner and Mrs Ambrose (Brooklands), Mr R Gracey and Mr M Warriner (Ravenswood), Mrs Beryl Gordin, Mrs B Bear and Miss Bull (Our Lady's Convent), and Mrs Dudeney, Mrs Dewhurst and Mrs Barlas (Fosse Bank). I am particularly grateful to Mrs Brenda Bentall, who not only supplied a great deal of information herself, but also tracked down numerous friends and relations to do the same. The information on Yardley Court was passed to me by the Editor from N. J. Crompton's *Yardley Court 1898-1973* (1973).

Sport

Laurence Johnson

With arguably the best publicly-owned sports ground in the south of England, together with a county cricket ground and numerous private sports facilities, it is not surprising that the main leisure occupation of the people of Tonbridge in the first half of the century should be sport in its many forms.

The Sports Ground, commonly known as the Racecourse, was originally used for horse racing. Although it was no Kempton Park or Goodwood it attracted large crowds; the nature of the crowds, which included some of the worst and roughest elements of the times, disturbed the members of the Tonbridge Urban District Council and it was resolved to exercise some control from the Council. Initially 14 acres of the Racecourse Meadows were leased from the Tonbridge Water Works Company and Mr Streeten, a private owner. By 1923 the whole of the Sports Ground was purchased. Before the purchase, the Council, wisely had decided to entrust the administration of the sports ground to a separate organisation. Thus the Tonbridge Sports Association, comprising representatives of all the clubs who would use the ground, was set up to collect rents from the clubs and to allocate grounds.

The Association is the oldest such organisation in the country and has proved to be a great success, being the envy of many other municipalities. The sports catered for were many and varied from cricket and football (both codes), via hockey and tennis to quoits, lacrosse and stoolball. A putting green was added and let to a private operator.

Members of the Association took great pride in the work of running a successful administration. This is expressed very clearly in their Annual Report dated May 1929: 'The Committee in issuing their Ninth Annual Report and Balance Sheet are pleased to state that sport on the ground has been a success, almost every branch of sport being played there. Clubs have done their best to make this a success and are making the grounds more attractive by creating several new pavilions. The delegates of the clubs who form the Committee have worked hard for the welfare of all the clubs concerned. The Committee are pleased to state that all cricket pitches are let this season and the prospect of the same can be said of the tennis courts available. In closing our report we appreciate the use of the grounds which are such a valuable asset to the town'.

Possibly the most imposing of the pavilions mentioned in the report was the grandstand and changing facility erected by Tonbridge Football Club, a very successful amateur side for which Frank Woolley and other Kent cricketers played. Unfortunately, the stand was burned down in 1936 and after rebuilding was severely damaged in a strong gale.

Throughout the life of the Association one of the keenest issues to be argued between Town Council and the Association each year was that of Sunday play. It became an annual ritual for the Association to present the Council with a request for permission to use the sports facilities on Sundays; each year this was refused. In 1936, Sunday play in afternoons only was permitted for the summer period only. Soon afterwards full Sunday play was allowed.

A wide variety of sports was played on the ground but there can be no doubt that the chief preoccupation of Tonbridgians was cricket. Cricket for Tonbridgians was not merely a Saturday afternoon pastime; it was a way of life: indeed for many Tonbridgians it provided a living.

Since the early days of cricket, Kent has always been a very strong cricketing county. This strength was due mainly to its seedbed in Tonbridge since the county nursery was located on the Angel Ground from 1897 to 1927. It was managed by Tom Pawley, also manager of the Rose & Crown hotel. He was an ex-Kent cricketer and had at one time been appointed to manage the Kent team.

The Angel Ground, which had been acquired by Tonbridge Cricket Club in 1905, following a public subscription to purchase the ground, became the very heart of sporting Tonbridge between the wars, when Sainsbury's was still a single shop in the High Street, with immaculate marble counters and one cashier's desk. Apart from cricket there were staged on the ground athletics meetings, military tattoos and other events.

The highlight of the year's activities on the Angel ground was the County Cricket week, when the High Street was decorated with flags and bunting and at night time lit up by fairy lights from Bordyke to the Angel hotel. Apart from two county matches, other events included musical concerts in the Public Hall (now used for Bingo and Snooker). Of the many events that filled the week the most popular was the Venetian Fête consisting of illuminated coloured floats on the river. An early fête made a great impression on the *TFP* reporter, who waxed lyrical in his account of the event. He tells us that 'as dusk falls it is delightful as many lights of many hues spring up in all directions until one could imagine that a corner of Venice had been dropped in our midst'. In addition to the county cricket week, the Tonbridge Club hosted annually a secondary cricket week of a very high standard, when three two-day matches were played against such well known fashionable clubs as I Zingari, The Free Foresters, The Band of Brothers and others.

Sadly the Army took over the ground in 1939, when the playing surface was damaged too severely to enable restoration to cricketing standard, bearing in mind the cost involved. The Town Council bought the ground and the new tenants were the Tonbridge Football Club, a professional team. That this change is regretted not only in Tonbridge but throughout the county is shown in a report in the Kent Cricket Club's Annual for 1985 to the effect that 'volumes could be written about the Angel Ground; cricketing history hangs about the place and it is doubly sad that of all grounds used by Kent, only the Angel has succumbed to the developers'.

Whilst the County nursery was based in the town a large number of Tonbridgians became outstanding cricketers for both County and England. Frank Woolley must take pride of place. The brothers Frank and Claude Woolley were born and brought up in Tonbridge, living next to the old Baptist Church in the High Street (the site now occupied by Somerfields supermarket). Frank achieved world wide fame. This tall, elegant left-hander played 64 tests for England, scored 3283 runs, took 83 wickets with his medium-paced spin bowling and was credited with 61 catches. His best years for both County and England were just before the outbreak of the First World War, but he continued to play for Kent until 1938. Claude, although overshadowed by his brother developed into a reliable opening bat for Northamptonshire. Colin Blythe of Tonbridge made an excellent foil for Woolley with his slow bowling. Their best effort was the destruction of the Warwickshire side for 16 in June 1913 at Tonbridge (each taking 5 wickets for 8 runs). Tragically, Colin Blythe was killed in the 1914-18 War.

Tonbridge School had an excellent reputation as a cricket school and some very entertaining matches were to be seen on the 'High', the ground next to the school buildings. The school cricket captain, F. H. Knott played for Kent scoring a total of 426 runs. His namesake C. H. Knott did exceptionally well

Tonbridge representing England in 1930: Frank Woolley (right) opens the batting against Australia at Lords (from O. Warner: Frank Woolley, Phoenix House, 1952).

for Kent, scoring 4,026 runs, with a highest score of 154 not out.

Local young men from all walks of life made their names at the sport. Doug Wright, 'Hopper' Levett, Alan Watt and Tich Freeman have all done well for county and England. Another outstanding player was Arthur Fagg, who, on leaving Sussex Road School (now Hayesbrook) soon established a place in the Kent side as an opening bat and followed this by playing for England. His long career spanned the Second World War and he remains the only first class player to score a double century in each innings of a match. Leslie Ames became one of the famous wicket keeper/ batsmen who played for Kent and England. (Although he was an import from Folkestone, Ames lived just round the corner from Arthur Fagg and was an adopted Tonbridgian.) His partnership with the bowling of Tich Freeman was a sight to attract the crowds to the Angel Ground.

Thus between the wars this combination of county cricket on the Angel and 13 or so smaller clubs carrying out a full programme of fixtures against other clubs on the Sports Ground and fixtures against nearby village sides, many with very attractive grounds such as Leigh on its charming village green and Penshurst in the historic park with a background of the Elizabethan mansion, gave cricket pride of place in the summer season.

Amongst clubs using the Sports Ground were Tonbridge Onward, Tonbridge Trade, Tonbridge Half Holiday and, perhaps deserving special mention was the YMCA Club which, apart from Tonbridge Cricket Club was the oldest cricket club in Tonbridge, having been founded in 1888. In the early years, the club played on the Racecourse and on the Angel Ground as tenants of the Tonbridge club. The club had a very strong side, being assisted from time to time by some of the younger players from the Kent Nursery, among them Frank Woolley, Wally Hardinge, J. C. Hubble, W. J. Fairservice and Claude Woolley.

Although cricket remained the most popular summer sport in Tonbridge, by the 1920s tennis was beginning to make inroads into its popularity. The influence of tennis coaching being given in the girls' secondary schools – the Girls County School (now Tonbridge Grammar School), Fosse Bank (commonly known as Madame King's), and the Convent – were the main sources of this impetus. The groundwork no doubt, had been laid by the private tennis party circuit generated by the large number of middle class houses possessing tennis courts. A very good insight into this circuit is contained in an account written by a well known local resident, who records that 'from the time we built Bourne Cottage in 1923 we had a lovely well kept tennis court till the war, and played regularly twice a week in the evenings and every fine Sunday afternoon and evening. We collected six or eight pretty good players and after 1924 played very jolly little matches against friends from nearby villages and small clubs in the town. It was great fun and we did not play mere garden party tennis and was good training for my husband before he joined the Tonbridge Club'. The Tonbridge Lawn Tennis Club referred to had six tennis courts and three croquet courts and a roomy pavilion. It was situated on London Road, Tonbridge, on the border with Hildenborough. Other private courts were available on the Angel Ground and used by the Angel Tennis Club. On the Sports Ground 30 grass courts and four hard courts were fully utilised by a number of small clubs. Some of the larger were UNA Tennis Club, the Eureka, the Technical Institute Tennis Club, and the Whitefriars Press Club. Most of these clubs, together with the Crystalate Club (with courts in Hadlow Road), competed in a Summer League. A well contested singles competition with a trophy provided the climax to the season.

It would be wrong to think that Tonbridgians relied only on the Sports Ground and the Angel for their sporting and leisure interests, since the Town has always possessed a fine natural resource in the River Medway, of which full use was made between the wars. The Tonbridge Boating Club, with a club house and boat houses up-river from the Castle Grounds, had a strong membership with a large fleet of punts, canoes and rowing boats, plus a few racing skiffs (single scullers). The Tonbridge Rugby Football Club was closely associated with the Boating Club and organised every year a very popular regatta with keen competition between teams of canoeists from various sports clubs, plus fun events such as pillow fights on the greasy pole and the obligatory pirate crew.

Keen swimmers and golfers may be thinking that their respective sports are being neglected in this account. But both sports were well supported despite their lack of the facilities of the present day.

The Tonbridge Swimming Club overcame the handicap of having only a primitive open air pool, depending for its water supply on a pipeline from the Electricity Works, supplemented when necessary from a nearby well. The club's 120-plus enthusiastic members produced some excellent results in inter-club competitions. Other swimming venues were just outside the town. One of them was the Ballast Pit, near Haysden, excavated by the South Eastern and Chatham Railway Company for their Redhill line, which was used by Sir Andrew Judd's Commercial School (now The Judd School) for a number of years for swimming lessons; they later moved to the town Swimming Pool for school sports and lessons. The second venue – the most popular – was the Weir Pool created by the weir on the river built by the nearby gunpowder works owned by Curtis & Harvey. During any fine summer weekend this looked more like Brighton Beach with family picnic parties, campers and swimmers intermingled. The main attraction of the Weir was no doubt the fact that no restrictions on mixed bathing existed, as they did in the Town Pool (see pages 173-75).

The Tonbridge Golf Club had a nine hole course between Tonbridge and Hildenborough, moving in 1910 to another, newly laid-out nine hole course at Greentrees Park Estate between Tonbridge and Hadlow. When the Greentrees Park Estate was sold in 1919, the Club moved to Somerhill Park, owned by its President Mr O. E. d'Avigdor-Goldsmid. The members enjoyed an annual subscription of 21s, but by 1932 the club was appealing for additional sums from its members. The Club had a membership of 200 in 1934.

A factor which produced a complete change in the town's sporting activities was the very severe weather, a succession of very hard winters being experienced which caused the town to become, temporarily, a winter sports centre. The

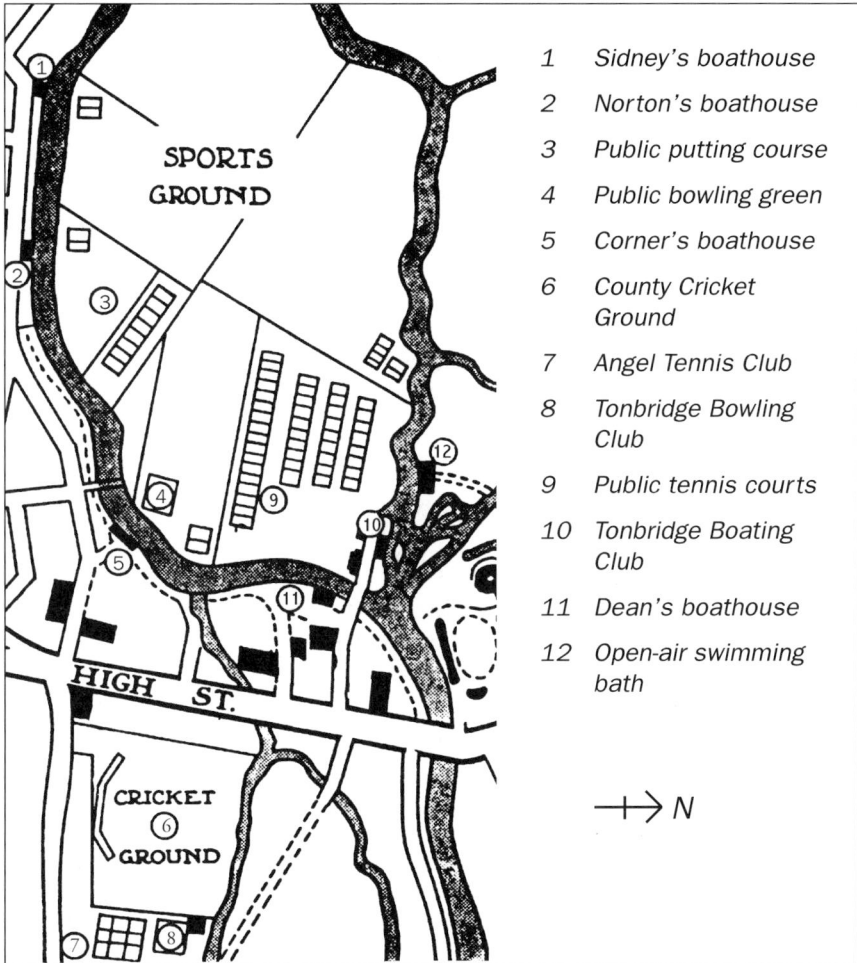

Sports facilities in the central part of Tonbridge in the 1920s (adapted from a map in the Tonbridge Official Guide*, c1924).*

Tonbridge Skating Club had a private pavilion and enjoyed skating and curling on the Ballast Pit near Haysden. For most people the popular skating area was the lake in Somerhill Park. For tobogganers, Lamb's Bank, off Quarry Hill, was the popular spot.

Given reasonable weather, however, the main activity in the winter on the

Sports Ground was dominated by some 13 or so football clubs competing in local leagues. This most popular sport was played in the local state schools. However, towards the 1920s soccer began to give some ground to rugby football, with two rugby clubs competing. The Tonbridge Rugby Football Club was formed in 1904, initially using the premises of the Boating Club for changing etc. By 1924 a most attractive club house was built on the river walk. In 1924 football at the Judd School switched to the rugby code and the Old Juddian Rugby Club was formed soon afterwards, with a ground initially on Haysden Lane. Later the club moved to the Sports Ground. By 1923 the town club fielded three regular teams.

They also ventured into foreign tours in various parts of the world. The Old Juddians fielded two teams and for the most part had fixtures with other old boys' sides in Kent and Surrey.

By 1938 despite the ominous gathering clouds of war the *Tonbridge Free Press* still carried reports of the very successful rugby clubs and the Hockey Club. Tonbridge Rugby Club was playing the Artists Rifles whilst the Old Juddian Rugby Club fielded two teams against Ashford. At soccer the Kent Amateur League was still going strong with seven Tonbridge teams playing in Division 1. The Sports Association reported a very successful year in 1939, despite the constraints of wartime. From that point onwards some ad hoc matches continued to be played, providing a playing opportunity for visiting players who might be available.

Appendix: Cricket Ball Making

Since Tonbridge was the centre of cricket in the Kent area it was natural that the industry devoted to manufacturing equipment for the game should be based in the Tonbridge area, particularly the manufacture of cricket balls. The town had the advantage of possessing a large reservoir of skilled workers accustomed to working in leather such as in the manufacture of saddlery and boots. Moreover the process of cricket ball making required a supply of hops for the dyeing process (changing white balls to red). Ball-making was a highly skilled trade with skills passed down from father to son. The organisations representing employers and workers both had their headquarters in Tonbridge. These were the English Cricket ball Manufacturers Association and the Cricket Ball Makers Trade Union (with more than 240 members).

The oldest cricket ball making firm in the country was Duke & Sons of Chiddingstone Causeway, established in the eighteenth century. Many Tonbridge people will remember the names of firms such as Twort, Farmer, Wibley, Hitchcock, Risley, Woodrow, Sayers, Mepham, Luff, Hearne, Lillywhite Frowd and Ives. From Tonbridge and its environs cricket balls were exported throughout the world. In the 1920s foreign competition in the form of machine stitched balls from Australia and low-wage production in India severely eroded our markets. Competitors were able to beat us on price but not on quality. The number of firms and the number of employees were substantially reduced as a result.

Sources

Copies of the *Tonbridge Free Press,* 1910 to 1939

Moore, D., *The History of the Kent County Cricket Club*

The *Tonbridge Free Press Centenary Book*

Barty-King, H., *Quilt Winders and Pod Shavers*

Minutes of the Tonbridge Sports Association

Personal memories of Mr S. Simmons, Mr J. Packham, Mr G. Mainwaring and the writer

Year Books of Tonbridge Urban District Council

Bentall, B., Church, G., Lawrence, A., Pettett, J., and Pierce, C., *The History of the Tonbridge YMCA Cricket Club*

Hales, B., *A Short History of the Tonbridge Rugby Football Club*

Taylor, G., *The Judd School 1888-1988*

Kelly's Directory, 1919

Acknowledgements

I am greatly indebted to a number of members and their friends for their help in preparing this essay. In particular, Mr A. A. Hams, Chairman of the Sports Association, was very helpful with information about the Association and loan of the Association's minutes, and, from his national sports contacts, the views of other authorities.

Thanks too, to Mr Sydney Simmons for a sight of the year books of the TUDC, to Mr J. Packham for information about Greentrees Park, and to Mr G. Mainwaring for Golf and Greentrees Park. For details of Tonbridge Rugby Football Club I was helped by Mr Tony Ward, who also provided a copy of *A Brief History of TRFC*. My thanks also to Mr A. Lawrence for a *History of the YMCA Cricket Club*, and for his general knowledge of Tonbridge sport.

Councillor Clark and Mixed Bathing

Gwenyth Hodge*

Donald Clark, a Scotsman by birth and former soldier, was one of the leading figures in Tonbridge political and municipal life between 1904 and 1921.

Born in the valley of Glencoe in 1857, his mother was a descendant of a victim of the Glencoe Massacre, and he believed his father had had Oliver Cromwell as an ancestor. As a youth he joined a regiment with local connections, moving to the Scots Guards in 1880. While stationed in Egypt he was a member of the force sent to relieve General Gordon at Khartoum. He served with distinction in the Boer War. He read extensively during barrack life. His studies included army regulations and their legal aspects, his knowledge enabling him to help his colleagues. Because of it he once had to complain about being accused of writing a letter in the London *Star* suggesting that political pressure had been put on certain soldiers and their relatives, contrary to regulations.

When he retired in 1904, Clark came to Tonbridge, occupying a house in the newly-built Mill Crescent. He was a Liberal and strong supporter of Free Trade against the wishes of Joseph Chamberlain and many Conservatives for duties on imported foodstuffs and Imperial Preference. He was a keen reader of Adam Smith and J. S. Mill. His activity contributed to the Liberal electoral victor in Tonbridge parliamentary constituency in 1906.

Donald Clark was a prominent member of the Urban District Council until 1921 apart from military duties in the First World War, and was Chairman between 1918 and 1920. In this office he was said to be noted for his strict impartiality during debates on which he sometimes held strong views. Two events showed his skill as a public speaker. In July 1919 he accepted a tank on behalf of the Council in the presence of 12,000 people. It was in recognition of the town's patriotic response to an appeal by the War Savings Committee 'to supply our soldiers with the sinews of war' (in his words). During the

---

*This essay was written by Gwenyth Hodge and, after its loss, rewritten by Christopher Chalklin.

Tonbridge Swimming Club's first Water Gala on Saturday, 17 June 1911.

Armistice Day Celebrations at the Public Hall, he was a leading figure addressing the gathering. The writer of his obituary notice mentioned that as an orator his words arrested attention, expressing ideas in an original way, and his flights of rhetoric were successful.

In the same year, Clark attracted national notice by opposing mixed bathing. Some councils which owned swimming baths had already accepted it, and it was a controversial issue in other towns at this time and later. On 2 June the Council considered a letter from the secretary of the Swimming Club, which used the municipally-owned bath opened in 1910. Its request to use it for 'mixed bathing' on Sundays led to a devastating speech in opposition by Clark.

Another Councillor named Skilton was a permanent opponent, but he was less vocal. Clark objected to mixed bathing because he believed women should be modest and virtuous. 'When a woman loses her modesty and recklessly exposes as much of her figure as she can, she loses one of her most precious possessions, the aura of mystery'. Women in bathing dress were less attractive to men than when they wore normal clothing, and made them unmarriageable. He also opposed sunbathing and watching mixed bathing from deckchairs. He proceeded to go to seaside resorts all over England, tramping the beaches to crusade against mixed bathing. He was mentioned in the national newspapers. He did not mince words. 'For one woman whose perfection of person can withstand the absence of clothing, there are dozens whose imperfections would be too glaring to overlook'. He objected to lack of clothing on women in general.

Despite his objection at the Council meeting, bathing by men and women together on Sundays at the Tonbridge pool was accepted. On 28 April 1921 it was also opened for this purpose on Wednesday afternoon.

Clark moved to Hildenborough in 1921 and ceased to be a councillor. After several seasons of mixed bathing, two cold summers were said to have stopped it altogether. In August 1928, the month of Clark's death, the Council reintroduced it with one dissentient, Councillor Skilton.

During the First World War and years immediately following, women's clothing changed dramatically. In a way it symbolised their efforts to achieve social and political equality with men. It is not surprising that many older men reacted instinctively against mixed bathing. Clark was courageous in speaking his mind in so forceful a way. His long experience in the Army and as a councillor was a helpful training for his unusual activity. While he may be accused of eccentricity in this special respect, one should not overlook his leadership of Tonbridge in other ways.

Sources

Tonbridge Free Press, April 1917, August 1928 and August 1937

Minutes of Tonbridge Urban District Council, 1919-22, including reports of the Parks, Museum and Bath Committee (Tonbridge Reference Library UD/To/Am 21)

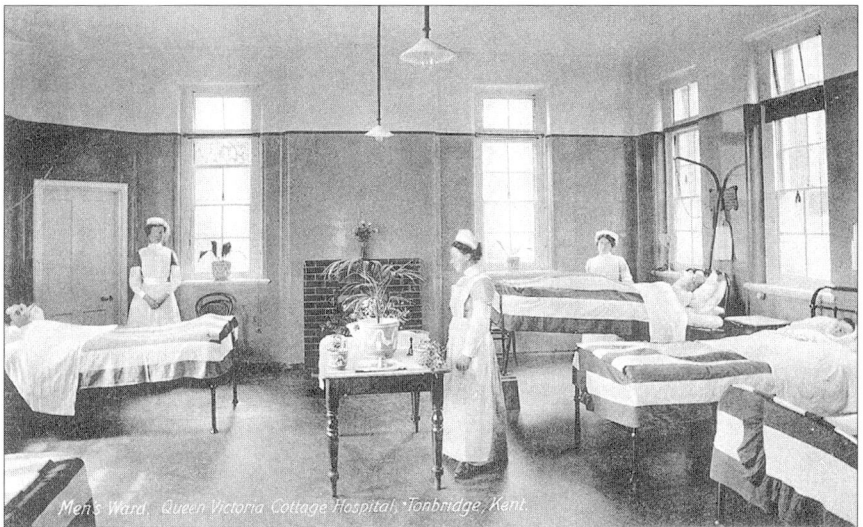

The Queen Victoria Cottage Hospital. Upper: *the hospital on its
Baltic Road site.* Lower: *the Men's Ward.*

Hospitals and Health

Pat Mortlock

Tonbridge between the Wars, like the country in general, moved from a period when disease and death were still too close acquaintances, to a time when there seemed, medically speaking, to be improvements on the horizon. At the end of the Great War diseases which had held sway for generations still existed. The town had been subject to epidemics of scarlet fever and diphtheria and the still largely incurable curse of tuberculosis existed. By 1939 the diseases were still there but the virulence had abated somewhat and the medical facilities provided in the town appeared to be coping with the situation. In many ways the Twenties and Thirties are a good time to study what life was like for the inhabitants of Tonbridge in that one is looking at the end of an era. The Second World War would soon disrupt ordinary people's lives and the advent of the National Health Service in 1948 would economically, socially and medically change things for ever.

In 1918 Tonbridge possessed two hospitals: the Isolation Hospital in Vauxhall Lane and the Cottage Hospital on the corner of Baltic Road and Quarry Hill. This of course changed in the mid 1930s when the Cottage Hospital took over the Isolation Hospital site and was replaced by the KCC Clinic in Baltic Road. However, when the war ended in 1918 the inhabitants of the town were used to the system whereby the Cottage was a permanently working hospital treating a variety of cases, while the Isolation Hospital was used only in the event of infectious disease. In addition, for a short period after the Armistice, a VAD (Voluntary Aid Detachment) Hospital on Quarry Hill was available for the treatment of soldiers.

The Isolation Hospital, sometimes referred to as the Hospital for Infectious Diseases, was the first permanent treatment centre in the town. The question of the foundation of a hospital first arose in 1876 when both smallpox and scarlet fever were being nursed in separate isolated cottages around the town. In February the Clerk of the Tonbridge Local Board wrote to the Tonbridge Guardians, who administered the Union Workhouse at Pembury, trying to organise a system whereby they would treat 'any infectious cases that may arise in the District on fair and liberal terms'. By 1878 the cost of nursing infectious cases convinced Dr Baylis, the Medical Officer of Health, that a permanent hospital for the reception of infectious cases should be built and after some discussion a site at Vauxhall Bridge Wood was chosen. By May 1879 a plan had been approved, three and a half acres of woodland had been cleared and levelled and a loan for £1650 had been negotiated. Everything was now ready for Tonbridge's first permanent hospital which was ready for use by December 1879.

By 1900 the Isolation Hospital had become an integral part of the town's health. The institution was still used only in cases of infectious disease, and the minutes of the Council give monthly reports on the state of affairs. There is often the satisfying entry that 'there are no cases in the hospital'.

Epidemics were obviously unpredictable and although all sensible precautions were taken, such as the purchase of a disinfection chamber for infected clothes and bedding, there were still unforeseen emergencies. 1893 had seen the hospital so full with scarlatina cases that it was seriously suggested that either one extra bed be placed in each ward or that two small children might share a bed. The ensuing discussions reveal that by this time the hospital could accommodate 24 patients, six in each of the four wards.

In 1895 the town was hit by further outbreaks of scarlatina and the hospital, unable to cope with more than 40 cases simultaneously, purchased 'an iron building' which became a permanent part of the buildings. The general problems of these years were aggravated by the fact that the Medical Officer of Health (MOH) recommended that a child with scarlet fever should remain in the hospital for seven weeks. Looking at treatment elsewhere in the country this seems to have been the norm and was the surest way of confining infection to as small an area as possible. However, by this time there was also a move to discourage infection at source and school closures became common.

There was no doubt that the Isolation Hospital played a vital role in the town, but one that was limited. Something else was urgently required for those needing emergency medical or surgical treatment. In 1897, the year of Queen Victoria's Diamond Jubilee, a public meeting was held in the town as a result of which it was agreed to erect a Cottage Hospital. Mr Goggs, the Hon. Secretary of the Committee set up to bring this about later wrote: 'there was no wish to divert the subscriptions from the Tunbridge Wells Hospital, as very much good work was being done for the town by that institution. It was thought that great relief might be afforded to it by our own management of many cases of accidents'. In February 1900 another meeting, presided over by Mr E. O. d'Avigdor Goldsmid (one of the town's great benefactors) was held and a definite decision made to build a hospital. Plans for this were published in the *Tonbridge Free Press (TFP)* for 3 March 1900. Six trustees were appointed to raise money to build on a site which had been donated by Messrs Catchpole, Potter and Powell. There was, however, a certain apathy in the town as a whole.

Enthusiasm for the whole project was revived when Queen Victoria died in January 1901, and in Tonbridge, as elsewhere in the country, there was a strong move to commemorate so long and glorious a reign. A public meeting held in May decided that contribution to the National Memorial was not enough and there should be some local scheme which would be both a worthy and permanent reminder of the late queen and something which would benefit the town.

The hospital was officially opened on 2nd February 1902 by Captain Boscawen, the local MP. A collection was organised at the actual ceremony and thanks to this it could be announced that the building opened free of debt. Later speeches alluded to the generosity of local individuals and tradesmen who had given money or discounts on goods so that the building could be furnished and supplied with surgical equipment. The practical advantages were also outlined: local accident cases would no longer have to travel the five miles to Tunbridge Wells and would thus be both more comfortable and stand a better chance. The representative of the Tunbridge Wells Hospital said that in the previous 12 months they had dealt with 20,000 outpatients and a new hospital in Tonbridge would relieve their caseload and help those who lived in villages like Hadlow and Hildenborough.

It should be remembered that the new Queen Victoria Cottage was, like the majority of the country's cottage hospitals, a Voluntary Hospital. Those patients who could afford to pay did so but their contributions could not cover the expenses of the poorer patients and the day to day running costs. As everywhere before the introduction of the National Health Service, there now began large numbers of money-raising events and more elaborate funding schemes.

The most well-known local hospital fund raising was already well established. In 1887, the Tonbridge Friendly Societies and Fire Brigades movement had begun the annual Hospital Sunday. Each July, on the designated Sunday, collecting boxes were placed all round the town to persuade those who could only afford the smallest contribution to make it then. Later in the day a procession made up of the Friendly Societies, the local Fire Service and then, as time went by, the Boy Scouts and Wolf Cubs, made its way along the High Street. In the early years the money raised went to a variety of good causes, including the General and Homeopathic hospitals in Tunbridge Wells, the London Throat Hospital and the payment for local patients to go to the Hastings Convalescent Home. After 1902 the Queen Victoria Cottage Hospital relied on this movement for some of its annual income. What had always been a good day out for the town also contributed a lot to the health of the area.

In the years that followed there were large numbers of money-raising events, from whist drives to theatre performances and flower shows, all to raise small but essential sums for the Cottage Hospital. The Trustees could also rely on the annual contributions of subscribers, together with larger one-off sums from the well off or the grateful. One annual event which brought fairly substantial help was the Alexandra Rose Day appeal. In addition there are numerous mentions of goods in kind, ranging from eggs, fruit and vegetables in season to gifts of tobacco and toys at Christmas.

By the outbreak of the First World War the two hospitals were an established part of local health provision. The Cottage Hospital had gradually increased both its accommodation and scope. In 1906 the number of beds had increased to twelve, while there were 69 admissions, but the AGM held to give an account of the hospital in1914 gave details of most satisfactory progress. Sir David Salomons had presented the hospital with a complete X-ray apparatus which had come just at the right time, in that, even in the early days of the war it had frequently been used to help wounded soldiers. The hospital had altered and improved its accommodation to house the new equipment and the new technology kept Tonbridge up to date with the latest in medical advances There were 145 inpatients during the year and many outpatients, several of them because of the availability of the new means of diagnosis.

Within days of the outbreak of War in August 1914 the town was preparing for the wounded. By October the VAD was mobilised and told to expect wounded Belgian soldiers immediately. Within days a proper VAD Hospital had opened at Quarry Hill House which Mr Deacon had placed at the disposal of the service. On 19 October, 45 men arrived at the hospital and the town began a war effort which would last into the first year of peace in 1919. Clothes were donated, a barber service provided and those who were convalescent were taken out for drives. When, very soon, the Belgian soldiers were replaced by the British, even more efforts were made and those recovering were taken to the Star cinema to see the latest films. Every week the *TFP* lists donations of food, cigarettes and money which helped the VAD to keep the hospital in good shape. As late as Spring 1918 cases were coming so fast that two marquees had to be erected in the grounds of the hospital.

Peace opened a new, but not always optimistic, chapter for the town. Spanish 'flu was already prevalent by the time of the Armistice in November and was responsible for several deaths, including three from one house in Rose Street. By December it had really begun to attack all levels of society. Edward le May, described as 'Tonbridge's most prominent citizen', died after contracting pneumonia as a result of the 'flu, and there were reports that undertakers could not cope with the number of dead. The *TFP* stated on 6 December that 'there have been more death notices in this paper during the last month than in any period during the worst times of the war'. The late winter of 1919 did see some return to normal. The VAD Hospital closed at the end of February and, although the 'flu lingered until March, there was the hope of better things to come.

However, there were changes as a result of the conflict. At the beginning of March 1919 malaria, dysentery and trench fever, together with acute pulmonary and influenzal pneumonia became notifiable diseases under the Public Health Act – an indication of how the war had changed what one might expect!

The immediate post-war years saw several attempts to improve the well-being of the town. It was decided that the National Kitchen, set up to help eke out supplies of food and fuel in the last months of the war, should continue. The Avebury Avenue centre could provide more than 2,000 meals a day, either to be eaten on the premises or taken home in a bowl. The *TFP* printed the following week's menus and prices, and there was a general feeling that nutrition, particularly that of children, must be benefiting.

As a national economic slump began to bite in the 1920s there is evidence that there was some distress in the town. A teacher at Sussex Road School complained that an examination by the school doctor showed that 70 per cent of one class were suffering from malnutrition. In the heated debate which followed the County MOH claimed that the figure was only 39.6 per cent. He also went on to point out that this was not an average figure since the class consisted of 'dull and backward' children and was therefore unrepresentative of the school and town as a whole. However, it is telling that in all the argument and justifications used, it is admitted that the alleged defects shown by the children did not include those whose only problem was 'uncleanliness or unsatisfactory clothing'.

The poverty of some sections of the town may not have seemed so obvious at a time when there was so much more to fear from frequent disease by all levels of society. In the early 1920s Isolation Hospital statistics show a small but steady number of both scarlet fever and diphtheria cases, together with notifications of typhoid, erysipelas and, most constant of all, tuberculosis (TB). After the War the Government began to concentrate on the problem of TB and official figures were collected frequently. The statistics for Tonbridge show no dramatic fluctuations, and figures for most quarters show a very gradual increase in line with the growth of population. The report for the third quarter of 1925, a representative selection, shows 125 TB cases in the town.

It is quite clear that the local authorities were not only well aware of the health problems but were extremely anxious to do something about them – not always with the co-operation of those at a higher level. In the summer of 1922 there were at least 16 children excluded from school with TB and the Council wrote to the County asking that open air treatment be funded for them. Little seems to have come of this. Again in May 1926 the Health Committee recommended the building of six outdoor shelters for the use of pulmonary tuberculosis patients. This plan had to be submitted to the Ministry of Health who replied that such shelters should be provided by the County Council. The latter announced that they thought the existing provision of rotating TB shelters (which could be turned to keep the patient out of the wind) was quite sufficient, unless Tonbridge could make a very good case for more. A subsequent survey of patients showed they were satisfied, though how fairly this conclusion was arrived at is not clear.

The County was also less than encouraging in its provision of Maternity Services. Immediately after the War the Council had asked for better maternity services. A clinic was in existence in a room at Sussex Road School but the accommodation was thought to be too restricted and not in an appropriate place. The County Council suggested the purchase of a 'better made army hut' since the provision of purpose-built quarters would cost somewhere around £2,000. For some time Tonbridge Council tried to get agreement and funding for a building on a site they owned in Lamberts Yard, a great deal more central for the mothers who would use it, but the necessary permission from the County was never forthcoming. After some time a temporary maternity clinic was opened at St Eanswythe's Church Hall and this remained until the original Cottage Hospital building on Quarry Hill became vacant in the mid 1930s.

Money was a constant problem in the 1920s, especially so in the case of the Isolation Hospital. The Council, usually short of money, had set up a Hospital Sub-committee, several of whose members were the wives of well known local figures, many of them councillors. By 1922 there appears to have been considerable tension between the ladies of the sub-committee and Mrs Shelton, who had been matron of the hospital since 1910. There was a lot of financial advice from the committee which Mrs Shelton obviously resented. In reply to a report which claimed the costs and quantities of hospital food were 'amazing to the ordinary housewife', she retorted, 'I had no idea I was compelled to do so [use half butter and half margarine]. Had I known I would have reported to the Health Committee the necessity of butter, as the nourishment supplied by the butter is needed for both patients and staff to keep them in good health to battle with the different diseases and trying cases we have at times'.

Staff troubles were also a cause of concern, and there were references to the difficulties of retaining permanent staff in a dark and lonely area well out of the town. Despite the hitches there is evidence that the Isolation Hospital was held in high regard. A letter of thanks from a resident in 1928 says, 'it must be a source of much confidence to the public to be able to see at first hand the efficient and effective service that obtains'. The committee may have been mollified by the comment that the administration and the staff 'both give most efficient and courteous service, and reflect the greatest credit upon your Authority'.

The years 1919 to 1929 saw the end of the old system of health and hospital care in Tonbridge, though of course this was not obvious at the time. In 1919 a new and very effective means of financing the Cottage Hospital came into being. Known as the Pay Day Fund it was introduced by

Mr H. J. Benham, the manager of the London County, Westminster and Parr's Bank. The scheme was very simple: the employees of local firms and businesses were asked to contribute one penny of their weekly pay to the Cottage Hospital Fund. This entitled the contributor to treatment at the Hospital when necessary. The first quarter of the scheme, which ended on 1 November 1919, brought in £45 and thereafter the total increased as businesses and shops with only a few employees joined the larger firms and works. The Annual Report for 1920 shows Pay Day Fund receipts at £421 and 72 patients being treated under the scheme.

Despite the depression, both financial and psychological, 1920 saw a more confident approach to health care. The Cottage Hospital continued to treat a rising number of cases with 257 inpatients during the year, an increase of 69 over the previous year. All departments, i.e. inpatients, outpatients and x-ray, extended the scope of their work. The only problem seems to have been an acute shortage of qualified nursing staff. The Isolation Hospital continued to treat infectious diseases which, though still too prevalent, were treated with few resultant deaths. Although not an exciting medical advance, the new tracheotomy equipment bought for this hospital was responsible for saving the lives of some diphtheria sufferers.

It was therefore with some pride that the local MOH presented his annual report for 1920. There were 353 births registered in the district, giving a birth rate of 23 per 1000 of the population, the highest rate since 1908. The number of deaths was 174, giving a death rate of 11.3 per 1000 of the population, compared with a national figure of 12.4. Infant mortality (registered deaths of children under one year), numbered 20, or 56.6 per 1000 registered births. This last figure was certainly a matter for congratulation since the Tonbridge infant mortality rate per 1000 had been 107.8 in 1918 and 94.8 in 1919. Although the statistic appears horrific in these days the national infant mortality rate for the whole country was still 80 per 1000 in 1920. It was generally agreed that the increase of births over deaths was very satisfactory – understandably so in days when many of those born were destined to die early.

The same report shows 19 cases of diphtheria notified during the year and relates that they were widely scattered through the town – with the roads listed, presumably to prove there was no one black spot. Scarlet fever had been lighter than usual and no cases of smallpox had been reported in the district since 1911. There were 21 new cases of TB notified in the year, not a large number by the standards of the time, and generally the incidence of serious infectious disease was not great.

In fact infectious disease was a considerably greater problem in 1929 when 105 cases of diphtheria were notified in the Tonbridge Urban area, 8 of them resulting in death. At the same time there were other health scares, at least for the officials. In 1928 a case of smallpox among wandering itinerants had raised the question of the right to enforce quarantine. A group of tramps, in transit between the coast and Bromley, had stayed overnight at the Pembury Workhouse and it was only when they had left the district that the smallpox had been diagnosed. When it seemed likely that the group might be about to return the MOH found an anomaly in the law. Those who lived in permanent accommodation could be compulsorily detained in their homes in cases of highly infectious disease, but this was not so in the case of those with no fixed abode. The group, however, was persuaded to move rather quickly through the district.

A more public concern, and one that arose quite frequently, was the dubious health of the hoppers who arrived from London every September. In September 1929 the *TFP* contained an interview with Dr S. Nicol Galbraith, the MOH for South-West Kent, in which he stated that the previous year's smallpox outbreak in Marden had been brought into the district by hop pickers from London. The reason for his concern was that history appeared about to repeat itself. The previous week he had heard from the Poplar Health Department that a woman and her child, both suffering from smallpox, had travelled to the local hop gardens by train and bus. This raised two points of contention locally. Firstly there was resentment against the influx of hoppers – who were not always welcome at the best of times – purely because of fear of infection, but secondly the local authorities wanted to know who would pay for the treatment and hospitalisation of these people. Over the next few years frequent, and sometimes tetchy correspondence with the London County Council meant that in cases of infectious disease that only became apparent when the hoppers reached Kent the London authorities would bear a large proportion of the treatment costs. Looking at newspaper reports from the period it is clear that local costs were still high, in that the local medical officers spent a lot of time investigating and testing any contacts.

The Local Government Act of 1929 was responsible for the important changes of this period. However, it was clear that some change was desirable anyway. The Annual Report and Meeting of the Cottage Hospital at the end of October 1929 called for a new hospital. Dr Bunting, the chairman of the House Committee, said that the noise from the road was so appalling that there were times when there was no point in him having a stethoscope, since he could hear nothing anyway. The medical conditions treated needed more wards so that they could be separated, there were increasing numbers of patients brought in from road accidents and all these required more peace and quiet than the site on Quarry Hill could provide.

Col. d'Avigdor-Goldsmid said that the committee had made careful enquiries from King Edward's Hospital Fund as to the approximate cost of a new hospital. Including administration costs, the sum was estimated to be £800 to £1,000 per bed but it was hoped that this might be reduced by acquiring a house conveniently situated, well built and somewhere near the centre of the town. The Committee had therefore taken an option on Marlfield, situated about 350 yards from Pembury Road and having direct access to The Drive. The house, built in 1870, would need adapting but that, and the addition of two ward blocks, could be put in hand for around £14,000. The meeting adopted this scheme.

A year later those at the Annual Meeting found that a number of decisions would have to be made if the scheme was to continue. The Chairman explained that the passing of the Local Government Act 1929 had brought about the possibility of dual control between the public authorities and the voluntary hospitals. Dr Bunting made it quite clear that in the matter of finance everyone must understand that the new hospital would, sooner or later, be under dual control, partly under the local committee and partly under the Public Assistance Council funded by the KCC. The advantage seemed to be that there would be some financial support from the Public Assistance Committee, partly with money from the rates. Whatever the decision, it would have to be understood that times had changed and that a truly local hospital, using only local money, was a thing of the past. After considerable discussion it was decided to go ahead with the planning of a new hospital, and the Chairman ended the meeting on a happy note with the news of a £500 donation.

While far-reaching decisions were being taken, the work of the hospitals continued much as usual, but there were some changes in the fund-raising schemes. In September 1933 the Pay Day Scheme was amalgamated with the Tunbridge Wells & District Association of Hospital Contributors. It was thought that, with a new and bigger hospital in mind, it would be sensible to consolidate and centralise the means of raising money. This was an idea which was acceptable in the town since it was felt to be fair and would allow Tonbridge to have a share of what was available. This was particularly important since local money was going to the new and well-equipped Kent and Sussex Hospital which had opened in Tunbridge Wells in 1928 and in which Tonbridge had some beds for more complicated cases. Nevertheless, the old Pay Day Scheme had served Tonbridge well. It was stated that since its inception in 1918 it had raised £6,500 and the total administrative costs in that time had been less than £1 per annum! Even by 1933 the weekly contribution rate was only 2d.

The changes of the early 1930s were more apparent at the Isolation Hospital than anywhere else. The Local Government Act gave the County Council considerable powers, and the financial responsibility and resources for implementing them. There was, therefore, a need to rationalise existing resources to keep costs in check and make sure that as many as possible had access to necessary services. In 1932 it was proposed to amalgamate some of the local isolation hospitals on the basis of a scheme originally put forward in 1924. Dr Galbraith, the MOH for South-West Kent, pointed out that, had the scheme been adopted when first proposed, it would already have saved the ratepayers of Tonbridge Urban and Rural Districts, together with Southborough, some £10,000. His figures showed that in 1931 only 73 patients had been treated in the three hospitals, costing about £56 per head.

The new arrangements were first set out in draft form in November 1932 when it was suggested that a Joint Committee of eight members, four from Tonbridge Urban and four from Tonbridge Rural be set up. Southborough no longer wished to be part of this plan. The Committee would concern itself with the two isolation hospitals for infectious diseases (other than plague and smallpox) under the Public Health Acts. It seemed sensible to amalgamate the two districts and it was agreed that the Capel Hospital be leased to the Joint Committee at a rental of £200 per year, with costs borne by both Councils proportionate to their populations. The Chairman of the Health Committee of Tonbridge Urban Council was then deputed to approach Mr O. E. d'Avigdor Goldsmid as to the terms on which he would release the Council from their lease on the Vauxhall Lane site since this was now redundant. As well as the more well-known local hospitals it should be pointed out that, since the County Council had decided that only four smallpox hospitals were required in Kent,

Dislingbury, near Capel, was to continue to exist for this purpose, and Sevenoaks and Maidstone soon agreed to send their cases there too.

The more human cost of this rationalisation is found in a letter from the Clerk to the Council to the County MOH enquiring whether he can find suitable engagements for the present employees at the Tonbridge Isolation hospital.

While all this was going on, Mr and Mrs Shelton, the caretaker and matron, went on with their usual jobs. As he always had, Mr Shelton fumigated infected bedding from both the hospital and those houses where disease had struck. He was responsible for the collection of the latter from the houses of patients and returning it in a decent, clean condition. In addition he not only kept the hospital buildings and equipment in good order but grew a large quantity of the fruit and vegetables used in the staff and patients' diets.

Mrs Shelton's work, while always of a variable amount because of the selective nature of epidemics, involved nursing – often 24 hours at a time during diphtheria outbreaks. In quieter times she organised a permanent staff, usually seven or eight, ordered supplies and kept the books, saw to the making of large quantities of jam, made from the garden fruits and generally ran a small but vital unit. The Urban District Council clearly recognised the Sheltons' service over 23 years since, when they finally became redundant in June 1933, they were awarded a gratuity of £350, though this was also to cover loss of wages and housing.

Just before the Isolation Hospital finally closed in 1933 a combination of factors changed the plans many had had for the town. The provision of a new Cottage Hospital on the Marlfield site had hung fire for some months while the Hospital Committee came to terms with the demands of the new regulations on provision and funding. In July 1933 a Special Meeting of the Subscribers was held at the Castle and decided 'that all necessary steps be taken for acquiring Vauxhall Lane Hospital for the remainder of its present lease and the Committee have the right to enter into an agreement for a new 80 years' lease at a yearly rental of £25 from the freeholder'.

The subscribers were given the whole picture, which was far from ideal in some aspects. Dr Bunting said that not to go to Vauxhall Lane, where there was the nucleus of a fine institution, would be nothing short of stupidity, but that such a move would be expensive. The wards required alterations, there was no theatre, no gas or electric light, the water supply (though not the quality) was doubtful, the kitchens were inadequate for the purpose and staff accommodation was insufficient. (One can only admire the Sheltons for doing such a good job there when their frequent demands for better lighting were turned down on account of the expense.)

The meeting was not put off by the inadequacies of the accommodation and took a decision to proceed at an estimated cost of £9,000. There was some hard bargaining over the site by the Council and the Cottage Hospital Committee which eventually resulted in the payment of £600 to the Council for the remainder of the lease. (The Council also received £145 for equipment needed at the extended isolation hospital in Capel.)

A frantic fund raising scheme now began throughout the town in an effort to make the plans for the new Cottage Hospital a reality. J. C. Elkington won the contract for the new buildings with a tender of £8,790 and, once this figure was known, a mass of fund-raising ideas were given full reign. It was impossible to be unaware of the need for funds since the *TFP* frequently allowed a banner headline to advertise functions. They were also persuaded to print poetry of a somewhat amateur kind: the following appears in an alphabetic appeal, from A to Z:

> T is for Tonbridge – I give you a toast –
> Here's to the sportsman who forks out the most.
> U are the people who have to get going
> For Tonbridge is growing, and growing and growing.

The Alexandra Rose Day Appeal continued to be a reliable source of money, with several record totals achieved in the mid thirties. There were also a number of very generous gifts of money from the more well off, together with collections from local organisations. In July 1933 the hospital's thirty-first annual report recorded a total of £480 1s 0d from the Crystalate Pay Day Fund, the Tonbridge Hospital Sunday Pay Day Fund, the Twopenny Fund and the ex-Servicemen's Welfare Committee.

By October 1934 things were going well enough for the foundation laying ceremony to go ahead. Only five minutes before this began there was a wonderful surprise for all concerned. Mr E. W. Meyerstein, of Morants Court, Sevenoaks, presented the fund-raising committee with £5,000 so that the new hospital could start free of debt. Mr Meyerstein was already a considerable hospital benefactor having recently given £85,000 to the Middlesex Hospital in London.

On 22 February 1935 'an imaginary bird's-eye view' of the new hospital drawn by the architect, appeared in the *TFP*, together with a description of what the buildings had to offer. There were to be three main wards – men's, women's and children's – as well as six private wards, an operating theatre, x-ray room, mortuary, and post-mortem room, together with kitchens and staff accommodation. The hospital would be able to accommodate 10 beds each for males and females, five children's cots and six private patients giving a total of 31. This showed a great improvement on the Quarry Hill site where there were 12 beds and one private ward.

The Building Appeal Committee, which had already received the very generous gift of £5,000, now made a massive effort to raise money for the Endowment and Equipment Fund, pointing out that the equipping of a modern hospital was a very expensive procedure. The propaganda aspects of King George V's Silver Jubilee were not lost. All over the town it was noted that it seemed extremely appropriate that a hospital which had come into existence as a result of Queen Victoria's jubilee should be improved with money collected in her grandson's jubilee year. The Chairman of the Council was asked to give his backing to the money-raising and one of his fellow councillors suggested, 'that you, Sir, as Chairman of the Council, be asked to open a Jubilee Fund of ten-shilling units.' This left him with little option and the unit scheme began in earnest; the money was collected at the Castle and the entire scheme had the backing of those in power. By April 1935 the Clerk to the Council was authorised to obtain two 'Contribution Barometers' for use outside Lloyds Bank and the Castle. so that the amount raised was obvious to almost every inhabitant.

The *TFP* was a very effective means of both publicising events and giving due thanks to those who had participated in the effort, however small their contributions. Readers could also see how their money was making an impact, since every week the newspaper gave figures of how many patients there were in the Hospital, how many had been admitted that week and the number of those treated as outpatients. The figures for the week ending on Wednesday 1 July 1936 show 12 patients in the general wards and four in the private ones. Of those, six had been admitted to the general wards that week and one privately. Eight outpatients had been treated and two X-rays done.

*Architect's imaginary bird's-eye view of the new Cottage Hospital in Vauxhall Lane (*Tonbridge Free Press, *22 February 1935).*

Contributions for that week had been £13 6s 6d. With this wealth of information each week, few could be unaware of the scope and needs of their hospital.

Balls, theatre performances (raising money through sales of both tickets and programmes), flower shows, gymkhanas and jumble sales, together with dozens of other ideas helped raise a large sum, and when the hospital buildings were finally ready in September 1935 any inhabitant of Tonbridge, guided by a map and data in the *TFP*, could, for 6d, have a tour round the hospital on an open day on the Sunday preceding its official opening.

What they saw must have both impressed them and reassured them that treatment locally was of the highest standard available at the time. It was certainly an improvement on what had gone before. Each bed had a range of electric plugs for bedside lights, doctor's inspection light, wireless and an emergency help bell. The ward lighting could be full light, or on a dimmer switch, and there were emergency gaslight fittings throughout the hospital in case of a electricity power failure. The whole building was equipped with central heating, synchronised electric clocks in each ward and emergency fire

The Cottage Hospital in Vauxhall Lane as it appeared in the 1940s.

hydrants in case any of this went wrong. For times when only occasional heating was needed there was provision for a coal fire at the end of every ward. The Princess Margaret Rose Ward for children contained five cots and up to date equipment. The committee felt that they had also learned from the mistakes of others in that the windows were provided with blue blinds which was not so trying to the eyes as the red ones recently installed at the Kent and Sussex Hospital.

The operating theatre was very well lit and meticulous attention had been devoted to its ventilation; the sterilising room gleamed with its stainless steel equipment. There was also an emergency telephone for the use of the surgeons. Domestic appliances were not forgotten: the kitchen had the latest 'Frigidaire' refrigerator and enamel surfaces for cooking. There was a staff of 14 to be accommodated whose needs were well catered for. The Matron had her own sitting room and bedroom and most of the nurses had single rooms with wash basins, Lloyd Loom chairs and full length mirrors. There was a separate room for the night nurse, and a cottage just outside the main building for the caretaker and the porter.

The only important equipment which was not in place at the time of the open day was that in the X-ray unit, which was to arrive immediately after the official opening, though whether this was for medical or financial reasons is not clear. If it was the latter this problem would again be solved by a benefactor. The Queen Victoria Cottage Hospital was officially opened on 23 October 1935 by the Marchioness Camden in the presence of many of those who had worked so hard for this day. Once again those at the official ceremony were to hear some good news. A gift of £860 for X-ray equipment was donated 'in memory of Charles James Rae from members of his family', and a purse presented by children from local schools and other organisations amounted to £466 10s 9d. Despite this the President of the Hospital announced the need to raise a further £5,000 to pay off various extra debts that had accumulated since the foundation stone had been laid. All present seemed to agree that this would be something worth working for, since the President said, 'you have here as well-equipped a hospital as any in England. You have unrivalled medical and nursing skill, and you have a cause in which we are all united, that makes a claim on every single person in the town and area'. It was a view reiterated by the *TFP* which enthused that 'the only sounds they (the patients) will hear will be the song of the birds and the breeze in the trees. What a difference from Quarry Hill'.

All this emphasis on money should not obscure the fact that the hospital facilities were available to everyone whatever their social standing. In answer to a question posed in the *TFP*, 'Does the hospital only take in patients who can pay and turn away those too poor to pay?', the answer was an unequivocal 'no'. The townspeople were assured that all proper cases would be admitted 'irrespective of creed, cash or circumstances'. Hospitals were said to exist for these very people. However, where possible, those treated who had the means to pay should do so in proportion to their income, on a scale ranging from one to three guineas a week. Private patients' fees would be four guineas a week.

The outstanding debt did however still exist and in the years before the war there were admirable money-raising ventures, including the help of the famous Pea-Nut Club which had contributed so much to the Kent and Sussex funding. The Pea-Nut Club fête held at the Castle in July 1938 raised a sum of £331 4s 6d for the Cottage Hospital. 'Aunt Agatha' of the Pea-Nut Club was responsible for several more contributions over the next year or two. Yet the tried and tested methods still yielded appreciable income. One third of the Cottage Hospital's revenue was still coming via the contributory schemes started at the beginning of the inter-war period.

A study of the Hospital, from the Committee reports, the Urban District Council Minutes and the *TFP*, from 1935 until the start of the war shows it working efficiently and with purpose. The Annual Meeting held in February 1939 heard that the Hospital Building Fund debt had been reduced from almost £5,000 in 1936 to £155 4s 11d. The number of inpatients treated was around 630 per year with over 220 'casual cases'. In 1938 there had been 363 major operations and 214 minor ones, and 609 patients had been x-rayed. On average each in-patient remained in hospital for 13 days, at a daily cost of 10 shillings.

The relatively rosy picture painted above may have appeared less encouraging at the time. Disease still struck suddenly and it is sobering to find frequent obituaries of children and teenagers in the local press. There were also startlingly high figures for a new cause of death: road accidents. As early as 1932 the MOH for South-West Kent reported 27 people killed and 534 injured in the year as a result of road accidents. Compared with 167 cases of notifiable infectious disease resulting in only one death, it seemed one type of disaster was being replaced by another.

Certainly by 1939 the annual Public Health Report for the South-West Kent area showed subtle changes in the health of the district compared with the period immediately after the Great War. Though scarlet fever and diphtheria were present and still treated with isolation, the number of cases had decreased. Death and fever after childbirth continued to strike, but less frequently, and infectious disease notifications were well down. However, there was a case of poliomyelitis and three mild cases of typhoid. The commonest cause of death was heart disease, with 346 out of 1027 deaths in the district attributable to that. Yet it must be pointed out that this was in the very large area of South-West Kent; the number of deaths in Tonbridge itself was 173.

Figures for 1938 show a healthy trend, with births outnumbering deaths by 49. The birth rate for Tonbridge was 13 per 1000 compared with 13.5 for South-West Kent, 13.4 for London and 15.1 for England and Wales. The Tonbridge death rate was especially impressive at only 9.9 per 1000, compared with 12.3 in South-West Kent, 11.4 in London and 11.6 in England and Wales. In fact the unusual figure in this set is that for South-West Kent.

There are many reasons for the improving health of the area. Some are a result of national policies, some local initiatives. There is no doubt that local effort helped substantially to get national policies implemented. The advance in the scope and effectiveness of the local hospitals could not have occurred without the wholehearted involvement of the townspeople. But there was a great deal of local achievement which there has been no time to acknowledge in this article. The vastly better housing available on the new estates at Barden, Cage Green and Hectorage Road, often as a result of slum clearance, was something of which the local council could be proud. By the end of the 1930s private developments in areas like Deakin Leas, Kings Road and Thorpe Avenue also raised housing standards well above those of the early 1920s.

Babies and schoolchildren were also better catered for. The provision of maternity services and a nurse to offer advice and help to mothers was an asset in both childcare and the nursing of infectious disease. One of the main concerns of the 1930s was the provision of tuberculin-tested milk to schools, and there are several references to the testing of milk from school premises. After the Cottage Hospital was moved to the Vauxhall Lane site the KCC took over the old Quarry Hill buildings as a clinic which was used for both babies and school medical services for decades to come. For years it also served as a treatment centre for tuberculosis.

Finally one must mention National Rat Week which was held in the first week of November from the end of the First World War. This annual event was clearly needed both in the town and the county. The *Kent Messenger* ran a competition for the greatest number of vermin killed by any one person, and sums of money were offered for a certain number of tails. In 1937 one of the Council's employees caught 435 rats on the refuse tip just working in the evenings during the five days of Rat Week, and was rewarded by five shillings extra on his wages and the promise of two shillings for every hundred he continued to catch after the week was over. This certainly did the trick: the following year saw a massive decline in the rat population – a decline which seems to have been permanent.

The marked improvement in health by the end of the thirties was something that the town might have been happy to contemplate had other considerations not started to cloud the horizon. By 1938 air raid preparations for an approaching war were well under way. By October, 16,600 civilian gasmasks had been received and Air Raid Wardens enrolled. It seems that whatever had been decided at Munich had made little optimistic impression on Tonbridge. On the eve of the Second World War the local hospitals were back in the news, but with no hope of medical improvements this time. The KCC clinic on Quarry Hill, the original Queen Victoria Cottage Hospital, was about to be adapted as a First Aid Post in the coming emergency, and the Ministry of Health had directed that a mobile first aid unit must be based at the new Cottage Hospital in Vauxhall Lane. The Dislingbury smallpox hospital at Capel was also set aside for infectious diseases among the evacuated.

As further sites round the town were earmarked for more first aid posts, evacuation centres and mortuaries, it was apparent that Tonbridge had done well to get its hospital improvements in place when it had. The opportunity for further development was about to be seriously curtailed.

Sources

Minutes of Tonbridge Local Board, up to 1895

Minutes of Tonbridge Urban District Council, from 1895

Annual Report of the Registrar General for England and Wales

Tonbridge Free Press

Kelly's Directory

Acknowledgements

I am grateful to the staff of Tonbridge Reference Library for all their help.

List of Subscribers

Presentation Copies

The President of Tonbridge Historical Society, Dr Joan Thirsk, CBE
The Mayor of Tonbridge and Malling, Councillor Anita Oakley
The Editor and Authors

Subscribers

Of the nine hundred copies of this book printed in November 1999, three hundred and seventy-five were for advance subscribers, among whom were:

Mr A. W. Alder
Robert Albert Alder
Peter Allan
Mr & Mrs N. G. Allen
James Angell
N. Ashwell
Barbara Baldock
Terry Ball
Audrey R. Barber
John D. Barber
Mr & Mrs A. J. Barden
Mrs D. Beach
Margaret Beech
Connie Bell
Mrs John Bickmore
Lawrence Biddle
Mr & Mrs G. M. Bishop
Mr R. J. Bishop
Mr & Mrs F. G. Blundell
Mr & Mrs R. F. Bolam
K. J. H. Bonner-Williams

Mr & Mrs S. Boorman
Mrs Kim Botten
Mrs Trudy Botten
John Boulding
Clare Bowerman
Keith & Susan Brackley
Mr & Mrs C. Bristow
Mr & Mrs D. C. Brooker
Mr & Mrs John E. Brooker
Mr & Mrs John J. Brooker
Mr & Mrs W. H. Brooker
Mr & Mrs R. Broomfield
Shiela Broomfield
C. Browne
Frank C. Brownhill
I. Browning
Geoffrey Lewis Bullard
Mr & Mrs A. J. Bumstead
Jonathan Burgess
Mark Burgess
Peter & Yvonne Burgess

Sandra & Terry Burgess
Mrs G. Burton
Marie Burton
Maureen Buss
Mr & Mrs A. B. G. Capel
Mr & Mrs Francis Cazalet
Andrew & Dorothy Chalklin
Mr & Mrs D. F Chapman
Margaret Child
T. M. Chivers
Inga Churchman
Mrs & Mrs R. A. Churchman
Mr & Mrs T. Cooper
Irene & John Cox
The Crouchers
Chris & Joy Croucher
David Croucher
Anne Curling
Mrs B. J. Curnock
Mrs B. D'Alton
Mr & Mrs A. K. Dane
Mr & Mrs D. O. Davis
John & Joanne Davis
Mrs T. J. Dawson
Miss J. M. Debney
Peter Diggens
Jean Durrant
Mr T. Dwyer
John R. Dyson
Christopher Easeman
Dr Elizabeth Edwards
Michael Edwards
Mr J. G. Ellis, MA
Mrs J. W. Etherington
Mr H. G. Fahy
Dr J. M. T. Ford
Susan Ford
Stuart & Jean Forsyth
Robin Foster
Eric & Olive Francis

Mrs M. Fraser
Mrs G. Fry
John & Neil Ghosley
Mr & Mrs M. Gilham
Mr & Mrs G. Gillespie
Ian Goodacre
Anne & Roger Goodman
W. D. Gowin
Joyce Graf
Daniel Christopher Grant
Mrs & Mrs D. J. Green
Mr M. A. Green
R. G. Greenhill
Patricia M. Greenslade
Michael & Benedict Guttman-
    Kenney
Hadlow Historical Society
Mrs J. R. Haffenden
Mr & Mrs Robert A. Hales
Pearl Hall
Mrs Gillian Hankey
Brian Hanson
Hugh Hanson
Janet Hanson
Mr & Mrs R. H. Harding
David & Diane Hardy
Martin J. Hardy
Paul & Corinne Hardy
Stella Hardy
Tony & Shirley Hardy
Anthony & Annabelle Hayward
Mr & Mrs R. J. Hedley-Jones
Alex J. Heggie
Anita & Patrick Hemeon
Diana Hemeon
Sally Hemeon-Brooks
Mr & Mrs K. B. Hemsley
Mr & Mrs N. J. Hemsley
Marian Hemsted
Mrs Christine J. Higgs

A. Hillen
Hillview School for Girls
Mr Guy Hitchings
Mr & Mrs R. T. Hollingsworth
Brenda Hook
Darrell & Rebecca Howard
Dr P. L. Humphries
Dennis Ingram
Maureen Jackson
Ken & Toni Jarrett
Alec R. Jeffery
Shaun A. Jeffery
Hazel Johnson
Wilfred & Joan Jones
Mr G. J. Kemp
Susan & Diane Killick
Pauline Kingswood
Mrs Pat Large
Mr & Mrs S. J. Larkin
Christina Lawrence
Miss Phyllis Luff
J. C. Maidman
Alexander Mallett
Philip & Anne Mallett
Mr & Mrs A. W. Mankelow
Sidney R. Marfleet
Mrs M. J. Marsh
D. R. & G. M. Martin
Mr & Mrs D. C. L. Marwood
Linda J. Marwood
Thelma Maunsell
Richard T. Maylam
Mr & Mrs R. N. Millman
Miss C. E. Mills
Mrs J. L. Mills
Barbara Mitchener
Jack & Linda Moore
Mr & Mrs K. Moore
Heather & Callum Morgan
Mr & Mrs G. E. Mortley

Graham & Margaret Mungeam
Keith Nicholson
Michael & Elizabeth Norrie
Jack K. Nutley
Richard & Glennys Obbard
J. M. O'Mordha
Brenda & Peter Overton
Mrs Mary Page
Mr & Mrs D. Parker
W. K. Parkin
Derek & Barbara Payne
David Penny
Ann Philp
Mrs J. Pink
Marion Pointer
Mr & Mrs A. M. Porteous
John R. Potter
Nora J. Potter
Davyd Power
Jared Prakash
Michael & Pam Price
Mrs Eileen E. Reynolds
Mr & Mrs M. Rhodes
Marjorie Riley
Eric E. Rogers
Mr & Mrs P. R. Rogers
Mr & Mrs S. H. Ruck
Arthur Ruderman
Mrs M. Sales
Mr A. J. O. Saunders
Mr A. O. W. Saunders
Mrs L. M. Saunders
Mr N. C. Saunders
Mrs S. A. Saunders
M. F. Sawyer
Mrs V. Scrotton
C. F. Sergison
Mr Nigel Shaw
Brian & Shirley Sheppard
Mrs Lily Sheppard

Russell Sherwen
Jean Simmons
Sydney Simmons
K. M. Simms
Evelyn Sivers
Mr & Mrs E. E. Skeates
Don Skinner
Mr & Mrs J. D. Small
Mr & Mrs E. J. Smalman-Smith
Geoffrey & Elizabeth Smethurst
Monsignor Michael Smith
Emily & James Smithers
Mr & Mrs K. C. Smithers
Mr & Mrs G. J. Spencer
Dorothy Stammers
Roger Stanley
Mr & Mrs J. Stephens
Colin Stevens
Peter Stibbard
David & Diana Sturmer
Graeme & Clare Thompson
Nicholas M. Thompson
Mrs G. W. Todd
Darren Tolton
Del Tolton

Tonbridge Civic Society
Tonbridge School Library
Tonbridge Tourist Information
  Centre
Frank Tullett
Peter Tunstell
Mrs D. Turley
Mrs Margaret Turnbull
Jane Waldron
A. P. Waterhouse
Clive G. Waters
John & Gillian Watt
Rupert & Mary Weld-Smith
Mr & Mrs B. G. Wheeler
J. Wheeler
Mr & Mrs S. C. Wiles
Mrs M. A. Wilkinson
Dr & Mrs A. W. Wilson
Mr & Mrs R. J. Wise
Mollie Woodrow
Peter F. Woods
Mr & Mrs Peter York
Colin Young
Mr & Mrs G. Young
Malcolm Harvey Young

Indexes

General Index

Index of People

Index of Places